MEN *of the* BIBLE

Books by Ann Spangler

MEN *of the* BIBLE

A One-Year Devotional Study
of Men in Scripture

ANN SPANGLER &
ROBERT WOLGEMUTH

ZONDERVAN®

ZONDERVAN.com/
AUTHORTRACKER
follow your favorite authors

ZONDERVAN

Men of the Bible
Copyright © 2002 by Ann Spangler and Robert D. Wolgemuth

This title is also available as a Zondervan ebook.
Visit www.zondervan.com/ebooks.

Requests for information should be addressed to:

Zondervan, *Grand Rapids, Michigan* 49530

This edition: ISBN 978-0-310-32889-6 (softcover)

Library of Congress Cataloging-in-Publication Data

Spangler, Ann.
    Men of the Bible : a one-year devotional study of men in Scripture / Ann Spangler &
    Robert Wolgemuth.
        p. cm.
    Includes index.
    ISBN 978-0-310-23944-4
    1. Men—Prayer-books and devotions—English. 2. Men in the Bible. I. Wolgemuth,
    Robert D. II. Title.
    BV4843 .S68 2002
    220.9'2'081—dc21   2002007548

Printed in the United States of America

10 11 12 13 14 15 /DCI/ 23 22 21 20 19 18 17 16 15 14 13 12 11 10 9 8 7 6 5 4 3

TO MY GODSONS
Tim Scholand
Paul Lapczynski

—Ann Spangler

TO MY BROTHERS
Stanley G. Guillaume
Samuel C. Wolgemuth
Kenneth G. Wolgemuth
Daniel S. Wolgemuth
Randal G. Birkey
Douglas E. Shumaker
Kenneth R. Heise

Comrades in grace and loyal friends,
Joining me in their own faith-walks as men of the Bible

—Robert Wolgemuth

CONTENTS

Alphabetical
Index of Men

THEME INDEX

INTRODUCTION

Welcome. We're glad you've joined us in the adventure of this book.

Many different techniques can be used for studying and understanding the Bible—topical studies, systematic studies, and verse-by-verse studies. These are all worthy approaches.

Men of the Bible gives you a different approach, an overview of Scripture through the eyes—and hearts—of the men who lived it. Like its predecessor, the best-selling *Women of the Bible,* this book focuses on the lives of fifty-two men in Scripture whose stories offer a fresh encounter with the Bible. The cast of characters is long and colorful, including peacemakers and warriors, saints and scoundrels, kings and peasants, prophets and rebels. These are real men whose difficulties and victories often mirror our own struggle to believe and obey.

By reading about the many ways these men experienced their walk with God, you will gain a deeper appreciation for how God works in the lives of individuals as well as a greater understanding of his nature and character.

Men of the Bible offers a unique one-year devotional program, combining five elements: inspiration, application, Bible study, Bible promises, and prayer. Each week focuses on one man's life, providing five days of readings and reflections suitable for your own personal prayer and study as well as for use in study groups.

Even though the men you'll meet in this book lived in a culture vastly different than ours, you'll discover that their hopes, victories, defeats, and passions are remarkably similar to the ones you and I face every day.

Here's how each week is organized:

Monday: His Story—a portrait of something from his life
Tuesday: A Look at the Man—a closer look at his story and its application for you

Wednesday: His Legacy in Scripture—a Bible study on some of the
principles revealed through his life

Thursday: His Legacy of Promise—Bible promises that apply to his
life and ours

Friday: His Legacy of Prayer—praying in light of his story

By focusing on one man for an entire week, you will learn something new about the culture that surrounded him or about the pressures he faced. You'll see how his faithfulness was rewarded or how
his disobedience was punished. You will learn *about* these men, and
through the process of weekly Bible study and prayer, you will learn
something *from* them.

How to Use This Book

On Monday, you may want to begin by looking up the "Key Scriptures" to read something of the man directly from the Scripture. Then
we suggest that you read the narrative entitled "His Story." Although
we have relied on the biblical text for these accounts, we have done
some fictionalizing within these stories. Every effort has been made
to remain close to the original text, drawing reasonable implications
from the accounts in the context of the culture.

On Tuesday, "A Look at the Man" gives you an opportunity to
look more closely at the man and see life from his perspective.
Wednesday takes you into God's Word and helps you to pursue the
principles that marked this man's life—or those that were missing
from his character. Depending on the amount of time you have set
aside on Wednesday, you may want to select only a few of the passages
to read and questions to answer. That's fine. Also, there is a "Going
Deeper" question that is more challenging. Your ability to answer this
question may depend on your time availability. You can always come
back to the questions you have not answered at a later date.

On Thursday, you'll be encouraged by several biblical promises that
address the topic you've just studied. And Friday provides a brief summary of the week and brings you to a guided prayer. Here you can
express your gratitude to God and seal those things that have had a
particular impact on you from the week's experience.

However you use this book, our hope is that it will provide you
with a chance to slow down and soak in the wonder of the Bible and
the truths that fill its pages. We also pray that this experience will give

you a deeper understanding of the most important biblical story that winds its way through every account from Genesis to Revelation— the story of redemption.

It should be said that neither of us is a biblical scholar but a writer primarily interested in exploring the spiritual messages embedded in each man's story. Thus it is not our intent to present a scholarly analysis of the various texts we explore or to debate various interpretations of key passages, but to familiarize you with these important stories so that you may recognize the way in which God's grace has been manifested throughout salvation history. We do so with a keen awareness of our own limitations, remembering the words of Saint Augustine upon writing a commentary on the book of Genesis, which he had studied for more than thirty years: "If anyone is of the opinion that this passage should be explained differently and he is able to lay out a more likely interpretation, not only should I not resist him, I should thank him."

We are so thankful to those who joined us through the process and completion of this project. Thanks to our editor, Sandy Vander Zicht, for her advocacy, guidance, patience, insight, and encouragement. We are grateful to Dirk Buursma, Laura Weller, Sue Brower, Kevin Harney, and especially Lisa Bergren for all their excellent help.

And thanks to our families, who were forced to take up the slack while we sat quietly in our caves to write.

Any deficiencies in the book, of course, can only be traced to us. Whatever these might be, our sincere prayer is that this book will give you a greater understanding and love for God's Word and will renew your passion to spend time on your own learning from its timeless truth.

—Ann Spangler
Grand Rapids, Michigan

—Robert Wolgemuth
Orlando, Florida

ADAM

His Name Means "Of the Ground"

His Work:	Until his sin, Adam was naked and was the happy caretaker of the Garden of Eden. After succumbing to temptation, he tailored his own clothes and became a farmer.
His Character:	The first man, Adam, was initially God's perfect human creation. Adam was in harmony with nature and with his wife, who was formed from one of his ribs.
His Sorrow:	More tragic than any story in the Bible, Adam disobeyed God, was expelled from the Garden of Eden, and spent the rest of his life in hard labor.
His Triumph:	Adam was the firstborn of all creation.
Key Scriptures:	Genesis 2–3

Monday

HIS STORY

"What's that sound?" The tension in Eve's voice reflected the new feelings in Adam's gut. His mind and heart swirled with sickening sensations, ones he wished he had never experienced, born of deepest guilt and the terror of truth.

Until this moment, his life had been filled with remarkable delight.

It all began when Adam took his first breath.

The span of time between morning consciousness and gathering enough energy to open one's eyes usually takes just a few moments.

But for Adam, the prewaking experience of semiconsciousness must have taken some time. This was unlike anything that had ever happened before—or has happened since: a full-grown man literally sucking in his first gulp of air.

As he lay somewhere between sleep and full consciousness, Adam's first thoughts must have been, *Who am I? What are those sounds? Where am I? What is this?*

Brushing the sleep from his eyes, accepting life, Adam slowly sat up. He looked down at his own legs and arms and saw smooth skin and firm, strong muscles. He lifted his hands to his face, bending and stretching his fingers, studying the sinews. He drew his hands closer and touched his face, feeling the contours of his eyes and cheekbones, then briefly to his hair, thick and long.

Adam slowly stood to his feet. He tightened the muscles of his legs and stretched his new arms skyward. He drew in a deep breath of fresh, cool air that would rival a pristine, deep forest breath. And it was only then that Adam saw something of the breathtaking beauty that surrounded him.

The foliage was lush, the flowers a panoply of color. The fully orchestrated sounds of songbirds and animals filled his head with sheer ecstasy. *I am alive.* He took another deep breath. *Life is good.*

Adam began to walk. Slowly at first, then a jog, finally a dead run. Like a child turned loose, the man finally pulled up and spun around, his arms spread wide. He sang and shouted sounds from his own mouth, something he had never heard before.

And if the sounds and the beauty and the wind tousling his hair were not enough to flood his senses, Adam felt an indescribable Presence. Yes, there were lots of living things around him, but this was different—an inexpressible Someone. All about him. *Over there . . . over there . . . and over there.* Whoever it was, Adam inherently knew that he was not the only one in the garden. Yet he was not afraid; instead, he was comforted by the Presence.

Adam stopped in a small meadow, the soft grass cushioning his feet. The glowing yellow sun in the sky warmed his shoulders. He looked at the trees surrounding him and felt a vague emptiness in the pit of his stomach.

And then, for the first time, Adam heard a voice, a sound different from the sound of any of the other living things around him. He heard words—a language that took shape and became immediate knowledge in his mind. The voice was quiet and authoritative, and he recognized it as belonging to the Presence.

"You are free to eat from any tree in the garden," the voice said, "but you must not eat from the tree of the knowledge of good and evil, for when you eat of it you will surely die."

Adam nodded his willing compliance. He had noted again the tree to his left and decided he was more than willing to obey. *With all of this,* he thought, looking all about, *why would I miss the fruit of that tree? It's an easy promise.*

Walking to a small bush covered with red fruit, Adam pulled a berry from a reluctant stem and tentatively bit into it. Juice covered his tongue and ran down his throat, tickling his mouth with a delightful sweet-tart sensation. Eagerly, he gathered others and shoved them into his mouth.

Then from the woods and skies, animals and birds approached him. As though mysteriously commanded to organize, these living things passed by, and group by group, Adam called out their names. And once they were named, they scattered again.

If ever a man experienced satisfaction by his surroundings, it was Adam. There was the invisible Presence, the creatures, the vegetation, and the fruit. But they weren't enough. Deep in his soul, Adam longed for something—or someone—else by his side.

"It is not good for you to be alone," the voice spoke again. "I will make a helper suitable for you."

Adam sat down. The words warmed him. He knew that the Presence understood his longing.

First a drowsiness, then a complete fatigue overwhelmed Adam. He laid his head on the soft grass and closed his eyes.

In what seemed like a moment, he slowly opened his eyes, snatching consciousness from the mist of sleep. As his eyes took focus, he saw a form lying on the ground next to him. His heart raced at the beauty of the creature, like him in some ways, different in delightful other ways.

Rising to his feet, Adam took the hand of the woman, helping her to stand. Their eyes met. They smiled and gently extended their arms toward each other until they embraced. Feeling the warmth of her body against his own, Adam nestled his face on the woman's neck. And her presence filled the hollowness in his heart. *A perfect companion.*

Adam felt an unexplainable sense of completeness. Wholeness. This was someone with whom he could share the beauty and company of the garden. Joy filled him and spilled upward, causing him to smile.

"I'm Adam," he said.

She smiled with a silent understanding.

"And you're Eve."

Taking her hand once more, Adam walked with her into the woods. He spoke of his own "birth," the parade of living things, the taste of the fruit, and the beauty of their surroundings. Adam told her of the Presence and how she was the perfect answer to his yearning.

But later, as time went on, something happened. Something awful. What should have been enough became clouded with a new longing. It started with an innocent conversation with a serpent and a fascination of that forbidden tree. Whispers of untold pleasure and desire. Conspiracy between man and woman to blatantly disobey the Presence.

Now new feelings of fear and dread engulfed Adam's soul, eating away the peace and joy that once resided there. And when he and his mate heard the Presence—the sovereign Creator—walking in the garden, they instinctively cowered, ducking behind the brush.

Shame filled them, flushing their faces with heat, widening their eyes with fear at what was to come. The Presence. Judgment.

"What's that sound?" Eve whispered again.

But they both knew exactly who it was and why he had come.

Tuesday

A LOOK AT THE MAN

For the Man Who Has Everything

Try to imagine what it must have been like to wake up for the first time as a grown man—to rub the sleep from your eyes and not know anything about anything. This is exactly what happened to Adam. Everything was unfamiliar and new. His mind must have spun with possible scenarios of who he was and who put him in the garden.

The first few days of Adam's life were an indescribable sequence of extrasensory experiences, like checking into one of those opulent European hotels, all expenses paid—only much better and much more extravagant. Everywhere he turned he saw lavish beauty. And because no other man was in sight, Adam rightly assumed that all of this belonged to him.

And if that wasn't enough, Adam's great longing—for perfect human companionship—was completely satisfied with the creation of a woman, her face lovely and radiant, her companionship pleasing, her affection for him alone.

Every day the Life section of *USA Today* tells of the rich and famous, the accomplished and gifted, the successful and powerful— the beautiful people. But if ever there were such a person, Adam was surely the man who had everything. How could he possibly want for more?

But, incredibly, he *did* want more. He refused to be satisfied with what God had provided for his pleasure. His heart was piqued with a hint of discontent. He wanted to go his own way, to do what he wanted to do, to be his own man.

And so the only thing God had told him to avoid became the very thing he submitted to. Willing to sacrifice his abundance on the altar of this temptation, Adam, the man who had absolutely everything, lost absolutely everything. All of this ruin over a silly bite of fruit he was told to avoid. What a foolish wager. What a waste of paradise.

The man who has it all risks it all on something shameful and inconsequential. But doesn't this sound strangely familiar? Of course it does. Every once in a while the beautiful people in the Life section find their way to the News section—indicted for shoplifting, embezzlement, fraud, assault, and even murder. And so, by their own accord, they exchange their riches for the poverty of embarrassment and exile—a page right out of Genesis 3.

But before we jump to judgment against Adam and these fallen contemporary heroes, we have our own hearts to deal with, don't we? Our longing for more when we have enough. Our sin of discontent in the midst of plenty.

Wednesday

HIS LEGACY IN SCRIPTURE

Read Genesis 1:26–28. *BECAUSE HE KNOWS HIMSELF*
1. Why do you think God made men and women in his image? What does it mean to bear God's image? *TO BE LIKE HIM*
2. God told the first human beings to fill the earth and subdue it. What might that have involved before the fall? What about after the fall?

Read Genesis 2:15–24. *IT IS STRONGLY REQUIRED*
3. What role does obedience play when it comes to enjoying the good God intends for us? Think of instances in your own life that have required obedience. How have you experienced God's goodness during such times? *WHEN I AM OBEDIENT HE BLESSES ME*
4. God saw that Adam was incomplete without a partner. And Adam seemed delighted by the woman God made for him. When married couples blend their lives to do God's will, God's initial plan is carried forward. What makes couples who have a strong marriage so effective and happy? *IT IS BUILT AROUND GODS WILL AND THEY LOOK TO HIM FOR GUIDANCE OF THEIR MARRIAGE.*

GOING DEEPER

Read Genesis 3:8–24. *THEY SAW THEMSELVES FULL OF SIN*
5. Why did Adam and Eve suddenly become aware of their nakedness after they disobeyed God? What did their attempt to make clothing for themselves signify? *TRYING TO COVER THEIR SKIN*
6. Why did they hide from God? Think about ways you tend to "hide from God" when you do something wrong.

THEY WERE ASHAMED & FELT GUILT FOR THEIR SIN

Thursday

HIS LEGACY OF PROMISE

Adam's story offers a glimpse of the good life God intended for all of us. He was the first to commune with God, the first to look at everything beautiful, the first to enjoy an intimate relationship with his wife, the first to be given satisfying work at which he could certainly succeed. Utter peace, perfect health, supreme confidence—all these were his. Unfortunately, Adam, along with Eve, was also the first to lead the way into sin—into that dark tunnel full of misery and death. Still, Adam retained his status as a creature made in God's image, even though that image became suddenly distorted. Fortunately, God has initiated a plan to restore his image in the children of Adam (that's us) by making us the children of the new Adam (that's Christ).

Promises in Scripture

Because of the LORD's great love we are not consumed,
for his compassions never fail.
They are new every morning;
great is your faithfulness.

—Lamentations 3:22–23

For as in Adam all die, so in Christ all will be made alive.

—1 Corinthians 15:22

"Where, O death, is your victory?
Where, O death, is your sting?"

The sting of death is sin, and the power of sin is the law. But thanks be to God! He gives us the victory through our Lord Jesus Christ.

—1 Corinthians 15:55–57

Friday

HIS LEGACY OF PRAYER

The LORD God took the man and put him in the Garden of Eden to work it and take care of it. And the LORD God commanded the man, "You are free to eat from any tree in the garden; but you must not eat from the tree of the knowledge of good and evil, for when you eat of it you will surely die." —Genesis 2:15–17

Reflect On: Genesis 2:8–25

Praise God: For creating you in his own image.

Offer Thanks: For the work God has given you, whether it's easy or hard—or, more likely, a mixture of both.

Confess: Any discontent, disobedience, or mistrust that prevents you from enjoying the good things God intends for your life.

Ask God: To help you understand the link between obedience and blessing.

Every day offers us another chance. Either we can become more like Adam, the natural man who follows his own independent course, or we can become more like Christ, the supernatural man who depends on God for everything in his life. Take a few minutes today to slow down and ask yourself where God is requiring your obedience. Maybe he wants you to look for a new job, to keep putting up with your old job, to spend more time with your children, or to get help with a persistent sin. Whatever it is, don't hide from the truth, but face it, trusting that if God is showing it to you, he will help you make the change and bless you in the process.

Father, you know how hard it is for me to rely on anyone but myself. I don't like the idea of depending on someone else. Help me, God, to learn how to trust and obey you no matter how "unnatural" it may feel. Help me to remember the example of my brother, Jesus, who depended on you for everything and who never once went his own way.

Cain and Abel

CAIN

His Work:	As the first child of Adam and Eve, Cain chose farming as his profession.
His Character:	He failed to be generous and was quick to be defensive and outright violent.
His Sorrow:	Like his father, Adam, Cain discovered God's severe punishment for his sin.
His Triumph:	In spite of God's curse on Cain's livelihood, God also promised to protect the man from his enemies.
Key Scripture:	Genesis 4

ABEL

His Name May Be Related to a Hebrew Word for "Breath"

His Work:	Cain's younger brother, Abel, was the keeper of flocks.
His Character:	He was willing to offer the best he had to the Lord.
His Sorrow:	Brutally murdered at the hand of his brother, Cain.
His Triumph:	"Well done, good and faithful servant."
Key Scripture:	Genesis 4

Monday

THEIR STORY

Cain hurriedly wiped his fingers on his tunic, desperate to rid himself of the stain. But blood is more difficult to remove than common dirt.

"Cain, where's your brother?"

Cain spun around at the sound of the voice, the question reverberating in his chest. His heart raced with panic. Cain had carefully checked to be sure no one was about when he and Abel had walked into the field.

Apparently he hadn't been careful enough.

Cain scanned the meadow, as if looking for Abel himself. How can this be? Abel is dead! "I don't know," he said finally, pausing as an idea crossed his mind. Cain lifted his head, tilting it slightly in feigned confidence. "Am I my brother's keeper?"

"What have you done?" the voice spoke again, ignoring Cain's question.

Finally suspecting that whoever was addressing him already knew the answer to the question, Cain did not speak, could not speak. Terror flooded his heart.

"Listen! Your brother's blood cries out to me from the ground."

Cain absently lifted his stained hands to his tunic once again, instinctively trying to wipe them clean.

"Now," the voice continued, "you are under a curse and driven from the ground, which opened its mouth to receive your brother's blood from your hand."

Cain stopped trying to clean his hands and stood motionless before the sound of the voice. He tried to comprehend the impact of what he was hearing. *The earth is my life,* he thought to himself. *Without the land, my family and I will surely starve.*

The voice spoke once more, pronouncing the severest sentence. "When you work the land, it will no longer yield its crops for you. You will be a restless wanderer on the earth."

Cain fell to the ground in grief and shame. He knew the living God threatened him with the loss of all he knew, all he held dear. "My punishment is more than I can bear," he cried out. "Today you are driving me from the land, and I will be hidden from your presence; I will be a restless wanderer on the earth, and whoever finds me will kill me."

The gravity of Cain's sin raced toward him like a boulder tipped from the edge of a cliff, hurtling downward with gathering speed. The consequences were worse than he could have imagined. How long would he even be able to cling to his own life, if not his livelihood?

And then Cain heard the voice of the Lord once more. But this time he detected a hint of compassion. "If anyone kills Cain," God said, "he will suffer vengeance seven times over." Then the Lord put a mark on Cain to seal this promise.

Cain slowly walked from the field where he had just murdered his younger brother. His heart was heavy with remorse for what he had done. The Lord had declared Cain's terrible, costly sentence but had granted him mercy and protection on his life.

The man looked at his hands once more—hands that had taken his only brother's life and that had once caressed the earth, making it flourish with bounty, hands that now would be forced to learn a new trade.

So Cain began again, this time as a builder. He found a wife and started a family. His first son—and his first city—was named Enoch, or "consecrated."

Cain did not name his firstborn and building project haphazardly. His calloused hands would always remind him of the blood of his brother and the sentence tinged with mercy that a holy God had pronounced on his life.

Tuesday

A LOOK AT THE MEN

Boys Will Be Boys

How could two brothers turn out so different?

Adam and Eve's first two children were boys. And, as siblings often do when they grow up, they chose different vocations.

Cain became an agriculturist. Working the soil, planting, and caring for his crops were his greatest delights. Cain's brother, Abel, became a herdsman. Tending, feeding, and protecting livestock became his occupation. Two good choices.

Both of these men knew God, introduced by parents who must have told them many stories of their own encounters with the Creator. Some of these accounts would have been painful recollections of Adam and Eve's sin and corresponding punishment. And others would have included God's mercy and grace—his loving pursuit of his wayward children, their remorse, their sacrifice and restoration to fellowship. The boys must have known these stories very well.

And so Adam and Eve's sons offered the results of their vocations to the Lord. Cain brought fruits, and his younger brother, Abel, brought animals to offer to God.

When one of Abel's flocks or herds delivered her firstborn, that animal was earmarked. *This one belongs to the Lord,* he thought to himself. *It's the most prized and perfect.*

But like a man reaching into his pocket for a little loose change to toss into the passing offering plate, Cain only brought "some of the fruits of the soil." *This will have to be good enough,* he reasoned. The premier crops he wanted to reserve for himself.

The offering *might* have been good enough for Cain, but his brother had done better. So like the laggard in school who resented the one who prepared for the test and spoiled the curve, Cain became "very angry." This was compounded, of course, because the "teacher"—the Lord himself—looked with favor on Abel's offering but with disfavor on Cain's.

Cain plotted against his faithful and obedient brother. "Let's go out to the field," he told his younger sibling. And there he killed him.

In the moments that followed, Cain heard God pronounce a life-long sentence on his life. But God also promised his protection on the man. For the remainder of his life, Cain must have wondered why God had not killed him after what he had done to Abel. Instead, his life sentence was to live with the memory of his sin, while never forgetting the mystery—and the bounty—of God's grace and mercy.

Wednesday

THEIR LEGACY IN SCRIPTURE

Read Genesis 4:8–16.

1. Genesis 4:7 indicates that God was primarily concerned with the attitude of each brother's heart. What does this say about God's ability to discern our motives? About the difference between true worship and mere religious behavior? *They come from the heart. True worship is from heart*

2. God told Cain that "sin was crouching at your door" and admonished him to "master it." It's easy to picture a hideous creature lunging at Cain as soon as he commits the world's first murder. How can you avoid falling prey to sin? *Gods word, prayer, relationship w/God*

3. God warned Adam and Eve that eating from the tree of the knowledge of good and evil would result in death. How tragic that their firstborn son would follow in their footsteps, shutting his ears to God, and that their second son would be the world's first fatality (v. 8). What does this say about the rapidly escalating power of sin and its ability to thread its way through families? *It knows no boundary*

4. Adam and Eve, the first mother and father, must have been close to despair when they learned they had lost both of their sons—one to death and the other to exile. How do you feel when you see one of your own children straying from God? What can you do to help prevent this? *It would break my heart. Show them my own relationship w/ Him*

GOING DEEPER

5. Cain's sin, stemming from anger at God and his brother, resulted in alienation—from God, from the land, from his brother, from his entire family. When, if ever, have you experienced this kind of alienation? How did it happen? *Right after H.S. walked away from God.*

6. Even though God drove Adam and Eve from the Garden of Eden, he did not abandon them. Where can you find evidence of this in the story of Cain and Abel? How have you experienced God reaching out to you despite your sin? *He came to Cain and told him he was still there. Yes after being away God came to me and reminded me he was still there*

Thursday

THEIR LEGACY OF PROMISE

Abel enjoyed the Lord's favor. Nevertheless, God did not protect him from the consequences of his brother's sin, and he became the world's first murder victim. If any comfort can be taken from Abel's story, it is that God knows our suffering ("Your brother's blood cries out to me from the ground," he tells Cain in Genesis 4:10). Human beings are easily deceived when it comes to justice, but God has no trouble distinguishing the guilty from the innocent. If you or someone you love has been brutalized by another's sin or violence, you can be confident that God knows all about it and that he will certainly do something to punish the guilty. Sooner or later, now or hereafter, there will be a price to pay.

Promises in Scripture

> The LORD has become my fortress,
>   and my God the rock in whom I take refuge.
> He will repay them for their sins
>   and destroy them for their wickedness;
>   the LORD our God will destroy them.

—Psalm 94:22–23

> He will judge the world in righteousness
>   and the peoples in his truth.

—Psalm 96:13

> A righteous man will be remembered forever. . . .
> in the end he will look in triumph on his foes.

—Psalm 112:6, 8

Friday

THEIR LEGACY OF PRAYER

Then the LORD *said to Cain, "Why are you angry? Why is your face downcast? If you do what is right, will you not be accepted? But if you do not do what is right, sin is crouching at your door; it desires to have you, but you must master it."* —Genesis 4:6–7

Reflect On: Genesis 4

Praise God: Because nothing escapes him. He knows the state of our hearts.

Offer Thanks: That God hasn't left us in the dark, but speaks clearly to us about what he requires.

Confess: Any patterns of anger that make you more vulnerable to sin.

Ask God: To search your heart and free you from the root causes of your anger.

Anger is an emotion common to everyone on the planet. In itself, it's neither right nor wrong. But if we lean into our anger and it becomes the energy that fuels us, then we need to repent and find ways to defuse it before it consumes us and everyone around us. If you detect patterns of anger in your own life, ask God to help you overcome them. He may lead you into a special time of prayer and fasting. He may want you to confide in a trusted friend or a minister on a regular basis. He may want you to talk to your spouse or to a professional who can help you as you try to form new patterns of responding to life. Let the Lord lead you. Believe that he will. When he tells you to master sin, he doesn't mean that you should simply grit your teeth and stop sinning. Instead, he wants you to depend on him so that you can experience his power at work, making you more like him.

Father, I admit that anger has sometimes controlled me, spilling over and hurting other people—my spouse, my children, those I work and do business with. Please help me to learn how to express my anger in healthy, not hurtful, ways. I know that all the willpower in the world won't make a bit of difference unless you give me the grace to change.

NOAH

His Name Means "To Rest"

His Work:	We don't know what Noah did for a living before he heard from God, but following that encounter, he became an accomplished carpenter.
His Character:	Noah was a righteous man, obedient and faithful.
His Sorrow:	In spite of his admonitions and warnings, Noah was unable to convince his neighbors, friends, and extended family to repent. As a result, they were all drowned in the flood.
His Triumph:	Noah's obedience saved not only his life but the lives of his wife and children.
Key Scriptures:	Genesis 6–7

Monday

HIS STORY

The sound of muffled weeping awakened the woman. Reaching out, she gently touched her husband's shoulder. Pulling her body close to his, she held him until the sobbing subsided.

No words were spoken. No explanation was necessary. Over the years, she had slowly watched her husband become isolated from his family and friends. His righteous life was enough to keep him at arm's length from most people. But he had "heard God's voice" and undertaken the most massive—and ridiculous—building project anyone had ever seen. Her husband had built an enormous boat—in their backyard.

She had questioned him many times, gently at first, then more and more pointedly as the years had passed. Frankly, this undertaking had been an embarrassment to her. But in time she had learned to trust her husband and their God, and so she had supported and loved Noah.

Tonight she held him close as she had through the years and years of frustration and fear and wakeful nights. This time, however, the methodical rocking motion of the boat in which they were lying brought them welcomed sleep.

From the time his father, Lamech, had told him of the immortal God and the need to live righteously, Noah had sought to be obedient and to follow the God of his father. Most of the time, Noah could ignore the derision and segregation from others—others who noted his loyalty to God's ways and hated him for it. But sometimes the loneliness became too much to bear, especially during the solitude of the night.

Nine generations had passed since Eden. The unsullied garden and the pristine world surrounding it had become a cesspool of debauchery and sin. Violence, corruption, and sexual lewdness were not only commonplace but were so prevalent they were going unnoticed—except by the mournful eye of the Creator himself.

Early one day as Noah walked through the morning mist, he heard the voice of God. There had been other times when Noah had sensed or felt the voice of the Lord, but this time was different. This time God's voice was audible and clear—and his words were shocking.

"I am going to put an end to all people, for the earth is filled with violence because of them. I am surely going to destroy both them and the earth." Then the Lord laid out his plan to his servant, who cowered in fear at God's awful words and crazy directions. "Collect your tools ... gather supplies ... and build a boat. A very big boat. I am going to bring floodwaters on the earth to destroy all life under the heavens, every creature that has the breath of life in it. Everything on earth will perish."

Noah struggled to comprehend such a thought. *Total destruction of the earth?* But God wasn't finished. God instructed Noah to collect two of every kind of bird and animal and to place them in the boat along with his family.

Completely dazed by what he had just heard but determined to be obedient, Noah did everything just as God commanded him.

But as the days melted into weeks and the weeks into months . . . and the months into years, Noah grew tired. The physical labor took its toll on the man, but the incessant mocking from many whom he had once called friends found a foothold in his soul.

"What's the matter, Noah?" they jeered. "Did you forget that you live in the desert? How are you going to get that monstrosity to the sea?"

"Have you gone mad?"

Noah wondered if they were right. But over and over, he went back to the words he had heard from God, determined to remain true to his original mission.

Decades passed, and finally the work was finished. Built to God's precise specifications, the ark was ready for its occupants—and the flood.

Diligently Noah collected two of every creature, shepherding them into the craft. Finally, the ominous task was complete. Each living thing nestled in its rightful cubicle in the massive boat. Noah's ark rose from the desert floor like a great and mighty monument to his obedience.

Then the Lord spoke to his faithful servant, "Go into the ark, you and your whole family, because I have found you righteous in this generation. . . . Seven days from now I will send rain on the earth for forty days and forty nights, and I will wipe from the face of the earth every living creature I have made."

Finally, once everyone—including Noah's own precious children—was on board, the Lord shut him in.

And the rains fell.

Noah's neighbors and friends and cousins died, groping for air, some clinging to the boat until they could no longer hold on. Now every single one was drowned and gone.

And in the darkness of the night, aboard a massive, noisy ship floating on an endless sea, the thought of that brought Noah to tears.

Tuesday

A LOOK AT THE MAN

All Aboard

Once in a while a man comes along who's not afraid to obey.

We cannot imagine what it must have been like to be Noah. He lived in a culture that was corrupted by immorality and violence. According to the story, the earth was literally "full" of it.

So reprehensible were people's lives that God regretted having created these divine image-bearers. So much so that he decided to remove every living thing from the face of the earth, like a man clearing a table with the back of his hand. Can you imagine?

But on his way to starting all over again, the Lord looked at Noah. His life was so exemplary that in the middle of all this debauchery, he found favor in God's eyes. This man, Noah, was righteous and blameless among the people of his time. Because of his faithfulness, he was the one man whom the Lord chose not to destroy.

We don't have to look very far to find a lesson in this man's life. Like Noah's culture, the one that surrounds us is drowning in immorality, corruption, and violence. And like Noah, we can choose to quietly capitulate or to stand against it. Once we decide to stand firm—to live in obedience to God—the tricky part comes with trying to understand how. What does submission to him look like? And what should we expect as the result of this obedience?

Tucked away in this story is the secret to Noah's success. Noah walked with God. For Noah, surrender was not a single decision or noteworthy event; it was a process. A routine. A journey. A walk. Obedience was the natural result of this methodical approach. Walking with God meant knowing him. Knowing God meant loving him. Loving meant hearing. Hearing, obeying.

And obeying God meant salvation.

We can imagine that decades of subtle and overt ridicule may have led Noah to question God. There had to have been moments of loneliness and genuine doubt. But taking one step at a time along the path God had laid out for him kept Noah on track.

Noah's obedience led to the preservation of not only his own life, but of the lives of his wife and children. Once the project was complete and everyone around him had rejected the notion that God would actually destroy the earth with a catastrophic flood, Noah and his whole family entered the safety of the ark. Then the Lord shut him in. Noah's obedience not only led to the preservation of his own life but the lives of his wife and children.

In fact, Noah's faithfulness—in the form of a great ark—became one of the early church's symbols for refuge. The interiors of many great cathedrals were built to resemble the inside of a boat—a shelter in the time of storm, a reminder of an obedient man who went before us and was saved.

Wednesday

HIS LEGACY IN SCRIPTURE

Read Genesis 6:5–22. *DISAPPOINTED / HURT*

1. How do you think God feels when we distort his image in us by our selfishness, greed, and violence? Do you think God is injured by sin? Why or why not? *NO . HE CAN'T BE INJURED*

2. Put yourself in Noah's place (vv. 9–11). What does it feel like to follow God even though everyone around you is heading in the opposite direction? *IT IS HARD . TEMPTING TO GO WITH THE FLOW*

3. God did not completely destroy the world but carried out a plan to renew it. What does this say about his mercy? How can you reflect mercy to those who are not living for God? *HE HAS ALOT . EVERY DAY WERE ALIVE . GOD SENDING HIS SON TO DIE*

4. God saved not only Noah but his wife, his sons, and their wives. What does this say about the way God's blessings work within a family? How have you experienced God blessing your own family? *IT INVOLVE EVERYONE . MY JOB, HOME , HEALTH*

Read Genesis 9:8–16.

5. God promised to "remember" his covenant whenever a rainbow appeared in the clouds. "To remember" in the Bible refers not simply to recalling something but to being concerned for or caring for it. How does Noah's story speak about God's care for the world after the flood? *HE WANTS WHATS BEST FOR US EVEN IF HE HAS TO DISCIPLINE US*

INTERESTING FACTS

See Genesis 5.

- It's tempting to dismiss genealogies in Scripture as long, boring lists of unfamiliar names. But careful reading often yields interesting insights. Keep in mind that the most important names in any biblical genealogy are usually the first and the last, in this case Adam and Noah (along with his sons). The meaning of Noah's name is connected to ideas of "rest" or "bringing relief." When Noah's father named him (v. 29), he associated the name with relief from the curse originally placed on Adam.

- Scholars believe that some of the numbers in this genealogy may be interpreted symbolically; for example, Enoch's 365 years parallel a full year and may therefore signify a full life.

See Genesis 8:11.

- Olive trees grow only at lower altitudes. When the dove returned to the ark with a freshly plucked olive leaf in its beak, Noah realized how far the water had receded. The dove with an olive branch in its beak has become a universally recognized symbol of peace.

Thursday

HIS LEGACY OF PROMISE

To many of us the word *rainbow* conjures up a picture of something trite, a colorful poster tacked onto the wall in a little girl's bedroom or a happily-ever-after ending pasted onto a fairy tale. But as a natural phenomenon, rainbows are far more impressive than their "greeting card" counterparts. The next time you see one, let it remind you of a supernatural phenomenon—of God's promise to remain faithful to his covenant. If you have suffered your own "personal flood," a time of difficulty that has washed away an old way of life and ushered in a new one, let it be a reminder that God has a plan to give you a future that is full of his goodness.

Promises in Scripture

Whenever the rainbow appears in the clouds, I will see it and remember the everlasting covenant between God and all living creatures of every kind on the earth.   —Genesis 9:16

There is a future for the man of peace.   —Psalm 37:37

> *"Though the mountains be shaken*
> *and the hills be removed,*
> *yet my unfailing love for you will not be shaken*
> *nor my covenant of peace be removed,"*
> *says the LORD, who has compassion on you.*
>   —Isaiah 54:10

Friday

HIS LEGACY OF PRAYER

Noah found favor in the eyes of the LORD. . . . Noah was a righteous man, blameless among the people of his time, and he walked with God.
—Genesis 6:8–9

Reflect On: Genesis 8

Praise God: For using his followers to accomplish his purposes.

Offer Thanks: For God's mercy toward the human race.

Confess: Any tendency to care more about what the world thinks of you than about what God thinks.

Ask God: To show you what it means, not just to obey a set of laws, but to stay close to him throughout your life— to walk with him.

What would have happened had Noah not found favor with God, if his heart had been as wayward as every other man's? Would God have spared the human race even though he couldn't find a single person worth saving? Or would the world simply have vanished? End of story. *Finis. Caput.* Noah's experience of God reminds us of the importance of one good life. No matter how difficult it may be to remain faithful, no matter how insignificant your life may sometimes seem, no life is small in God's sight. It doesn't matter what your natural gifts are or how much money you make or how fit you seem or how clever you may be. God looks at your heart. Nothing else. If he finds his own reflection there, he will use you—and it will surprise you to someday realize just how powerfully his grace has been at work through you— transforming your family, your work, and the world around you.

Lord, give me the courage to follow you even when those around me are heading in another direction. Help me to stay close to you, not walling you out of my life, but inviting you in. Help me to listen for your voice. Make quick obedience part of my character. Use me in ways that will help others to celebrate your faithfulness.

ABRAHAM

His Name Means "Father of a Multitude"

His Work:	A tender of livestock.
His Character:	Abraham was a man of faith who followed God even in the most challenging of circumstances.
His Sorrow:	At times Abraham compromised God's instructions.
His Triumph:	Abraham obeyed God, and God blessed him with a son in his old age.
Key Scriptures:	Genesis 12–23

Monday

HIS STORY

One by one, Abraham took the pieces of wood he had cut, stacking them on his young son's back. Then he slipped his knife into his belt, took the torch from his servant, and began walking up the steep slope of the mountain—just he and his boy.

Then, almost as an afterthought, he turned and said to his servants as they prepared to follow, "We will worship and then we will come back to you."

Abraham and Isaac walked along in silence. Since they had left on their journey three days before, Isaac could tell that something was troubling his father. The spontaneity and camaraderie that marked their relationship was gone. Conversation had seemed strained and wooden.

Unknown to Isaac, the day before they left home, God had ordered Abraham to sacrifice Isaac as a burnt offering on one of the mountains. Abraham had waited a lifetime for this son. Now God was asking the most terrible sacrifice a man could imagine, a sacrifice that seemed to contradict the promise God had made so many years before, to give him a son and heir, to make of him a nation uniquely blessed.

Along the journey, Isaac hadn't had the courage to ask if anything was wrong. In fact, something told him that this awkward silence had something to do with him, so it was best left unexplored. He'd learn soon enough.

"Father," Isaac finally said as they made their way up the trail.

"Yes, my son."

"The fire and the wood are here ... but where is the lamb for the burnt offering?"

Like spears, Isaac's words must have plunged themselves into Abraham, deepening his distress—even panic—but he wasn't going to let his son in on any notion of uncertainty. Mustering all the courage he could, Isaac's father spoke. "God himself will provide."

When the man and his son reached the spot God had told Abraham about, they stopped. Propping the burning torch against a rock, he took the wood from Isaac's back and carefully laid it out over a heap of stones to form an altar. Neither of them spoke, but the emotion of the moment must have been overwhelming. *God himself will provide. God himself will provide. God himself will provide.* The cadence of this assurance repeated itself in Abraham's mind as he put the wood in place.

Pulling the thong from his sandal, Abraham nodded toward his only son. Silently and without resistance, the boy stepped forward. With the leather string, Abraham tied his son's hands together and lifted him onto the altar.

Did God not promise? Abraham must have reviewed God's promise as he removed his knife from its sheath. *Your wife Sarah will bear you a son. . . . I will establish my covenant with him for his descendants after him.* And then he must have wondered, *How can this be if this covenant son is dead?*

Extending his arm above the boy, Abraham lifted the knife, ready to plunge it into the chest of his precious son.

God himself will provide, Abraham breathed one last time.

"Abraham! Abraham!" The words from an emissary of the sovereign God literally shook the ground.

"Here I am," Abraham responded. His arm did not move.

"Do not lay a hand on the boy. . . . Do not do anything to him."

The sinews in Abraham's arm released as it collapsed to his side, the knife dropping harmlessly to the ground.

"Now I know that you fear God, because you have not withheld from me your son, your only son."

At that moment, Abraham looked and saw a ram that had tangled its horns in a thicket. He walked to the bush, released the ram, and brought it back to the altar. Picking up his knife, Abraham cut the strap that had bound Isaac.

The boy crawled down from the altar as his father laid the ram on the same spot where Isaac had just been lying. Pulling the sharp knife across the animal's throat, Abraham and Isaac watched as the ram's blood spilled down the wood and onto the ground.

Emotion welled up in Abraham's soul. God himself had provided.

Once again God's messenger spoke in an audible voice. "Because you have done this and have not withheld your son, your only son, I will surely bless you and make your descendants as numerous as the stars in the sky and as the sand on the seashore. . . . All nations on earth will be blessed, because you have obeyed me."

Once the sacrifice was finished, the final embers extinguished, Abraham and his son descended the mountain. Going down a hill is always easier than climbing up, but without the burden of the wood and the anguish of heart, the ease of the downward slope was even more wonderful. Abraham's obedience would be bountifully rewarded.

Tuesday

A LOOK AT THE MAN

God Will Provide

The life of Abraham is a study in faithfulness, obedience, and sometimes blind trust. It's also the story of a God who keeps his covenant promises.

Abram (later named Abraham) and his wife Sarai (later named Sarah) lived in Haran where Abraham was a prosperous livestock owner. By all accounts, he was comfortable. But an order from the living God changed all that.

"Leave your country, your people and your father's household and go to the land I will show you." God did not mince his words. He didn't even ask Abraham to consider moving. He *told* him to go. And to make it even more of a challenge, God didn't specify Abraham's destination. He only said, "Go." And then God made Abraham a promise. "I will make you into a great nation and I will bless you."

It's hard to imagine how shocking this news was to Abraham. And when Sarah heard Abraham's report of what God had said, she must have been overwhelmed. "Leave our home? Go on a journey to nowhere? Have children even though we are barren?"

But Sarah trusted Abraham, just as Abraham trusted God. They said good-bye to their families and, along with their nephew, Lot, their possessions, and a caravan of servants, they set out southwest toward Canaan, the area where Abraham's descendants would call "home" to this day.

Time and again, throughout his life, God tested Abraham's resolve to obey him. And, time and again, God reconfirmed his promise to Abraham—a land, a nation, and a blessing.

Abraham is the most revered of the patriarchs. His name and God's promise of a nation were even recalled as Mary accepted her call to be the mother of Jesus. "God has helped His servant Israel, remembering to be merciful to Abraham and his descendants forever even as he promised."

But Abraham's place in history is not only well established because of the millions who count themselves as his offspring. Nor is Abraham honored because he was a perfect man. He wasn't.

Abraham is the most significant patriarch because of God's call and covenant with him and Abraham's remarkable courage to be obedient.

Wednesday

HIS LEGACY IN SCRIPTURE

Read Genesis 22:1.
1. What did it mean for Abraham to be "tested" by God? When have you ever felt that God might be testing you? How did you respond?

Read Genesis 17:15–16 and Genesis 22:2.
2. By commanding Abraham to sacrifice his "only son," "the son whom you love," God seemed to be both emphasizing the difficulty of what he was asking and contradicting the promise he had made to Abraham. When have you ever had difficulty believing God's promises? What in Abraham's story can help you believe and obey God regardless of your circumstances?

Read Genesis 22:6–8 and John 19:16–18.
3. Compare these passages. How many similarities can you find between the story of Abraham and Isaac and the story of God and Jesus?

Read Genesis 22:9–14, 16–18.
4. Put yourself in Abraham's place. Consider how difficult his obedience must have been. Then consider his relief and joy as Isaac is spared. How has God's provision affected your life?
5. Faith runs along the lines of God's promises. In other words, our faith will not be disappointed if we put it to work in connection with the promises God has clearly made. But God's promises often have conditions attached to them. How is that evident in Abraham's story?

INTERESTING FACT

Moriah signifies the "place of provision of Yahweh." Though scholars have not been able to identify the exact location of the mountain where Abraham brought his son to be sacrificed, some ancient sources identify it with a site in Jerusalem, on which the Dome of the Rock (a Moslem mosque) currently sits. Interestingly, the Dome of the Rock, located on the Temple Mount, is just a few hundred yards from the Church of the Holy Sepulchre, traditionally identified as the site of Jesus' crucifixion.

Thursday

HIS LEGACY OF PROMISE

More than any other in the Old Testament, Abraham's story is linked with the promises of God. He leaves his homeland because God promises to give him another. He is amazed when God promises him a son at the age of one hundred, especially since his wife, Sarah, will be ninety when she gives birth! He leads his son up a mountain to be sacrificed even though this child is the living embodiment of God's promise. As a result of his faith, he sees the incredible provision of God. As the result of his obedience, Abraham becomes the father, not just of one child or even one nation, but of a multitude of people across time and space, as numerous as the stars in the sky and the sand on the seashore.

Promises in Scripture

> *I will make your name great,*
> *and you will be a blessing.*
> *I will bless those who bless you,*
> *and whoever curses you I will curse.*
>
> —Genesis 12:2–3

> *I will establish my covenant as an everlasting covenant between me and you and your descendants after you for the generations to come, to be your God and the God of your descendants after you.* —Genesis 17:7

> *Through your offspring all nations on earth will be blessed, because you have obeyed me.* —Genesis 22:18

Friday

HIS LEGACY OF PRAYER

"Do not be afraid, Abram.
I am your shield,
your very great reward."

—Genesis 15:1

Reflect On: Genesis 12:10–20

Praise God: For not hiding his plans but revealing his intentions through the promises he has made.

Offer Thanks: For the way you have benefited from this one man's obedience.

Confess: Your failure at times to believe God's promises.

Ask God: To enable you to make faith visible through your obedience.

The story of Abraham and Isaac on Mount Moriah is one of the most moving in the Bible. But Abraham's story begins well before that, revealing a man who sometimes displayed very little faith. His failures and compromises are key to his story because they show us we are dealing with a human being rather than a cardboard cutout. His responses convince us that faith grows not in the absence of struggle but in the midst of it. Like Abraham, we too face setbacks and successes in our life with God. The key to growing more mature in faith is not to focus on our failures but to focus on God's patient, enabling grace.

Lord, you blessed Abraham with land and children and wealth. You used him in ways he could not imagine. But the best promise of all was that you would be his shield and his very great reward. Lord, be my shield too, as well as my very great reward.

ISAAC

His Name Means "He Laughs"

His Work: Isaac was an accomplished farmer and herdsman.

His Character: The only son of Abraham and Sarah, Isaac at a young age witnessed, through the faithfulness of his father, the meaning of obedience. He was gentle and hard-working.

His Sorrow: As an old and feeble man, Isaac was victimized by the deception of his son Jacob and to his later dismay gave him the blessing that he had intended for his older son, Esau.

His Triumph: Isaac is considered one of the three great patriarchs. For millennia his progeny have revered him.

Key Scriptures: Genesis 25–27

Monday

HIS STORY

Isaac always kept an eye on the sky. When there was plenty of rain, his crops flourished. But when there was no rain, there was no harvest. And when there was no harvest, it was time to move on.

The rain had stopped falling. Months passed and the soil turned to dust. Famine settled like a cracked, leathery hide over the gaunt bones of Canaan. Isaac packed up his belongings and moved with his wife to the region of Gerar, a territory of the Philistines, to the place the Lord had sent him.

As a courtesy, Isaac called on King Abimelech to tell the Philistine monarch of his plans and to obtain his consent. "My king, I ask for your permission," Isaac said. "We would like to make a home in the northern portion of this beautiful land."

"You and yours are welcome here," Abimelech greeted him.

Isaac studied the king, wondering at his ready greeting. Was it because he had heard of Isaac's former successes as a farmer? Did he know of Isaac and Isaac's God from the notoriety of his father, Abraham? Or was it because of the beautiful woman who accompanied him?

As Isaac watched, the king's eyes scanned Rebekah from head to toe. "And who is this woman beside you?"

Afraid that someone might kill him to get to her, Isaac tore a page from his father's playbook. "She is my sister," he lied, ignoring her puzzled expression and shielding her from the king and his men.

It didn't take long for the truth to be known, however. One day Abimelech glanced through a window and caught Isaac and Rebekah in a tender embrace.

"She is really your wife!" he said. "Why did you say, 'She is my sister'? What is this you have done to us? One of the men might have slept with your wife, and you would have brought guilt upon us."

With this deception discovered, Abimelech could have thrown Isaac out of his domain. Or worse, he could have executed Isaac for lying to him. But he did neither. Instead, the king issued a decree: "Anyone who molests this man or his wife shall surely be put to death."

Utterly relieved, Isaac went back to work planting crops and raising livestock. Season by season, his success brought him great personal wealth, spreading his borders, outdistancing his neighbors. The king's decision to honor Isaac and keep him in business in the land proved wise.

But Isaac had plenty of detractors. Their jealousy over the king's kindness to Isaac coupled with this outsider's great success—and stunning wife—made these small-minded enemies miserable. And so they filled his wells with dirt, hoping to put him out of business.

Knowing of his people's growing animosity toward Isaac, Abimelech asked Isaac to leave. "Move away from us. You have become too powerful for us."

So, in honor of the king's request and for their own safety, Isaac and Rebekah moved to the valley of Gerar. There Isaac found wells, cisterns that his father had dug and that the Philistines had also stopped up. But Isaac ran into opposition once more. The locals were not happy to have Isaac settle in their land. "This water is ours," they quarreled. As he reopened the wells, Isaac gave them names signifying the antagonism he faced. One he named "Esek," which meant contention. Another he named "Sitnah," which meant hostility.

Isaac christened another one of these wells "Rehoboth" (meaning "broad places"), saying, "Now the LORD has given us room and we will flourish in the land." Nothing could have more thoroughly summarized Isaac's vision.

After some time had passed, King Abimelech and two of his advisers paid Isaac a visit. He was understandably shocked to see the king and asked, "Why have you come to me, since you were hostile to me and sent me away?"

Their answer may have been as bewildering to Isaac as their surprise visit had been. "We saw clearly that the LORD was with you; so we said, 'There ought to be a sworn agreement between us' . . . that you will do us no harm, just as we did not molest you but always treated you well and sent you away in peace.'"

Then they added, "And now you are blessed by the LORD."

Isaac called his servants together and ordered them to prepare a feast for Abimelech and his advisers. The evening must have been filled with great celebration, because early the next morning the men swore an oath to each other. Then Isaac sent them on their way, and they left him in peace.

Isaac's heart was filled with gratitude and joy. Even these pagan leaders recognized God's blessing on his life—the result of covenant promises fulfilled.

Tuesday

A LOOK AT THE MAN

A New Address for Success

When a man is hugely successful in his work, everyone notices. Some of those people celebrate his prosperity; others hate him for it. That is what Isaac experienced. He is one of the early farmers in the Scriptures with a remarkable green thumb. "Isaac planted crops in that land and the same year reaped a hundredfold." But Isaac had a secret—something more powerful than a precise crop rotation strategy or specially formulated fertilizer: The Lord blessed him.

Godly excellence in the marketplace and the generous compensation that often follows it have been subjects of controversy among believers for centuries. Surely Christians are supposed to aspire to serving professions like physicians, missionaries, nurses, and teachers. But is there a place for successful, competitive businesspeople in God's plan as well?

The story of Isaac and Rebekah's years in the land of the Philistines illustrates the answer to these questions—and the reason why. As Isaac and Rebekah were leaving Canaan and looking for a new home, the Lord appeared to Isaac. "Do not go down to Egypt; live in the land where I tell you to live. Stay in this land for a while, and I will be with you and will bless you."

Isaac listened to God's voice and obeyed.

It didn't take too long for him to see that his neighbors were envious. The first time Isaac's servant brought word to him that one of his wells had been filled in with dirt would have been a strong indicator! Nothing specific is said about Isaac's reaction to this act of treachery, but there is no indication that Isaac was angry or vengeful. Instead, he simply sent his servants out to redig the wells or to find places for new ones.

Next, it was the king's turn to pay Isaac a visit. He asked Isaac to move, sounding much like an Egyptian pharaoh hundreds of years later. Once again Isaac could have been upset at such treatment. "After all I've done for you and your people," Isaac could have said to Abimelech, "this is the way you treat me?"

But he didn't. Instead, Isaac and Rebekah moved on, setting up yet another successful business in a new location.

Then Abimelech paid a visit to Isaac. As he greeted Isaac, the Philistine king summarized why he had come and why he wanted to establish a peace treaty with Isaac. "We saw clearly that the LORD was with you."

Why would a man pursue excellence in business?

The story of Isaac clearly gives us the answer: God had called (and gifted) Isaac for this work, and he was obedient; Isaac had shown respect for those in authority over him; he worked hard, and his efforts were productive; and Isaac did not allow the sabotage of his enemies to discourage or distract him.

What was the result of Isaac's faithfulness? God received the glory, and his name was honored among those who previously did not know or revere him.

Wednesday

HIS LEGACY IN SCRIPTURE

Read Genesis 22:6–12.

1. The story of Isaac's near death at the hands of his father is most often considered from Abraham's point of view. But think about Isaac for a moment. What would it have been like to lie on that altar? To escape death by a fraction of a second? To watch as a ram is killed in your place? How do you think this moment shaped the rest of his life?

Read Genesis 26:1–14.

2. What similarities do you note between Isaac's experience and his father Abraham's (Genesis 12:10–13) in this passage (vv. 1–6)?

3. Isaac apparently had enough faith to stay in the land of the Philistines but not enough faith to believe God would protect him while he was there (vv. 7–11). Why do you think he wavered? Have you ever experienced similar wavering in your own life? Reflect on what happened during your time of wavering.

4. Why do you think God blessed Isaac even though Isaac lied about Rebekah (vv. 12–14)?

GOING DEEPER

Read Genesis 21:9–14 and Galatians 4:28–31.

5. Isaac was the child of a promise God had made to two people who were long past childbearing age. As Christians, how are we also children of the promise?

Thursday

HIS LEGACY OF PROMISE

If Abraham was a man whose life was linked with the promise of God, Isaac was the living embodiment of the promise, the first install-ment of all that was to come. He was the first star in the sky full of stars that God had promised to Abraham. For the most part, Isaac enjoyed a peaceful and prosperous life even in the midst of a famine, even while living as a stranger in a strange land. In fact, he became so rich that his envious neighbors spitefully stopped up his wells with dirt and stones. But no amount of ill will could stop the blessings that God was determined to pour out on Abraham's son, child of the promise. And no amount of ill will will prevent the Lord from bless-ing those who belong to him, who are also children of the promise.

Promises in Scripture

I am the God of your father Abraham. Do not be afraid, for I am with you.   —Genesis 26:24

The LORD blesses his people with peace.   —Psalm 29:11

*The blessing of the LORD brings wealth,
and he adds no trouble to it.*
                                                          —Proverbs 10:22

Friday

HIS LEGACY OF PRAYER

Isaac planted crops in that land and the same year reaped a hundredfold, because the LORD blessed him. —Genesis 26:12

Reflect On: Genesis 25:1–31

Praise God: For his generosity.

Offer Thanks: For the ways God has already blessed you and for all the ways he yet intends to bless you.

Confess: Any tendency to take credit for what God has given you.

Ask God: To richly bless your life as you seek to follow him.

If you look at the divine equation in Isaac's story, it's clear that he received much more than he gave. God required only his obedience, which Isaac gave, though imperfectly. In return, Isaac enjoyed the fulfillment of God's promise in the form of land, children, peace, wealth, and long life. The divine equation still works that way. God gives us everything—shelter, daily provision, his own Son to save us. Only a fool would refuse such an offer.

———————

Father, I thank you for all the ways you have promised to bless your people. Help me to understand these promises and to put my faith in you as one who is able to bring them to fulfillment. Whatever you ask of me, help me to obey, trusting that you are who you say you are and that you will do what you say you will.

ESAU

His Name Means "Hairy"

His Work:	An outdoorsman, Esau was an accomplished hunter.
His Character:	The desire for instant gratification was one of Esau's greatest failures. It cost him his birthright.
His Sorrow:	When he realized that Jacob had secured his father's blessing, Esau wept aloud.
His Triumph:	Years later Esau demonstrated the ability to forgive his conniving brother.
Key Scriptures:	Genesis 27; 33

Monday

HIS STORY

"I'm famished," Esau said, setting down his pack with a dull thud. "Give me something to eat or I'll die." The physical rigors of hunting—negotiating the terrain, stalking his prey, and returning home with the trophies draped over his shoulders—had rendered him ravenous, his last meal a distant memory. As he stepped closer to the fire, the aroma of lentil stew overwhelmed his senses. His younger brother, Jacob, stirred the pot, having learned the craft from their mother.

In their finer moments, Esau and Jacob had a worthy partnership—Esau trapped dinner and Jacob turned it into a meal. But on this day, Esau's hunger was predatory. Jacob hungered for something far greater than food.

Jacob hesitated. An opportunity unfolded in his mind and a wry smile formed on his face. "First sell me your birthright," Jacob demanded, lifting an empty bowl toward his fraternal twin as though baiting a hungry fish.

"Give me some of that stew, and you may have it," Esau chortled. "What good is the birthright to me?"

Jacob seized the opportunity. He had his brother exactly where he wanted him. He ceremoniously ladled a portion of stew into Esau's bowl and again lifted it toward his brother, filling the air with the pungent fragrance of onions and herbs. "Swear to me first," he said, holding it just out of reach.

"I swear," Esau muttered as he mockingly raised his hand, "the birthright is yours." Then he swiped the stew from his brother's hand and ate.

So it was.

Esau, a rugged outdoorsman, lorded his stature over his brother. Jacob was never—nor would ever be—a physical match for his brawny twin. But now, without knowing or acknowledging it, Esau had become his younger brother's victim. Esau's appetite didn't have a chance against Jacob's cunning.

One of Esau's greatest joys was to bring his kill home to his adoring, aging father. Throughout his life, it was Esau's way of rewarding Isaac for his father's shameless favor. As he had many times before, Isaac one day called to Esau, "Get your weapons—your quiver and bow—and go out to the open country to hunt some wild game for me. Prepare me the kind of tasty food I like and bring it to me to eat, so that I may give you my blessing before I die."

Many years had passed since Esau's bowl of lentil stew. The promise to his brother of the birthright, along with many other promises, had faded into a landscape of watercolor commitments, of convenience now barely discernible.

Esau headed out on the hunt without further thought.

Unfortunately for Esau, his mother had eavesdropped on the conversation between him and his father. Seeing an opportunity, she conceived an elaborate plan that would swindle Isaac into giving the blessing to his younger son, Jacob. So while Esau was outdoors looking for Isaac's favorite wild game, Jacob was playing his own game of deception, dressing and sounding like his older brother. Because Jacob's performance was not flawless, age-blind

Isaac was suspicious. But lie upon lie finally won the day, and Isaac gave Jacob the blessing.

When Esau returned from his quest for his father's meal, he went to Isaac. "My father," Esau said, "sit up and eat some of my game so that you may give me your blessing."

Isaac was understandably confused. "Who are you?" he asked.

Esau's heart raced. *Has my father lost his senses? Have I been gone so long that he has forgotten who I am? How will I receive the blessing he promised?*

Flustered and shocked at the news, Isaac thundered, "Who was it that hunted game and brought it to me?"

When Esau discovered his brother's deception, he first pleaded with his father. "Haven't you reserved any blessing for me?" Then his pleading turned to tears. This rough-hewn man of the earth began sobbing like a child. Finally, his tears turned to fury. His only recourse was to murder his brother—once his father had died.

But before Isaac expired, Jacob fled. And for twenty years the brothers had no contact with each other. They both raised families. They both built successful enterprises. And they both lamented the day they would see each other again. Never would be too soon.

Then one day several men approached Esau who was living in the land of Seir. They identified themselves as Jacob's messengers. "Your servant Jacob says, 'I have been staying with Laban and have remained there until now. I have cattle and donkeys, sheep and goats, menservants and maidservants. Now I am sending this message to my lord, that I may find favor in your eyes.'"

Esau's heart may have swelled with conflicting emotions: (1) My brother is alive and well, and (2) So, the sniveling deceiver has finally dared to return!

Esau also had a choice to make: forgive his brother or kill him for what he did to him. Esau told Jacob's messengers that he wanted to see his brother, so they hurried off to tell their master.

Jacob was terrified. He divided his family, livestock, and provisions into two groups. He told his messengers, "If Esau comes and attacks one group, the group that is left may escape."

But although Jacob was paralyzed with terror, Esau had no such treachery in mind.

Jacob looked up and saw Esau with four hundred of his men. Jacob then went on ahead and bowed down to the ground seven times as he approached his brother.

"But Esau ran to meet Jacob and embraced him; he threw his arms around his neck and kissed him. And they wept."

Tuesday

A LOOK AT THE MAN
O Brother, Where Art Thou?

Esau was a "man's man." He was ruddy, strong, impulsive, competitive, impetuous—quite a lethal mix.

As a young man he was not accustomed to holding anything back. He may have lived on the edge of danger, self-indulgence, and immediate gratification. Having his father's favor did nothing to inhibit this behavior. But Esau had a serious problem—his brother Jacob.

My twin brother has ruined my life, Esau must have fumed. *And he will pay for it.*

The most destructive dimension to this conflict was that Jacob fled to Haran without any conversation with Esau: no explanation, no confession, no resolution. So the battle between these grown siblings may have waged silently for twenty years. The discord gnawed at their hearts—Esau's need for revenge and Jacob's fear of his brother's reprisal.

There is some levity in the account of Jacob going to such extremes to meet his brother after two decades. First he divided his servants, his family, and his possessions into two groups so that Esau could only capture half of what Jacob owned—one group could run away while the other was being attacked. Then Jacob prepared a gift to assuage his brother's fury: two hundred female goats and twenty male goats; two hundred ewes and twenty rams; thirty female camels with their young; forty cows and ten bulls; and twenty female donkeys and ten male donkeys. All in all, a very expensive transaction for Jacob! And completely unnecessary. Forgiveness was granted without charge. Esau's words tell the whole story: "I already have plenty, my brother. Keep what you have for yourself."

The image of these two grown men embracing and weeping is one of the most powerful in all of Scripture. It is, in fact, the echo of the prodigal standing guilty as his father runs to meet him. It is the image of our heavenly Father doing the same for us.

Esau's forgiveness was not offered reluctantly. He was not arrogant nor did he require that Jacob verbally review his transgressions against him, groveling with words of repentance. In his eagerness to forgive, Esau ran, he embraced, and he wept. Twenty years of apprehension and fear were erased in that incredible moment.

Wednesday

HIS LEGACY IN SCRIPTURE

Read Genesis 25:27–34.

1. How do you think Isaac's and Rebekah's favoritism affected Esau's relationship with his younger brother, Jacob? Have you experienced favoritism in your own life or observed it in others? How did it affect relationships?
2. What does this passage reveal about the brothers' character?
3. When Esau sold his birthright, he was holding God's promise to his grandfather Abraham and then to his father Isaac in contempt. What does this imply about the consequences of devaluing the promises of God in Scripture?

Read Genesis 27:30–41.

4. Jacob and Esau are the second set of brothers whose stories are told in detail in Genesis. The first set was Cain and Abel. What similarities do you see in their stories?
5. In the ancient world a blessing once spoken could not be retracted. Isaac's blessing over Esau is really more like an "antiblessing," the opposite of the bountiful blessing he bestowed on his younger son. Was Esau totally innocent of the deception inflicted on him by Jacob? Why or why not?

GOING DEEPER

6. Not only did Esau despise his birthright, thus holding God's promise in contempt, but he offended his parents by marrying foreign women. Just as Isaac foretold in his "antiblessing" over his eldest son, Esau's descendants, the Edomites, suffered periods when they were subject to Israel and periods when they managed to break free of them. The struggle between the two brothers foreshadowed the struggle between the peoples descended from them. What does this say about the root causes of many of the struggles we see today between ethnic groups and nations?

Thursday

HIS LEGACY OF PROMISE

Not many of us would trade the promises of God for a bowl of stew. The story of Esau's lost birthright might seem a bit far-fetched at first. But consider how the story might have played out in modern times. For instance, Jacob could have offered Esau a delicious blend of stocks and bonds, enough to insure a life of ease so that Esau could savor whatever pleasures he desired. The point is that Esau cared little for the promise God had made and instead gave away his birthright merely to indulge a fleshly desire.

Promises in Scripture

Hear, O Israel, and be careful to obey so that it may go well with you and that you may increase greatly in a land flowing with milk and honey, just as the LORD, the God of your fathers, promised you.

—Deuteronomy 6:3

If you faithfully obey the commands I am giving you today—to love the LORD your God and to serve him with all your heart and with all your soul—then I will send rain on your land in its season, both autumn and spring rains, so that you may gather in your grain, new wine and oil . . . and you will eat and be satisfied.   —Deuteronomy 11:13–15

How sweet are your words to my taste,
sweeter than honey to my mouth!

—Psalm 119:103

Friday

HIS LEGACY OF PRAYER

"Look, I am about to die," Esau said. "What good is the birthright to me?" . . .

Then Jacob gave Esau some bread and some lentil stew. He ate and drank, and then got up and left.

So Esau despised his birthright.   —Genesis 25:32, 34

Reflect On: Genesis 33:1–9

Praise God: For every earthly blessing.

Offer Thanks: For the basic ways God has cared for you, giving you food, water, and shelter.

Confess: Any tendency to pursue earthly pleasures at the expense of God's blessings.

Ask God: To help you rightly value the promises he has made to you in Scripture.

Make no mistake about it: God intends to bless you. And make no mistake about it, someone else intends to rob you of that blessing. His name is Satan, also known as "the great deceiver." If you want to receive all the good things God has planned for you, don't be seduced by promises of pleasure or power that may tempt you. Don't compromise your life in Christ by letting worldly desires smother your hunger for God. If you feel that your appetite for the things of God has diminished, take one day this week to fast from food as a sign that you want God to be first in your life.

Father, you know what I need even before I ask for it. Thank you for all the ways you care for me, for feeding me, clothing me, and giving me a good place to live and work to do. Help me to keep my eyes on the things that are above, where you are, remembering that your blessing is not just for this earth but for eternity.

JACOB

His Name Means "He Grasps the Heel" (Figuratively, "He Deceives")

His Work: As an indentured servant of his Uncle Laban for fourteen years, Jacob was a herdsman.

His Character: With a mother who encouraged it, Jacob learned the art of cunning and deception. In stealing the paternal blessing from his older brother, Jacob was forced to run, experiencing the consequences of his behavior.

His Sorrow: After seven years of hard labor as payment for Rachel, Jacob was deceived by her father, Laban, and was forced to work seven more. During these years he learned firsthand what his own deception had brought on his brother. Later in his life he thought he had lost his son Joseph to an attack by a wild animal.

His Triumph: One of the greatest moments in Jacob's life happened when he was reconciled to his brother, Esau. At the end of his life, he recovered another relationship that appeared to have been lost forever—he discovered that his son Joseph was not only alive, but very successful in Egypt.

Key Scriptures: Genesis 27–31

Monday

HIS STORY

Jacob hadn't planned this journey. A trip to Haran, over four hundred miles from his home in Canaan, was not something he had ever wanted to undertake—especially as a fugitive. But Jacob was in trouble. The conspiracy between him and his mother to wrest the blessing from his older brother had created a deep and painful schism in the family. With Rebekah's encouragement, Jacob had successfully masqueraded as Esau in the presence of his blind father and received the irretrievable blessing.

So awful was the clash between the brothers, Esau made a vow that when their ailing father died, he would kill Jacob. To cool Esau's rage and preserve Jacob's life, Rebekah told Jacob to leave home. His destination was his maternal grandparents' land in Paddan Aram. His objective was twofold: flee from the peril of his irate brother and find a wife from among Uncle Laban's daughters.

Endless hours of travel for this lonely man provided ample opportunity for him to review the recent sequence of events and the prospect of living the rest of his life running from his bloodthirsty brother. *This isn't what I had in mind,* Jacob thought to himself. *But I have no one to blame but myself.*

The city of Luz, about fifty miles from Beersheba, lay along the road to Haran. When Jacob finally reached it, he found a place to camp for the night. Spreading his blankets and cloak on the ground for a bed, he found a stone just the right size for a pillow and lay down.

But what started out as an ordinary night of slumber from a full day's journey turned into an unforgettable experience. Once asleep, Jacob had a celestial vision he would remember for the rest of his life. In his dream, Jacob saw a stairway. Its first step touched the ground near him and its treads rose into the heavens—like the sloping side of a mighty ziggurat—and Jacob could see angels descending and ascending. His eyes followed the staircase upward until, at the very top, he saw the Lord.

A sighting of the Creator of the universe would have been breathtaking enough, but then the Lord spoke: "I am the LORD, the God of your father Abraham and the God of Isaac. I will give you and your descendants the land on which you are lying. . . . All peoples on earth will be blessed through you and your offspring. I am with you and will watch over you wherever you go, and I will bring you back to this land. I will not leave you until I have done what I have promised you."

The power of the dream awoke the sleeping Jacob. *Surely the Lord is in this place, and I was not aware of it,* Jacob thought. Then as his mind began to embrace the stunning reality of what had happened, he nervously added, *How awesome is this place!*

As sunrise broke the night's hold, Jacob scrambled to his feet, lifted the stone he had used as a pillow, and turned it on its end like a pillar, naming the place Bethel, or "the house of God." As he gazed on his makeshift monument, Jacob made a vow. "If God will be with me and will watch over me on this journey I am taking and will give me food to eat and clothes to wear so that I return safely to my father's house, then the LORD will be my God and this stone that I have set up will be God's house, and of all that you give me I will give you a tenth."

Two decades later Jacob had another divine encounter after Jacob's uncle, who became his father-in-law, had given him a strong dose of his own medicine. Laban's multiple deceptions must have reminded Jacob of his own propensity to trickery, especially when Laban promised one daughter in marriage and secretly substituted another. But Jacob stayed there until he secured both sisters as brides, then gathered his family and possessions and slipped away.

Jacob was on the run again. To add to his anxiety, he was about to face his brother, Esau, for the first time since he had fled from Canaan. The day had come for Jacob to face the man whom he had robbed of his father's blessing.

Camped en route to do so, in the middle of a sleepless night, Jacob was startled by the presence of another man. Surprised by the intruder, Jacob wrestled the man to the ground. Strong in both spirit and muscle, Jacob was not overpowered by the man, even though they tussled until dawn. It didn't take long before Jacob realized that his contender was no mere mortal.

When the man realized that he was not going to prevail, he touched Jacob's hip, throwing it out of its socket. Even through the pain, Jacob hung on, grimacing but determined to remain.

"Let me go, for it is daybreak," the man finally said.

But Jacob replied, "I will not let you go unless you bless me."

The man studied him for a moment. "What is your name?"

"Jacob."

"Your name will no longer be Jacob, but Israel, because you have struggled with God and with men and have overcome."

In that moment, his name changed from "Jacob the deceiver" to "Israel the struggler with God," the perfect caption for the rest of his life.

Tuesday

A LOOK AT THE MAN

A Taste of His Own Medicine

Some people's lives seem to glide along with hardly a bump. Like a jockey in parallel cooperation with his horse, they are able to negotiate life's inevitable ups and downs in perfect sequence. No jaw-cracking collisions. No bone-jarring clashes.

And then there are folks like Jacob.

Like a puppy hanging on to someone's pant leg with his teeth, Jacob (meaning "deceiver" or "heel grabber") got dragged and jarred and slammed from one experience to another throughout his life. Of course, he could have let go and lived in relative peace. But that wasn't Jacob.

So what did God do with someone like him? Did he put him in the corner like a naughty child or forever consign him to life's detention hall? No. Instead of putting him away or hiding his adventure-packed story from us, God loved Jacob (Romans 9:13), paid attention to his growth by sending adversaries to challenge him, cared enough to make several personal visits to the man himself, and finally changed his life's course by changing his name.

Another great argument that has plagued intellectuals and lay-people alike is this one: Why does God elect some and not others? Why did God, for example, put his sovereign hand on the Jews in the Old Testament to the obvious exclusion of other peoples? Libraries are filled with volumes dealing with this worrisome question.

However, the real question should not be why God seems to overlook some but, considering our sinfulness and mutinous desires, why he chooses to favor *anyone at all*?

As we look back at Jacob's life, we see a man whom God loved with a special kind of affection. God saw Jacob as a paradigm of his people, capable of equal amounts of rebellion and repentance, disobedience and confession.

One of the confirmations of God's peculiar love for Jacob was his adversity-filled life. The conflicts within his family were obvious. Forever the younger brother, Jacob must have been slighted by his father's favoritism of his older brother. He may have felt manipulated by his mother's schemes as she used him to fulfill her own plans. He understood frustration in the house of Laban. And he knew the relentless dread of living as a fugitive. In all of these, Jacob was culpable, but God was preparing him for greatness.

For believers, God's presence through the person of the Holy Spirit is constant. But there are only a handful of times when Scripture records a face-to-face encounter between God and people. In his first dream, Jacob sees God standing at the pinnacle of the stairway to heaven. "I am with you and will watch over you wherever you go," the Lord said to Jacob. Twenty years later God meets Jacob in the form of a man. As a perfect template of Jacob's spiritual journey, Jacob grapples with a man sent from the Lord. And then, just before the man leaves the crippled Jacob, he gives him a new name and blesses him when he asks for it. At last Jacob learns that the blessing that counts comes from the Father of all.

You may know someone just like Jacob. You may *be* someone like Jacob. God loves you. Adversity is his gift to you. His presence through his Spirit is real. And he has given you a new name. You're a Christian.

Wednesday

HIS LEGACY IN SCRIPTURE

Read Genesis 25:22–26.

1. Like Isaac's mother, Sarah, Isaac's wife, Rebekah, seemed incapable of bearing children. The two had been married twenty years before she finally gave birth to twins, Jacob and Esau. It was almost as if God were setting up obstacles to the fulfillment of his own promise. Why do you think God allowed things to unfold in this way?

2. God made an unconventional choice, choosing the younger son over the firstborn. What does this say about the surprising way God chooses to fulfill his promises?

Read Genesis 27:1–13, 27–35.

3. What does this plot between mother and son reveal about their character? Did God need this kind of help to insure that the promised blessing was passed on through Jacob and not Esau? Why or why not?

4. What kind of family dynamic was at work in Jacob's home that allowed him to steal the blessing from his older brother? What does this say about God's ability to achieve his purposes despite human weakness and sin?

Read Genesis 29:16–27.

5. Soon after deceiving his father and robbing his brother of his blessing, Jacob fled for his life to Paddan Aram, the home of his Uncle Laban. Soon Jacob became the deceived rather than the deceiver, tricked by Laban into marrying his older daughter. Does this story have implications regarding how our actions toward others may come back to haunt us? If so, how?

GOING DEEPER

Read Genesis 32:22–31.

6. This scene takes place twenty years after Jacob fled his home to escape his brother's wrath. By now his life has been marked by a series of struggles. In this passage we see him struggling, not with mere men, but with God, insisting, "I will not let you go unless you bless me." Why do you think Jacob received the new name Israel? What is the significance of the limp he incurred during this supernatural wrestling match? Have you ever felt that you have been engaged in some kind of struggle with God? If so, how?

Thursday

HIS LEGACY OF PROMISE

God allows us to make our own choices. Jacob chose deceit rather than trust as his preferred method for getting what he wanted. As a result, he was forced to flee his home, and he spent twenty years struggling with his deceitful uncle. When Jacob finally returned, his mother was dead, and he wondered if his brother, Esau, would make good on his threats to kill him. But despite Jacob's difficulties, God persisted in blessing him. But why couldn't God's promise have been fulfilled in a less painful way? Why did there have to be so much running, so much struggling, so much division? Why couldn't Jacob have enjoyed a lifetime of peace and prosperity just as his father Isaac had? As we think about his story, it's difficult not to wonder how different things might have been had Jacob responded to God with peace and confidence.

Promises in Scripture

> *May God give you of heaven's dew*
> *and of earth's richness—*
> *an abundance of grain and new wine.*
> —Genesis 27:28

I am with you and will watch over you wherever you go, and I will bring you back to this land. I will not leave you until I have done what I have promised you. —Genesis 28:15

This is what the Sovereign LORD, the Holy One of Israel, says:

> *"In repentance and rest is your salvation,*
> *in quietness and trust is your strength."*
> —Isaiah 30:15

Friday

HIS LEGACY OF PRAYER

When Jacob awoke from his sleep, he thought, "Surely the LORD is in this place, and I was not aware of it. . . . This is none other than the house of God; this is the gate of heaven." —Genesis 28:16–17

Reflect On: Genesis 28:10–22

Praise God: For being with you even when you didn't know it.

Offer Thanks: For God's determination to keep his promises.

Confess: Any tendency to "help" God by using the wrong means.

Ask God: To give you greater confidence in his ability to provide for you as well as for those in your care.

One of the most famous dreams ever recorded is the one Jacob had when he fled from his brother. Alone in the wilderness, using a stone for a pillow, he dreamed of a stairway connecting earth and heaven. In his dream he saw angels moving up and down. He awoke with a sense of awe, pledging to give back to God a tenth of everything God would give him in the future. For a moment, Jacob was no longer scheming and striving to get ahead. Instead, he was simply responding with worship and thanksgiving and trust to the God who promised to care for him.

Lord, help me to sense your presence in my life and to rest in the confidence that you can take care of me far better than I can take care of myself. Thank you for everything you've given me. Please give me the faith to set aside some of these blessings so that I can give them back to you.

JOSEPH

His Name Means "May He [the Lord] Add"

His Work:	As governor of Egypt he saved many lives, including those of his own family, thus preserving God's people during a time of famine.
His Character:	Other than committing the youthful indiscretion of sharing dreams that made his brothers jealous, it is hard to find fault with Jacob's favorite son, Joseph. A dreamer and an interpreter of dreams, he overcame great adversity to rise to a place of prominence and power in the land of Egypt. A great-hearted man, God blessed him with wisdom and success.
His Sorrow:	To have been sold into slavery by brothers who hated him and to have been imprisoned for a crime he did not commit.
His Triumph:	To be reconciled with his brothers and reunited with his father and then to be used by God to preserve their lives and the lives of many others.
Key Scriptures:	Genesis 37; 39–50

Monday

HIS STORY

Shut up in an Egyptian prison, Joseph had time enough to mull over the events of his life. How his mother, Rachel, had died giving birth to his younger brother, Benjamin. How Jacob, his father, had favored him over his half brothers. And how his brothers had hated him for it.

He recalled the handsome coat his father had given him and the dream that had caused him so much trouble, the one he had foolishly shared with his older brothers: "We were binding sheaves of grain out in the field when suddenly my sheaf rose and stood upright, while your sheaves gathered around mine and bowed down to it." After that came another dream. "Listen," he had said, "I had another dream, and this time the sun and moon and eleven stars were bowing down to me." But even his father scolded him: "What is this dream you had? Will your mother and I and your brothers actually come and bow down to the ground before you?"

A short while later, the favored life Joseph had enjoyed since his youth was altered forever. It happened in an isolated field far from Jacob's watchful eye. Now, as he sat in his dungeon prison, the scene replayed itself across his mind.

He was just a boy, sitting at the bottom of a dry well, stripped of the robe his father had given him. He could hear his older brothers plotting his murder and then changing their minds, deciding instead to sell him to traders bound for Egypt. The fear, the sense of betrayal, the anguish of believing he would never see his father or his brother Benjamin again—the old emotions felt red and raw, as though they were brand-new.

But even in Egypt he had experienced God's favor. Hadn't he landed in Potiphar's household? Hadn't his work so pleased the captain of the guard that he had been placed in charge of everything Potiphar owned? But then Potiphar's wife had cornered him, pestering him to sleep with her. But how could he betray his master, how could he turn his back on God? Angered by his refusal, she accused him of raping her, and Potiphar had him thrown into prison.

But Joseph had felt God's blessing even in prison, where the warden recognized his abilities and put him in charge of the other prisoners.

Joseph's memories were suddenly interrupted by keys clanging in the lock. Pharaoh was summoning him to court. He had heard of Joseph from a former prisoner whose dream Joseph had accurately interpreted.

"I had a dream," Pharaoh told him, "and no one can interpret it. But I have heard it said of you that when you hear a dream you can interpret it."

"I cannot do it," Joseph replied, "but God will give Pharaoh the answer he desires." Joseph proceeded to explain the dream that had troubled Egypt's ruler, saying it predicted seven years of abundance

followed by seven years of famine. Then Joseph advised him to store
a portion of the food produced in the seven good years to prepare for
the seven difficult years that would follow. Pharaoh was so pleased by
Joseph's counsel that he declared, "Since God has made all this known
to you, there is no one so discerning and wise as you. You shall be in
charge of my palace, and all my people are to submit to your orders.
Only with respect to the throne will I be greater than you." So Joseph
became responsible for preparing Egypt for the coming famine.

The years passed just as Joseph had said. Before long, famine had
struck a wide region of the world, including Egypt and Palestine.
When Joseph's father, Jacob, learned there was food in Egypt, he sent
every son but Benjamin to buy grain. As soon as they arrived, they
bowed down before Joseph, the governor, without realizing who he
was. Pretending not to know them, Joseph accused them of being
spies. In return for selling them grain, he took Simeon hostage,
instructing his remaining brothers to prove their honesty by returning at some later date with their youngest brother, Benjamin.

Without realizing that Joseph could understand them, the brothers
turned to each other in dismay, saying, "Surely we are being punished
because of our brother Joseph. We saw how distressed he was when he
pleaded with us for his life, but we would not listen; that's why this distress has come upon us." Joseph turned to hide his tears, and the brothers returned home with the grain. Sometime later, after their food was
nearly gone, they returned to Egypt, this time with Benjamin in tow.

Joseph greeted his brothers warmly but instructed his steward to
plant a silver cup in the bag of grain belonging to his brother Benjamin. In the morning, shortly after his brothers left to return home,
Joseph sent men to chase after them. His steward accused the brothers of stealing Joseph's silver cup. If it was found on one of them, that
man, he assured them, would become Joseph's slave.

When Benjamin was identified as the guilty party, he and his
brothers were dragged before Joseph. But Judah pleaded with Joseph
for mercy, saying, "If Benjamin is not with us when I go back to my
father, my father will die of grief. Please let me remain here as your
slave in place of the boy, and let the boy return with his brothers."

Judah's willingness to enslave himself for the sake of his younger
brother broke Joseph's control. Weeping loudly, he exclaimed to them,
"I am Joseph! Is my father still living?"

Terrified by the realization that the most powerful man in Egypt, save Pharaoh, was the brother they had betrayed, his brothers were unable to speak. So Joseph calmed them: "I am your brother Joseph, the one you sold into Egypt! And now, do not be distressed and do not be angry with yourselves for selling me here, because it was to save lives that God sent me ahead of you to preserve for you a remnant on earth. You intended to harm me, but God intended it for good to accomplish what is now being done, the saving of many lives. So don't be afraid. I will provide for you and your children."

So Joseph was reconciled with his brothers and reunited with Jacob and his younger brother, Benjamin. The patriarch Jacob moved his family to Egypt, and his favorite son, Joseph, lived to be 110 years old. Before Joseph's death he made the younger generation of his family promise to carry his bones out of Egypt when, he reminded them, God would take them to the good land he had promised to Abraham.

Tuesday

A LOOK AT THE MAN

Reversing Adam's Mistake

After suffering so much misfortune, Joseph prospered in remarkable ways, governing the land he had entered as a slave and being reunited with his family. It's almost a storybook ending, in which the hero lives happily ever after. God's hand of blessing was so firmly on Joseph that nothing could keep him down—not the jealousy of his brothers, not slavery, not false accusations, not imprisonment. He was like the bar of soap that keeps rising to the top no matter how many times it's shoved beneath the water.

Was there something about Joseph that made it easy for God to bless him? Consider his position in Potiphar's house and his response to Potiphar's wife's attempt to seduce him: "No one is greater in this house than I am. My master has withheld nothing from me except you, because you are his wife. How then could I do such a wicked thing and sin against God?"

Now consider the first temptation of the first man, Adam: "The LORD God took the man and put him in the Garden of Eden to work it and take care of it. And the LORD God commanded the man, 'You are free to eat from any tree in the garden; but you must not eat from the tree of the knowledge of good and evil, for when you eat of it you will surely die'" (Genesis 2:15–17). Like Joseph, Adam was put in charge of everything. His master, God, had withheld nothing from him, except one thing—fruit from a tree in Eden. But, unlike Joseph, it was the one thing Adam could not refuse himself. And his disobedience ruined him for paradise.

It seems clear that obedience is a key to experiencing God's blessing. A life of obedience, coupled with God's power, is what enabled Joseph to provide deliverance for so many people. A life of obedience is what enabled Jesus to restore our relationship with God and open the gates of paradise. Like Jesus and like Joseph, we all are called to counter Adam's sin by living our life in loving obedience to God, realizing that his blessings are a taste of the paradise that awaits us.

Wednesday

HIS LEGACY IN SCRIPTURE

Read Genesis 37:3–8, 23–33.

1. Like it was in the story of Jacob and Esau, how is the theme of favoritism once again played out in Joseph's story? Was God showing favoritism by giving the seventeen-year-old Joseph a dream that seemed to indicate that he would rule over his brothers? Why or why not?

2. What do verses 23–33 say about the character of Joseph's brothers? Could Reuben and Judah have found another way to circumvent their brothers' plot to kill Joseph? What else might they have done?

Read Genesis 39:1–4, 6–23.

3. Already in his young life, Joseph had been severely and unjustly punished, not once but twice. What does his story say about God's faithfulness?

4. Unlike Adam in the Garden of Eden, who gave in to the temptation to eat what God had withheld (the fruit from the tree of the knowledge of good and evil), Joseph resisted the temptation to take the one thing his master, Potiphar, had withheld (his wife). Think about all the good things God has given you. Then ask yourself whether you have been more like Adam or Joseph regarding the things he has withheld.

Read Genesis 42:1–24.

5. How does this passage show the beginning of the fulfillment of Joseph's dream?

6. Why do you think Joseph didn't reveal himself right away to his brothers?

Read Genesis 45:4–8.

7. Joseph not only forgave his brothers but said that God, not they, had sent him into Egypt. What does this say about Joseph's faith? About God's surprising ways?

GOING DEEPER

8. In many ways, Joseph's life mirrors the story of Israel as it will unfold in the future. Like Joseph, the Israelites will first be blessed in Egypt and then cast into bondage as Joseph was unjustly cast into prison. Finally, through the leadership of Moses, they will be raised up again in the eyes of the Egyptians. But Joseph's life also bears similarities to Jesus' life. What resemblance can you find between the two?

Thursday

HIS LEGACY OF PROMISE

Joseph must have suffered extraordinary anguish and loneliness as the result of his brothers' betrayal. Though he had every reason to be bitter, there is no indication that he ever allowed himself to hate those who mistreated him. Instead, he saw God blessing him in the most unlikely places, in the most unlikely ways. Remarkably, his long ordeal had made him not a victim, weakened by what he suffered, but a strong man, whose character was forged by hardship. He was wise enough to lead a nation, big enough to forgive his brothers, understanding enough to see that God was doing something much larger with his life than merely giving him a "good life" free of struggle. Joseph reminds us of all the things we want our own lives to be: blessed by God for the sake of many others.

Promises in Scripture

Do not be afraid to go down to Egypt, for I will make you into a great nation there. I will go down to Egypt with you, and I will surely bring you back again.   —Genesis 46:3–4

> *From six calamities he will rescue you;*
> *in seven no harm will befall you.*
> *In famine he will ransom you from death.*
>
> —Job 5:19–20

> *The faithless will be fully repaid for their ways,*
> *and the good man rewarded for his.*
>
> —Proverbs 14:14

Friday

HIS LEGACY OF PRAYER

"God has made me fruitful in the land of my suffering."
—Genesis 41:52

Reflect On: Genesis 45:1–13

Praise God: Because he can use what others intend for evil to accomplish great good.

Offer Thanks: For his persistent blessings.

Confess: Any tendency to doubt God's love because you equate blessing with ease.

Ask God: To make you a person whose life will bless many others.

Genesis closes with Joseph's death at the age of 110. Because the Egyptians considered 110 years to be the ideal life span, this would have seemed further proof of divine blessing on the Hebrew slave who was lifted up to become ruler of the nation.

There is much in Joseph's life to feed our prayers. His forgiveness of those who tried to destroy him. His belief in God's help regardless of what was happening. His loyalty and his strength in resisting temptation. His wisdom in leading a nation through a time of great difficulty. Like few other men in Scripture, he stands out as a man who moved from strength to strength, helped as he was by his God.

Father, I can only imagine what a man like Joseph must have felt, to be betrayed by his own brothers, to be sold as a slave, and then to be imprisoned for something he didn't do. The next time I go through something difficult, help me not to waste time complaining about my life or wondering if you care about what's happening to me. Instead, remind me of Joseph. Give me his courage, his faith, and his patience. Bless me so that I will be a blessing to many others.

JUDAH

His Name Means "The Praise of the Lord"

His Work:	A leader among his brothers, he was head of the tribe from which both King David and Jesus would come.
His Character:	The fourth son of Jacob and Leah, he saved his brother Joseph's life and offered to take his youngest brother Benjamin's place as a slave in Egypt.
His Sorrow:	To have lived for many years with the knowledge that he and his brothers had sold Joseph into slavery.
His Triumph:	To have received a choice blessing from his father, Jacob, promising that Judah would be the greatest of the tribes of Israel.
Key Scriptures:	Genesis 37:26–36; 38; 42–45

Monday

HIS STORY

Judah lay on his back unable to sleep. He could see stars like bright holes puncturing the sky, as though light from another world were seeping through the firmament. Yet thoughts of other worlds brought little comfort, especially on sleepless nights when he could think of nothing but what had happened when he and his brothers had left their own world to travel to Egypt for the first time.

In those days, only the grain of Egypt had kept them alive. But Egypt's governor had mistaken them for spies, men who were not after grain but secrets that would undermine the kingdom. Judah should have been glad to escape with his skin and enough grain to feed his family, but he could not forget the brother he had left behind. Simeon had been jailed, the governor vowing to hold him until the brothers returned to their own land and brought back their youngest brother, Benjamin, as proof of their honesty.

But as soon as his father, Jacob, learned about Simeon, he complained bitterly, "You have deprived me of my children. Joseph is no more and Simeon is no more, and now you want to take Benjamin. Everything is against me. My son will not go down there with you; his brother Joseph is dead and he is the only one left. If harm comes to him on the journey you are taking, you will bring my gray head down to the grave in sorrow."

But the grain did not last forever, and Judah prevailed with his father, saying, "Send Benjamin along with me to return to Egypt for more grain and we will go at once, so that we and you and our children may live and not die. I myself will guarantee his safety; you can hold me personally responsible for him. If I do not bring him back to you and set him here before you, I will bear the blame before you all my life."

So the old man relented, and Judah and his brothers returned to Egypt, bringing Benjamin with them. But their brother Joseph, the one they had sold into slavery and the one who was now governor of Egypt though they did not know it, tricked them by selling them more grain and then planting his silver cup in Benjamin's sack to make him seem a thief.

When Judah discovered Benjamin's trouble, he begged the governor to punish him instead. "Let me remain here as your slave in place of the boy." How could he possibly return home without his father's youngest son? But then came the governor's startling response: "I am your brother Joseph," he said, tears choking his voice, "the one *you* sold into Egypt!"

It seemed to Judah as though the blood of Abel had come rushing up from the ground again, accusing him before God and man. Why had he not had the courage to stand against his brothers when they wanted to kill Joseph and he had instead suggested they sell him to slave traders? Perhaps slavery was better than death, but not by much. What would God do to him? What would Joseph do?

But before Judah or his brothers could speak, Joseph said something that startled them as much as the revelation he had just made.

"Don't be angry with yourselves for selling me here, because it was God, not you that sent me in order to save lives. Now hurry back to my father and say to him, 'This is what your son Joseph says: God has made me lord of all Egypt. Come down to me; don't delay. You shall live in the region of Goshen and be near me—you, your children and grandchildren, your flocks and herds, and all you have. I will provide for you there, because five years of famine are still to come. Otherwise you and your household and all who belong to you will become destitute.' Bring my father down here quickly."

Judah had expected harsh words from his brother, not these soft, forgiving words that fell like a sword against his chest, cutting his heart wide open and filling it with mercy. Against these there was no defense. Before Judah could find the words to reply, Joseph, the brother he had betrayed, threw his arms around him, and both men wept and held each other. The secret that had festered so long in Judah's soul was finally exposed, and his healing had begun.

Tonight as Judah looked up at the stars, he blessed God for his provision, for bringing him to live in Goshen in the land of Egypt, where there was plenty of food for his family and safety under Joseph's protection. He rolled over in bed and closed his eyes, the sound of his gentle snoring a sign that he had once again found peace.

Tuesday

A LOOK AT THE MAN

Finding Forgiveness

Though not the firstborn, Judah was a leader among Jacob's unruly sons. His leadership saved Joseph's life, and probably the lives of his extended family as well, because he was able to persuade Jacob that Benjamin needed to come with him to procure more grain in Egypt. His most impressive act of leadership was offering his own life in pledge for Benjamin's freedom, in a way reversing his earlier act of betrayal toward Joseph.

But Judah's leadership was flawed by the act of selling his own flesh and blood into slavery and by lying to his father about what happened to Joseph. It was also marred by what happened between him and his daughter-in-law, Tamar. After Tamar had lost her second husband, Judah's second son, he had promised to arrange a marriage with his youngest son, as the custom prescribed. But Judah failed to keep that promise and then falsely accused Tamar of being a prostitute, threatening her with death. To his credit, as soon as he discovered his error, he admitted that Tamar was more righteous than he.

Like so many of the Bible's best-known characters, and like so many of us, Judah was a man in need of forgiveness. He was a leader who needed mercy, and he found it in the arms of his brother Joseph and in the providence of a God who knew the secret that he and his brothers had kept for so many years.

Wednesday

HIS LEGACY IN SCRIPTURE

Read Genesis 38:13–26.

1. By right, Judah's daughter-in-law, Tamar, was entitled to marry his third son, since her first two husbands (also Judah's sons) had died and left her without a son. But Judah prevented her from doing so. The story of his tryst with the woman he thought was a prostitute immediately precedes the story of Joseph and Potiphar's wife. Contrast the character of the two men based on their actions.

2. Judah was ready to punish his daughter-in-law for her presumed guilt by burning her to death, yet he showed no remorse for visiting a prostitute. What does his readiness to judge her indicate about himself? About the culture of his day?

Read Genesis 43:7–9.

3. Judah's father, Israel (Jacob), balked at allowing Judah and his brothers to take Benjamin with them when they returned to Egypt for more food. How is Judah's leadership evident in this passage?

Read Genesis 44:18–34.

4. What does Judah's concern for Benjamin say about his character? Why do you think his plea had such a strong effect on Joseph?

Read Genesis 49:8–12.

5. Jacob blessed Judah and compared him to a lion, promising him "the obedience of the nations." Discuss the significance of the fact that both King David and Jesus of Nazareth were members of the tribe of Judah.

INTERESTING FACTS

- According to the custom of the time, which later became part of the Law of Moses, a deceased man's brother or nearest male relative was required to marry his widow if she had no sons to provide the dead man with an heir. This practice became known as "levirate marriage." Because it entailed considerable financial obligation, some men refused to comply with the law. In that case, the woman's only recourse was to haul the guilty party in front of the city's elders and remove a sandal from his foot and spit in his face, thus shaming him in front of the entire community.

- Judah was one of the two kingdoms into which Israel was divided after the death of King Solomon. Its capital was Jerusalem. Of the two kingdoms, Judah and Israel, the former was the most religiously faithful and maintained its independence a century and a half after the fall of the northern kingdom.

Thursday

HIS LEGACY OF PROMISE

Though Judah had obvious weaknesses, he seems less flawed than his older brothers, one of whom slept with his father's concubine and two of whom murdered the men of an entire city because one of them had raped their sister Dinah. Clearly, this was a troubled family.

But regardless of the size of their problems (maybe even because of them, in order to show his power), God chose the twelve sons of Jacob as heads of the twelve tribes of his people, the people from whom would be born the Savior of the world. And of all these flawed men, Judah received the choicest blessing from his father, Jacob, who said: "You are a lion's cub, O Judah; you return from the prey, my son. Like a lion he crouches and lies down, like a lioness—who dares to rouse him?"

Promises in Scripture

> *The scepter will not depart from Judah . . .*
> *until he comes to whom it belongs*
> *and the obedience of the nations is his.*
>
> —Genesis 49:10

> *"From Judah will come the cornerstone."*   —Zechariah 10:4

> *But you, Bethlehem, in the land of Judah,*
> *are by no means least among the rulers of Judah;*
> *for out of you will come a ruler*
> *who will be the shepherd of my people Israel.*
>
> —Matthew 2:6

Friday

HIS LEGACY OF PRAYER

Judah replied, "God has uncovered your servants' guilt. We are now my lord's slaves."
                                                   —Genesis 44:16

Reflect On: Genesis 44:14–16

Praise God: Because he knows the state of our hearts.

Offer Thanks: For ways God has strengthened relationships in your family.

Confess: Any sins against brothers or sisters, father or mother.

Ask God: To show you how to make amends for anything you've done wrong.

Judah spoke more truly than he knew, for at that moment God was uncovering the sin that he and his brothers had committed years earlier against their brother Joseph. A terrible family wound was suddenly and painfully reopened. Such wounds are unfortunately common in many families today. Set aside time this week to think and pray about your own family. Do unhealed wounds lie beneath the surface of any of your relationships? If so, ask God to give you the courage to admit whatever guilt you may bear for the situation. Then pray for wisdom to know how to take the first step toward those you have hurt. If the offense has nothing to do with you, pray that other family members will be able to resolve their differences through the grace of God.

Lord, I know that time can heal many things. But time alone never heals sin. It only makes it worse. Forgive me for the hurts I've inflicted on others, and give me the strength to do the right thing now. I especially ask that you will heal any and all of my family relationships that have been broken by sin.

His Work: To lead God's people out of Egypt and into the Promised Land.

His Character: Moses enjoyed a depth of relationship with God that set him apart from every other figure in the Old Testament and enabled him to intercede powerfully on behalf of his people. Though a reluctant prophet, he obeyed God as he led the Israelites out of Egypt. Through him God communicated his plan to forge a people unique in history, a people who belonged to him.

His Sorrow: To have been burdened with the leadership of a "stiff-necked" people whose failure to believe and obey God resulted in delaying their entrance into the Promised Land while they wandered for forty years in the desert wilderness. Moses died before entering the Promised Land.

His Triumph: On numerous occasions Moses encountered both the power and the love of God to such a degree that his face shone. Unlike other men, Moses spoke with God directly, face to face.

Key Scriptures: Exodus 1–20; Numbers 13–14

Monday

HIS STORY

Three hundred years had passed since Joseph's death in Egypt. By then a new ruler had come to power, one who knew nothing of Joseph.

Fearing that the Hebrews would soon outnumber and overpower his own people, this pharaoh put slave masters over them to oppress them with forced labor. But the more they were oppressed, the more they multiplied and spread; so the Egyptians came to dread the Israelites and worked them ruthlessly, making their lives bitter with hard labor.

The king of Egypt, still fearful of how rapidly the slave population was multiplying, gave the order to his people: "Throw every boy that is born into the Nile, but let every girl live." But three-month-old Moses was hidden away by his mother and placed in a floating basket among the reeds along the bank of the Nile. When Pharaoh's daughter went down to the Nile to bathe, she rescued the baby and made the child her own, naming him Moses and saying, "I drew him out of the water."

One day, after Moses had grown up, he saw an Egyptian beating a Hebrew slave. Glancing around to make certain no one could see him, Moses killed the Egyptian, burying his body in the sand. But Pharaoh learned what had happened and tried to kill Moses. So Moses fled to the desert of Midian, where he lived for forty years. During that time, the king of Egypt died. Meanwhile, the Israelites groaned in their slavery and cried out to God for deliverance.

Though Moses had married the daughter of a prominent man of Midian, forging a new life for himself in the desert, he still missed the sights and smells of Egypt—fresh fish baking in the fire pit, ripe melons sliced in glistening wedges, sleek white leeks and savory onions that made even simple food a splendid meal. He feasted on such memories, recalling Egypt's palaces and monuments and long days spent sitting on the green edges of the Nile watching the muddy river swirl by and wondering what the future held for a privileged son of one of Pharaoh's daughters.

But even the life-giving water of the great river could not tempt Moses back to the land he had fled as an outlaw. His life now was in the desert. The Midianites had taught him how to live well enough in the sparse land. Today, as he led his father-in-law's flocks to the far side of the desert, he could see Mount Horeb looming before him. Suddenly, through waves of heat rising from the desert floor, Moses noticed a bush engulfed in flames. He wondered how it was that this bush, though on fire, was not burning up.

"Moses! Moses!" the words came like sudden thunder from the midst of the flames.

"Here I am," he said.

"Do not come any closer," the voiced warned. "Take off your sandals, for the place where you are standing is holy ground. I am the God of your father, the God of Abraham, the God of Isaac and the God of Jacob."

Moses shook as he buried his face in his arms, as though hiding from a vision that might destroy him.

"I have seen the misery of my people in Egypt. I have heard them crying out because of their slave drivers, and I am concerned about their suffering. So I have come down to rescue them from the hand of the Egyptians and to bring them up out of that land into a good and spacious land, a land flowing with milk and honey. So now, go. I am sending you to Pharaoh to bring my people the Israelites out of Egypt."

Shaking still, Moses wailed, "Who am I, that I should go to Pharaoh and bring the Israelites out of Egypt? And why should the elders of Israel listen to me? Besides, I have never been good at speaking. O LORD, please send someone else to do it."

Instead of giving in to Moses' fears, God told him to throw his staff on the ground, and at once it turned into a snake so real that he ran from it. "Reach out your hand and take it by the tail," God said. Fearing God more than he feared the snake, Moses grabbed it by the tail, and it turned back into a staff. Then God relented and told Moses: "Your brother Aaron can speak to the people for you, and it will be as if he were your mouth and as if you were God to him. Take this staff in your hand so you can perform miraculous signs with it."

So Moses returned to Egypt, one man against an empire. But when he went to Pharaoh, saying, "This is what the LORD, the God of Israel, says: 'Let my people go,'" Pharaoh merely scoffed: "Who is the LORD, that I should obey him and let Israel go? I do not know the LORD, and I will not let Israel go."

After that, God sent ten terrible plagues on the Egyptians, the last of which was the worst. Finally, Pharaoh relented, and Moses heard the words he had been waiting for: "Up! Leave my people, you and the Israelites! Go, worship the LORD as you have requested." So Moses, the reluctant prophet, led the people out, carrying the bones of Joseph with him, just as Joseph had requested long ago when he lay dying.

A short while later, Pharaoh, whose stubbornness had no doubt made him stupid, pursued the Hebrew slaves, thinking to overtake them at the banks of the Red Sea. As his army drew near, the terrified Israelites cried out to Moses: "Was it because there were no graves in Egypt that you brought us to the desert to die? What have you done to us by bringing us out of Egypt? It would have been better for us to serve the Egyptians than to die in the desert."

"Do not be afraid," Moses shouted to the crowd. "Stand firm and you will see the deliverance the LORD will bring you today. The Egyptians you see today you will never see again. The LORD will fight for you; you need only to be still."

Then Moses raised his staff and stretched out his hand over the sea, and a strong east wind began blowing, turning the water into dry land and enabling the Israelites to cross over with a great wall of water on their right and on their left.

As the Israelites neared the eastern edge of the sea, Moses looked back again. Incredibly, Pharaoh's army was still pursuing them—into the sea itself. Suddenly, inexplicably, the wheels of their chariots fell off, throwing horsemen and chariots into confusion. Once the last Israelite had crossed over, Moses again stretched out his hand, and the sea rushed back to its place. All that was left of the pursuing army were the corpses of horses and men floating in the water.

Standing on dry land, Moses threw up his hands to the sky and sang this song:

I will sing to the LORD,
　　for he is highly exalted.
The horse and its rider
　　he has hurled into the sea.
The LORD is my strength and my song;
　　he has become my salvation.
He is my God and I will praise him,
　　my father's God, and I will exalt him.

Moses and all the people had watched the defeat of an enemy who had seemed invincible, a military power that had oppressed them year after year, decade after decade. Their bondage, so brutal and harsh, had finally come to an end, brought about by the wondrous love of a powerful God.

Tuesday

A LOOK AT THE MAN

Staying Faithful

When Moses witnessed how God had demolished the enemies of his people, he must have been filled with the knowledge of the greatness of God, utterly convinced that no one and nothing was beyond the reach of the Lord's power. That day Moses may have thought the worst was over in his struggle to lead the Israelites to freedom and into the land of promise. He couldn't have known how hard it would be to lead them across the Sinai Peninsula and into Canaan, a journey that would take not months but years.

For though God had freed the people, they were still in bondage—not to any military power but to their own way of looking at the world, to their stubbornness, and to their fear of taking the risks that inevitably accompany a life of faith.

When Moses appointed a contingent of leaders, one from each of the twelve tribes of Israel, to conduct a reconnaissance mission in Canaan, all but two (Joshua and Caleb) came back with a bad report: "We went into the land to which you sent us, and it does flow with milk and honey! But the people who live there are powerful and the cities are fortified and very large. The land we explored devours those living in it. All the people we saw there are of great size. We seemed like grasshoppers in our own eyes, and we looked the same to them."

The spies' report incited the people to rebellion, and they grumbled and complained, saying: "If only we had died in Egypt! Or in this desert! Why is the LORD bringing us to this land only to let us fall by the sword? Our wives and children will be taken as plunder. Wouldn't it be better for us to go back to Egypt?"

Because the Israelites entertained an evil vision of God's intentions toward them, making it impossible for them to obey him, he punished them by making them wander in the desert until the last of their generation (except for Joshua and Caleb) had died off. The Israelites who had left Egypt as slaves were not yet ready for the full freedom God intended for them.

But though Moses was frustrated by their response, he did not abandon his people. He did not shrug off the burden of leadership God had given him. Instead, he led them, taught them God's commandments, judged their disputes, prayed for them, and stayed with them until a new generation had grown up that was no longer burdened by a slave's mentality. And God loved Moses and praised him for his faithfulness and strengthened him with everything he needed to stay faithful throughout his long ordeal.

Wednesday

HIS LEGACY IN SCRIPTURE

Read Exodus 1:6–11.

1. Why do you think God allowed the Israelites to stay in Egypt only to become enslaved? Remember that God told Jacob (Israel) not to be afraid to go down to Egypt (Genesis 46:3–4).

2. What things in your own life have been accomplished in the midst of difficult circumstances?

Read Exodus 7:1–7.

3. What does God's "hardening" someone's heart mean? (The book of Exodus speaks nine times of God hardening Pharaoh's heart, and it also says nine times that Pharaoh hardened his own heart.)

4. Think about the condition of your own heart. Would you want God to harden it right now, that is, to set the attitude of your heart in stone for the rest of your life? Why or why not?

Read Exodus 20:1–17.

5. The Ten Commandments have sometimes been called the *Decalogue*, meaning the "Ten Words." What would it be like to be part of a community of people who faithfully observed these words?

6. Just before Moses delivered the Ten Commandments, God gave him this message to convey to the people: "If you obey me fully and keep my covenant, then out of all nations you will be my treasured possession" (Exodus 19:5). What are the benefits of belonging to God in this way?

GOING DEEPER

7. As the Old Testament's greatest prophet, Moses enjoyed a more intimate revelation of God than anyone who had ever lived. After meeting with God, his face radiated with light so much so that it actually frightened the people around him. Because Moses knew God so well, it is worth reflecting on a few of his descriptions of God:

    The LORD is my strength and my song (Exodus 15:2).

For the LORD your God is a merciful God; he will not abandon or destroy you or forget the covenant with your forefathers (Deuteronomy 4:31).

The LORD our God, the LORD is one (Deuteronomy 6:4).

He is the faithful God, keeping his covenant of love to a thousand generations of those who love him and keep his commands (Deuteronomy 7:9).

He is the Rock, his works are perfect, and all his ways are just (Deuteronomy 32:4).

Thursday

HIS LEGACY OF PROMISE

The promise of rest and a land to call their own must have stirred the hearts of the weary Israelite slaves, unaccustomed as they were to enjoying such blessings. Moses was a man uniquely chosen by God not only to set his people free and to bring them to a land to live in, but also to convey the deeper intention of God's heart—to make his people holy so that sin would no longer prevent them from knowing God as he longed to be known. God wanted not just to rescue his people, but to live in their midst, loving and caring for them. Then as now, anyone who wants to know God and experience his presence needs always to choose the path of loving him, which is also the path of obedience.

Promises in Scripture

I will redeem you with an outstretched arm and with mighty acts of judgment. I will take you as my own people, and I will be your God.

—Exodus 6:6–7

My Presence will go with you, and I will give you rest.

—Exodus 33:14

The LORD bless you
and keep you;
the LORD make his face shine upon you
and be gracious to you;
the LORD turn his face toward you
and give you peace.

—Numbers 6:24–26

Friday

HIS LEGACY OF PRAYER

"O LORD," he said, "why should your anger burn against your people, whom you brought out of Egypt with great power and a mighty hand?"... Then the LORD relented and did not bring on his people the disaster he had threatened. —Exodus 32:11, 14

Reflect On:	Exodus 32:30–32
Praise God:	For his mercy.
Offer Thanks:	That God hears our prayers on behalf of others.
Confess:	Any failure to regularly intercede for the needs of others.
Ask God:	To bring people to mind for whom he wants you to pray regularly.

Moses was always crying out to God on behalf of others. At Pharaoh's urging, he asked God to lift various plagues afflicting the Egyptians. Then he cried out in the desert wilderness for God to provide water for the people to drink. Later, when the Israelites were battling a band of Amalekites, he held God's staff in his hands until sunset, and his intercession won the day. After the Israelites betrayed God by committing idolatry, Moses begged the Lord to refrain from destroying them as he had planned. And God graciously spared them. Proverbs 15:29 assures us that "[God] hears the prayer of the righteous." Moses was a righteous man whose unselfish prayers saved a nation and advanced the plans and purposes of God.

Father, forgive me for any self-centeredness in the way I pray. Help me to be more sensitive to the needs of others and to show your love by faithfully intervening on their behalf through the power of prayer. Please help me to intercede for others based on what I know of your character and your promises.

AARON

His Work:	Aaron was the first in the line of Israel's hereditary priesthood.
His Character:	Aaron's role was primarily a passive one: to do and say whatever Moses told him to. Though he stood by Moses throughout his struggle with Pharaoh, he seemed unable to stand on his own as a leader. When Moses was absent for forty days, Aaron gave in to the people's insistent demands for a god to worship. On another occasion, however, he joined Moses in stopping a plague that threatened to destroy the Israelites because of their rebellion.
His Sorrow:	Aaron disobeyed the Lord by presiding over an incident of false worship. At another point he angered God by joining his sister Miriam in complaining against their brother's leadership.
His Triumph:	To have spoken God's word, entrusted to him through Moses, and eventually to have acted as a mediator between God and man, providing for the atonement of sin and the people's reconciliation with God.
Key Scriptures:	Exodus 20:1–6; 28; 32; Numbers 12:1–15

Monday

HIS STORY

Aaron was as perplexed as anyone by his brother Moses' long absence from the camp. Moses and his aide Joshua had been on the mountain forty days and forty nights. Had Moses been eaten by wild animals? Had he fallen off a cliff? Had he been consumed by the fire that covered the top of Mount Sinai?

Growing impatient and fearful, the Israelites in the valley below gathered around Aaron and demanded, "Come, make us gods who will go before us. As for this fellow Moses who brought us up out of Egypt, we don't know what has happened to him." Aaron opened his mouth to reply but nothing came out. What could he say? Moses had always supplied the words, straight from the mouth of God. But for more than a month there had been no words, and the people had grown restless, in need of assurance of the divine presence, fearful they would perish without a god to guide them on their wilderness journey.

Aaron had to act. The people were demanding it. So he told the Israelites, "Take off the gold earrings that your wives, your sons and your daughters are wearing, and bring them to me." Then he took the gold and made it into an idol cast in the shape of a calf, hoping that the bull would remind the people of God's power and strength.

But as soon as the calf emerged gleaming and golden from the fire, the leaders cried out, "These are your gods, O Israel, who brought you up out of Egypt." Attempting to redirect their worship, Aaron built an altar in front of the calf and announced, "Tomorrow there will be a festival to the LORD." So the next day the people got up early and sacrificed burnt offerings. But as the day wore on, they began to worship the calf in an orgy of drunkenness, behaving more like pagans than those who worshiped the Lord.

Meanwhile, on the mountain called Sinai, Moses had enjoyed forty days and nights in the presence of God, where the Lord had entrusted him with detailed instructions for shaping the life of his people. The first two of the ten commandments God had inscribed on two stone tablets were these:

> You shall have no other gods before me.
> You shall not make for yourself an idol in the form of anything in heaven above or on the earth beneath or in the waters below. You shall not bow down to them or worship them; for I, the LORD your God, am a jealous God, punishing the children for the sin of the fathers to the third and fourth genera-

tion of those who hate me, but showing love to a thousand generations of those who love me and keep my commandments.

Day after day, Moses conversed with God, but on the fortieth day,
he heard God's voice again, and this time there was anger in it: "Go
down, because *your* people, whom *you* brought up out of Egypt, have
become corrupt. They are a stiff-necked people. Now leave me alone
so that my anger may burn against them and that I may destroy them.
Then I will make you into a great nation."

But Moses pleaded with God, reminding him of his covenant: "O
LORD, why should your anger burn against *your* people whom *you*
brought out of Egypt with great power and a mighty hand? Why
should the Egyptians say, 'It was with evil intent that he brought them
out, to kill them in the mountains and to wipe them off the face of
the earth'? Turn from your fierce anger; relent and do not bring disaster on your people."

The Lord graciously relented, and Moses made his way down the
mountain carrying the two tablets containing the writing of God.

When Aaron saw Moses coming, he felt relieved and yet afraid of
what might happen next. As soon as Moses saw the calf and the dancing, he threw the tablets out of his hands, breaking them to pieces at
the foot of the mountain. Then he took the calf and burned it in the
fire and ground it to powder. He scattered the powder in water and
made the people drink it.

Then he turned his attention toward Aaron: "What did these
people do to you, that you led them into such great sin?"

Aaron tried to excuse himself: "Do not be angry, my lord. You
know how prone these people are to evil. When you didn't come
back, they demanded new gods."

To Moses, it sounded like the oldest of excuses, like the one Adam
had used to excuse himself for his disobedience in Eden, saying to
God: "The woman you put here with me—she gave me some fruit
from the tree, and I ate it."

That day Moses ordered the Levites to kill those who had been
unfaithful. Three thousand people perished as a result. Then Moses
spoke to God on behalf of all the people, saying, "Oh, what a great
sin these people have committed! They have made themselves gods

of gold. But now, please forgive their sin—but if not, then blot me out of the book you have written."

But God refused to punish Moses and said instead, "Whoever has sinned against me I will blot out of my book. Now go, lead the people to the place I spoke of and my angel will go before you."

After so great a betrayal, God led Moses and Aaron and all the people through the desert, still promising to be their God, still promising he would lead them to a land flowing with milk and honey. And all the days of his life Aaron remained a priest of God.

Tuesday

A LOOK AT THE MAN

An Imperfect Intercessor

After the incident with the calf, Aaron must have been aware of the seriousness of his failure to lead the people and of his own need for forgiveness. He would have realized that his life had been in jeopardy because of God's anger. But Aaron was spared because of God's merciful response to his brother's prayers. In the book of Deuteronomy, which depicts Moses addressing the Israelites prior to their entrance into the Promised Land, Moses says that "the LORD was angry enough with Aaron to destroy him, but at that time I prayed for Aaron too" (Deuteronomy 9:20).

Aaron was a man who had witnessed God's power over Pharaoh and who had for a time stood on the mountain with Moses and seen the glory of God. As one who was set apart by God to play an important role among his people, he had a unique part to play in the story of salvation. And yet even his kinship with Moses, even God's call to be a priest, did not spare him from the power of sin's temptation.

Thereafter, whenever Aaron performed his priestly duties as a mediator between a holy God and a sinful people, he would not be able to come before the Lord with any air of self-righteousness, as though only the people, and not he, were guilty of sin. Because of his own weakness, he would be capable of sympathizing with the weakness of God's people.

A priest who could sympathize with the people, as it turns out, was only half of what God had planned for his people. Centuries later there would be a man who would perfectly embody the role of the high priest, not only sympathizing with the weakness of his people, but also resisting the power of temptation. Because of him, we are now able to approach God, confident that his attitude toward each of us is marked by grace and mercy.

Wednesday

HIS LEGACY IN SCRIPTURE

Read Exodus 28:29–30, 36–38.

1. In these passages, the Lord instructed Moses how the priestly garments should be designed. What did these garments signify about Aaron's role as a priest?

Read Exodus 32:1–14.

2. What do Aaron's actions say about his character? About his leadership?

3. The Israelites had already seen incredible evidence of God's power—the ten plagues in Egypt, the parting of the Red Sea, the miraculous provision of manna in the desert. Why do you think they were still tempted by idol worship?

4. Why do you think God calls the Israelites "your" people in verse 7?

5. Moses interceded for Aaron and the people in very specific ways in verses 11–13. Comment on the nature and effectiveness of his prayer.

Read Numbers 12:1–15.

6. Moses, Aaron, and Miriam were all prophets through whom God had spoken. Yet Aaron and Miriam chafed under the leadership of their younger brother. What does this story say about sin's power to invade the community of God's people regardless of how powerfully God has been at work in their midst?

GOING DEEPER

7. In his role as priest, Aaron was a mediator between God and the people, making sacrifices before a holy God to deal with the people's sin and weakness. Imperfect as he was, his priesthood foreshadowed the perfect high priesthood of Jesus. The book of Hebrews makes this plain:

> Therefore, since we have a great high priest who has gone through the heavens, Jesus the Son of God, let us hold firmly to the faith we profess. For we do not have a high priest who is unable to sympathize with our weaknesses, but we have one who has been tempted in every way, just as we are—yet was without sin. Let us then approach the throne of grace with confidence, so that we may receive mercy and find grace to help us in our time of need (Hebrews 4:14–16).

Why is it important to have a high priest who can both sympathize with our weakness and resist sin?

Thursday

HIS LEGACY OF PROMISE

God called Aaron to be Israel's first high priest, to act as a mediator between God and the people, offering sacrifices to atone for sin. As an outward sign, he wore the words "HOLY TO THE LORD" on his forehead to remind himself and others of his essential role. Yet he was so weak, so human, so prone to sin. Thankfully, Aaron and his successors represented only a temporary measure for dealing with the problem of sin. God knew the remedy would have to be infinitely stronger if sin was to be finally defeated. By sacrificing his life, Jesus has opened the path to heaven, healing the rift that sin created in our relationship with God.

Promises in Scripture

If God is for us, who can be against us? He who did not spare his own Son, but gave him up for us all—how will he not also, along with him, graciously give us all things? —Romans 8:31–32

> *I will put my laws in their hearts,*
> *and I will write them on their minds. . . .*
> *Their sins and lawless acts*
> *I will remember no more.*
> —Hebrews 10:16–17

If we walk in the light, as he is in the light, we have fellowship with one another, and the blood of Jesus, his Son, purifies us from all sin.
—1 John 1:7

Friday

HIS LEGACY OF PRAYER

So Aaron did as Moses said, and ran into the midst of the assembly. The plague had already started among the people, but Aaron offered the incense and made atonement for them. He stood between the living and the dead, and the plague stopped.   —Numbers 16:47–48

Reflect On: Hebrews 4:14–16

Praise God: For providing us with a great high priest.

Offer Thanks: That God has made a way for us to return to him.

Confess: Any pride that makes you want to live life strictly on your own terms.

Ask God: To increase your confidence in his forgiveness.

God himself had called the Israelites a "stiff-necked people" because they were constantly complaining, questioning, resisting, and rebelling. On one occasion when the people were ready to mount a revolt and return to Egypt, Aaron stepped into the midst of them and stopped a plague that broke out as a result of God's judgment. Sin always carries its own set of plagues in the form of broken relationships and wasted lives. But Christ is ready to stand between the living and the dead, able to halt sin's deadly effects so that we can live in the presence of God.

Father, you already know how stiff-necked I can sometimes be. Don't let me get away with being stubborn toward you even in the smallest things. Help me come to the throne of grace confident that I will receive the help I need. In Jesus' name. Amen.

JOSHUA

His Name Means "Yahweh Is Salvation"

His Work:	He was Moses' aide and successor, a military commander and statesman.
His Character:	His remarkable military successes were achieved as a result of his attitude of trust and obedience toward the God who made them all possible.
His Sorrow:	That the Israelites failed to believe his good report of the Promised Land and that he and they were consequently prevented from entering it for forty years.
His Triumph:	To have led the Israelites to victory in Canaan, thus establishing them in the land God had promised their forefathers Abraham, Isaac, and Jacob.
Key Scriptures:	Numbers 14:1–38; Joshua 1–6

Monday

HIS STORY

Joshua shielded his eyes from the sun as he peered up the mountain, trying vainly to mark the path Moses, the man he had faithfully served and followed for forty years, had taken. The older man would not allow Joshua to go with him on this last journey up Mount Nebo, for the Lord had told Moses he would see the Promised Land from Moab's high mountain but die without entering it. All the old ones—Aaron, Miriam, Moses—were gone now. Joshua and his friend Caleb, the only two fighting men left alive from the multitude who had left Egypt, stood at Canaan's eastern border along with a new generation of Israelites awaiting the Lord's instructions.

Joshua had already been encouraged by the Lord's command: "Joshua son of Nun be strong and courageous, for you will bring the Israelites into the land I promised them on oath, and I myself will be with you." But now that Moses was gone, he felt the need for courage even more. What kind of man, he wondered, could lead this throng of people into Canaan without feeling a twinge of fear?

But God calmed Joshua with strong words and great promises: "Cross the Jordan River into the land I am about to give to the Israelites. I will give you every place where you set your foot. As I was with Moses, so I will be with you; I will never leave you nor forsake you. Today I will begin to exalt you in the eyes of all Israel, so they may know that I am with you as I was with Moses."

So, even though the waters of the Jordan had already breached its banks, making the river dangerous and difficult to cross, Joshua commanded the people: "This is how you will know that the living God is among you and that he will certainly drive out all your enemies in the land he is giving you. See, the ark of the covenant of the LORD of all the earth will go into the Jordan ahead of you. As soon as the priests who carry the ark of the LORD set foot in the Jordan, its waters flowing downstream will be cut off and stand up in a heap."

After Joshua's officers assembled the people, he watched as the priests stepped into the river, their robes swirling in the muddy water. He could almost sense Moses, the greatest of all the prophets, standing beside him, staff upraised, ready for God to open the waters once again, this time marking not the journey's beginning but its ending. Then he heard himself shouting and praising God because, incredibly, the priests were now standing on dry ground. The river had stopped flowing, just as God had said it would.

After the priests carried the ark into the middle of the river, the whole nation crossed over, tribe by tribe, clan by clan—the women clasping babies to their breasts lest the waters rush back and sweep them away, the men hurrying their herds forward, the children scampering across, oblivious to anything but the miracle and the adventure of entering a new land.

Then Joshua ordered twelve men, one from each of the twelve tribes of Israel, to take a stone from the middle of the river—twelve stones that would forever remind Israel of this miracle of God's faithful love.

Later, standing on the western bank of the river, just miles from Jericho, gateway to the Promised Land, Joshua glanced eastward a last time. Moses, the man who had been his friend and mentor, had vanished into the mountains. But Joshua no longer feared his absence. Instead, he felt invigorated, as though the soil of this new land was already yielding an abundant harvest to nourish him. Today's events had bolstered his faith, assuring him that God still held Israel's future securely in his hands, hands that were strong enough to overcome his enemies and plant his people firmly in the land he had promised to them.

Tuesday

A LOOK AT THE MAN

Tried and True

When God calls someone to play a part in the history of his people, he often begins by testing his or her faith. Joshua's first test was to return a faithful report after he had spied out the land of Canaan with its giants and strong cities. Later God told him to cross the Jordan despite the fact that the river was at flood stage.

But the challenges didn't stop. To enter Canaan, the Israelites would have to take the city of Jericho, which lay five miles west of the Jordan River. But there was one little problem. High-walled, well-fortified cities had discouraged Israel's spies forty years earlier, and Joshua knew that their desert wanderings had not rendered the former slaves any more physically capable of laying siege to the city than they had been.

But Joshua believed that God had already delivered Jericho into their hands. They had merely to march around it for six days. On the seventh day, seven priests carrying trumpets of rams' horns would lead the army seven more times around the city. When the priests blew the last blast of the trumpet, all the people were to shout at the top of their lungs and the walls of the city would simply collapse. To practical-minded people—to most of us—this would have seemed a ridiculous plan. But it was the strategy Joshua employed, bringing about a victory that terrorized the other peoples of Canaan, thus paving the way for Israel's future military successes.

As each test grew larger, Joshua's faith kept pace, his obedience nourishing his faith and his faith nourishing his obedience. The man who had witnessed Israel's deliverance from Egypt, who had walked across the Red Sea, and who had stayed alive by eating manna in the desert was not about to doubt God's power to do what he said he would. Because of Joshua's faithfulness, the Israelites experienced victory after victory as they swept across the land and made it their own.

Wednesday

HIS LEGACY IN SCRIPTURE

Read Joshua 3:5–13.

1. Why is it significant that the ark of the covenant was carried across the Jordan River ahead of the people?
2. Why do you think God told the priests to step into the water before parting the river? Have you ever felt God asking you to do something that involved taking a risk? What happened?
3. God parted the Jordan River while it was at flood stage. This miracle must have reminded Joshua and the people of the parting of the Red Sea at the beginning of their forty-year sojourn in the desert. But much had transpired since then. How different do you think the Israelites as a people were some forty years later?

Read Joshua 4:1–7.

4. Why do you think the Lord wanted Israel to build a memorial out of stones from the river bottom? What does this say about our need to find ways to remind ourselves of God's faithfulness?

Read Joshua 6:1–5.

5. Why do you think that the very first battle in the Promised Land began with God asking Joshua and the Israelites to do something that seemed to make little sense?

INTERESTING FACT

In biblical times, certain numbers held special symbolic significance. The number seven, a number that plays a significant role in the story of the conquest of Jericho, symbolized divine perfection or completeness. Consider a few additional mentions of this number in the Bible:

> By the seventh day God had finished the work he had been doing; so on the seventh day he rested from all his work.
> —Genesis 2:2

> Remember the Sabbath day by keeping it holy. Six days you shall labor and do all your work, but the seventh day is a Sabbath to the LORD your God.   —Exodus 20:8–10

If you buy a Hebrew servant, he is to serve you for six years. But in the seventh year, he shall go free, without paying anything.
—Exodus 21:2

I saw seven golden lampstands, and among the lampstands was someone "like a son of man," dressed in a robe reaching down to his feet and with a golden sash around his chest. . . . In his right hand he held seven stars.   —Revelation 1:12–13, 16

Thursday

HIS LEGACY OF PROMISE

Joshua was one of only two men of military age (the other was Caleb) who left Egypt as a slave and entered the Promised Land as a warrior. The rest died in the desert wilderness because of their sin and their unwillingness to believe God was capable of keeping his word. In contrast to fearful reports from the other spies who told of seeing giants and fortified cities on their initial foray into Canaan, Joshua rendered this report to Moses: "The land we passed through and explored is exceedingly good. If the LORD is pleased with us, he will lead us into that land, a land flowing with milk and honey, and will give it to us" (Numbers 14:7–8). Joshua knew the challenges ahead, but instead of dwelling on them, he focused on the Lord's faithfulness and his power. As Moses' successor, he heard God saying directly to him, "No one will be able to stand up against you all the days of your life." And no one did. His name, meaning "Yahweh is salvation," conveyed God's faithfulness to the Israelites as they battled to take hold of the Promised Land.

Promises in Scripture

The LORD himself goes before you and will be with you; he will never leave you nor forsake you. Do not be afraid; do not be discouraged.

—Deuteronomy 31:8

You know with all your heart and soul that not one of all the good promises the LORD your God gave you has failed.

—Joshua 23:14

He [the LORD] holds victory in store for the upright.

—Proverbs 2:7

Friday

HIS LEGACY OF PRAYER

On the day the LORD gave the Amorites over to Israel, Joshua said to the LORD in the presence of Israel:

> *"O sun, stand still over Gibeon,*
> *O moon, over the Valley of Aijalon."*
> *So the sun stood still,*
> *and the moon stopped,*
> *till the nation avenged itself on its enemies.*
>
> —Joshua 10:12–13

Reflect On:	Deuteronomy 31:1–8
Praise God:	For his power to do what he says he will.
Offer Thanks:	For the victories God has won in your own life.
Confess:	Any tendency to focus on your difficulties rather than on the God who promises to help you.
Ask God:	To strengthen your faith by helping you take the risks he is asking of you.

Joshua's audacious prayer, asking God to stop the sun and moon in their tracks so that he could win the battle, reminds us of the startling words Jesus spoke to his disciples about the power of faith: "I tell you the truth, if anyone says to this mountain, 'Go, throw yourself into the sea,' and does not doubt in his heart but believes that what he says will happen, it will be done for him" (Mark 11:23). Because Joshua believed every word God spoke and because he acted on that faith, he became Israel's deliverer, leading God's people into all the good land the Lord had promised.

Father, give me a faith like Joshua's, so that I can fight the good fight of faith no matter what obstacles I may face. Use me to encourage others in their own battles as well. Help me to be strong and very courageous, remembering your promise that you will never leave me or forsake me.

ACHAN

His Name Means "Troublemaker"

His Character:	Achan's greed for the spoils of war and his attempt to hide his sin led to a situation that endangered Israel's relationship with God. By disregarding God's command, he brought trouble and judgment on his own people.
His Sorrow:	His disobedience resulted in the loss of many lives, including his own.
His Triumph:	To have participated in the victory over Jericho.
Key Scriptures:	Joshua 7:1–8:2

Monday

HIS STORY

It was daybreak of the seventh day. During the past six days, Jericho had been under siege. But there were no battering rams, ladders, or axes. Nor were there chariots or well-armed soldiers ready to rush into the city as soon as the walls were breached. There were only men marching, day after day, in silent procession around the walls, trumpets blaring as they encircled the city. Each man held his tongue, exactly as Joshua had instructed: "Do not give a war cry, do not raise your voices, do not say a word until the day I tell you to shout. Then shout!"

At first there were catcalls from the men standing sentry on the walls, but after six days the siege had created a sense of dread among Jericho's inhabitants, so strong that it silenced even these. How long would the Israelites keep marching? Were they planning to take the city by magic or by trickery? When would they strike? The incessant blare of trumpets grated on their nerves and made them edgy.

As the sun rose over Jericho, Achan, of Judah's tribe, joined the rest of Israel's army, falling in line behind the priests, who marched before the ark. This time the soldiers proceeded around the city, not once but seven times, and Achan looked up at faces that had now grown familiar—Jericho's guards standing duty on the city walls. "All of them," he thought, "will be dead by sunset."

Earlier, Joshua had instructed the Israelites, telling them, "The city and all that is in it are to be devoted to the LORD. [Everyone and everything was to be destroyed.] No one but Rahab and her family [a woman who had protected Israel's spies] is to be spared. Keep away from the devoted things, so that you will not bring about your own destruction by taking any of them. Otherwise you will make the camp of Israel liable to destruction and bring trouble on it. All the silver and gold and the articles of bronze and iron are sacred to the LORD and must go into his treasury."

Suddenly Achan heard the sound of a trumpet blast followed by Joshua's urgent command: "Shout! For the LORD has given you the city!" A loud cry went up from all the people, and the walls of Jericho crumbled like day-old bread crushed between a man's fingers. Along with all the other Israelites, Achan rushed into the city, slaughtering the enemies of Israel and sparing no one. Even the animals were put to the sword.

After a time, once the chaos had diminished, he found himself alone in a house. Stepping over the bodies of the dead, Achan saw something that caught him fast and held him—spoils from the new land—a beautiful robe draped across a chair, a mound of silver, a wedge of gold. Perhaps the people who lived here had meant to escape with their treasures. He remembered Joshua's warning that the spoils belonged to the Lord. Any man who acted otherwise would bring trouble on Israel. But what trouble could come from merely touching the robe and feeling the heft of the silver and the gold? Surely the garment was the finest he had ever seen.

Did God really say that something as marvelous as this robe was to be destroyed? Hadn't he promised to give the land to his people, a land flowing with milk and honey? *Why,* thought Achan, *should I deprive my family of the good things my own hands have won?* He rubbed the robe against his beard, caressing it as though it were a lover he could not part with. Then he wrapped the gold and silver carefully inside the robe's folds, tucking the precious package beneath his tunic and fleeing the house just in time to see men running through the city setting fires.

After Jericho's defeat, Joshua sent three thousand men to Ai, a town fifteen miles to the west. But though his army should have scored an easy victory, they were defeated and thirty-six men were killed. Stunned by this sudden reversal in battle, Joshua fell on his face before the ark of the Lord, crying out: "O LORD, why did you ever bring this people across the Jordan to deliver us into the hands of the Amorites to destroy us? What can I say now that Israel has been routed? The Canaanites and the other people of the country will hear about this, and they will surround us and wipe us off the face of the earth. What then will you do for your own great name?"

"Stand up!" the Lord commanded. "What are you doing on your face? Israel has sinned; they have violated my covenant, which I commanded them to keep. That's why the Israelites cannot stand against their enemies. I will not be with you anymore unless you destroy whatever among you is devoted to destruction."

So Joshua ordered the Israelites to assemble early the next morning, and Achan stood with other men from the tribe of Judah. As the sun passed behind a cloud, Achan shivered, folding his arms across his chest as if to defend himself against advancing shadows. One by one, lots were cast to determine who had violated God's command. First the tribe of Judah was taken. Then the clan of the Zerahites. Then the family of Zimri—Achan's own family. He wanted to run but couldn't, as though stuck in a dream he could not escape. Man by man, each member of the family was called forward until, finally, inevitably, the lot fell to Achan, the son of Carmi, the son of Zimri, the son of Zerah, of the tribe of Judah.

"It is true," Achan confessed, words rushing from his mouth. "I have sinned against the LORD, the God of Israel. This is what I have done: When I saw in the plunder a beautiful robe from Babylonia, two hundred shekels of silver and a wedge of gold weighing fifty shekels, I coveted them and took them. They are hidden in the ground inside my tent, with the silver underneath."

Then Joshua, together with all Israel, took Achan; the silver; the robe; the gold wedge; his sons and daughters; his cattle, donkeys, and sheep; his tent and all that he had to the valley of Achor. And Joshua said, "Why have you brought this trouble on us? The LORD will bring trouble on you today."

Then the people of Israel stoned him, and after they had stoned his family, they burned them. Over Achan they heaped a large pile of rocks, which remained for many years. Then Joshua sent a force of thirty thousand fighting men to attack Ai, and God delivered the city into their hands.

Tuesday

A LOOK AT THE MAN

No Place to Hide

Achan may not have been a bad man, at least to begin with. While living for many years in the desert, he may even have fed himself on dreams of what life would be like in the Promised Land, where he could build a life for his family. He may have rushed into Jericho fully intending to follow the Lord's commands. But then came an opportunity to do otherwise. And that's when his resolve faded.

Achan's disobedience then produced a kind of foolishness in him; he attempted to hide what he had done, burying stolen goods beneath his tent. But he was hiding from the God who made him, from the same God who parted the Red Sea and the Jordan River, and from the God who had just caused the walls of a fortified city to crumble without a weapon being raised against it. Why was Achan foolish enough to think that God would find it hard to see through his little deception?

The truth is that it's sin's nature to hide. Consider your own experience. Isn't it hard to admit your sins to others? Isn't it difficult to admit them to yourself? Most of us have found ingenious ways to hide the ugliness of sin from ourselves and others, by rationalizing, excusing, and even forgetting things we've done wrong. But Achan's story tells us that God is never fooled by such foolishness.

Simple obedience and the cleansing power of God's grace are the best defense against sin. But when we fail to do the right thing, we should remind ourselves not to compound the problem by hiding what we've done. Instead, we can go directly to God, expressing our sorrow and asking his forgiveness, confident that he will give it.

Wednesday

HIS LEGACY IN SCRIPTURE

Read Joshua 6:16–21.

1. This practice of "devoting" everything in the city to destruction seems harsh to us. Moses advocated this approach, pointing out that otherwise the native peoples of the land would lead the Israelites into idol worship and other forms of corruption (Deuteronomy 16–18). Still, we must be careful to understand the context of this ancient story, which unfolded in a specific time and place. To use such a story to rationalize the unjust treatment of individuals or entire groups of people today would be to misread Scripture with terrible consequences. How then are we to apply the story? It might help to consider whether there is a spiritual parallel in your own life. What things need to be utterly destroyed before you can follow God wholeheartedly?

Read Joshua 7:1–25.

2. Why do you think verse 1 describes Achan in terms of his tribal relationships? Achan's sin highlights the truth that there is no such thing as private morality. How have you seen sin affect an entire community?

3. The ancient Israelites operated under different notions of justice than we do. In Achan's case, his entire family was destroyed for his sin. Read Ezekiel 18:1–4, 14–24 and comment on how God's unfolding revelation in Ezekiel helped the Israelites understand how God intends to deal with individual sin and righteousness.

4. Israel's defeat at the hand of a much smaller force of enemies points to the spreading effects of sin among the community of God's people. Why do you think Achan's sin affected everyone else? How do our own sins affect the community of believers?

5. Achan describes his temptation in detail—"a beautiful robe from Babylonia," "a wedge of gold weighing fifty shekels." We can almost imagine him fingering the robe as he marveled over its workmanship. *What a pity,* he must have thought, *to destroy such a beautiful garment.* At that moment, Achan succumbed to sin's central temptation: to do what he thought was right rather than what God thought was right. How can you guard against the temptation to base your actions on your own judgment rather than on God's?

GOING DEEPER
Read Joshua 7:25–26.

6. How does this memorial made of stones differ from the first memorial the Israelites made after crossing over the Jordan River (see Joshua 4:4–7)? What was God trying to convey to his people as they began their conquest of Canaan?

Thursday

HIS LEGACY OF PROMISE

Though we rarely like to think of it, God's promises often take the form of warnings. But warnings, like blessings, are a sign of his love, because he knows how vulnerable we are without them. He knows, for instance, that we often don't see people and situations very clearly. That as human beings our understanding is limited. That we have a propensity toward sin. He realizes how easy it is for us to be certain that something is good for us even when it's the very thing that will harm us. So he warns us to steer us away from the things that bring ruin and suffering. He warns us so that he can bless us. Achan is an example of a man who paid the ultimate price for disregarding the warning that was meant to keep him and the rest of God's people safe in the new land God gave them.

Promises in Scripture

> Do not be wise in your own eyes;
>> fear the LORD and shun evil.
> This will bring health to your body
>> and nourishment to your bones.
>
> —Proverbs 3:7–8

> This is what the LORD says:
>
>> "Stand at the crossroads and look;. . .
>> ask where the good way is, and walk in it,
>> and you will find rest for your souls."
>
> —Jeremiah 6:16

> But if you do warn the righteous man not to sin and he does not sin, he will surely live because he took warning, and you will have saved yourself.   —Ezekiel 3:21

Friday

HIS LEGACY OF PRAYER

"Oh, that their hearts would be inclined to fear me and keep all my commands always, so that it might go well with them and their children forever!" —Deuteronomy 5:29

Reflect On: Deuteronomy 6:1–3

Praise God: Because his commandments are meant to bless us, not to enslave us.

Offer Thanks: That God has not hidden his commands from us.

Confess: Any tendency to value your opinion about a course of action more than you value God's.

Ask God: To make you humble enough to realize that you do not always know what is best.

Fear is a healthy thing if it keeps a young child from crossing a busy street by himself. Similarly, fearing God, as a child might fear his parents, is a healthy part of the Christian life because it keeps us from dangers we often cannot see or understand. Achan's story drives home the consequences of a man's failure to fear God enough to keep a commandment he did not fully understand. May his life remind us of the good things we will certainly forfeit if we live in a way that shows our disregard for God's law.

Father, I want to obey your commandments—all of them. But I know from past experience that I can't just grit my teeth and leave it at that. The only way I can do what you ask me to is by relying on your Holy Spirit working inside me to strengthen me and change my heart. Lord, help me to fear you, love your Word, and act in a way that honors you.

GIDEON

His Name Means "Hewer, Slasher, Hacker"

His Work: A farmer called to bring Israel back to the Lord (a task in which he partially succeeded) and to deliver God's people from their Midianite oppressors.

His Character: A fearful man, living in a time when Israel had plenty to fear, Gideon questioned the Lord, demanding signs that would reassure him of God's faithfulness. Even though he was a reluctant warrior, he won a brilliant military victory and became one of Israel's greatest judges.

His Triumph: That God's vision for his life turned out to be far greater than his own.

Key Scriptures: Judges 6–8

Monday

HIS STORY

Instead of beating out the wheat on the hillside where the wind could carry off the chaff, Gideon had relocated his threshing floor to the bottom of a winepress, out of sight of Midianite raiders whose habit it was to strike quickly, stripping the lush fields bare and slaughtering the last of the sheep, cattle, and donkeys. That was where the angel of the Lord found him cowering from his enemies like all the other men of Israel.

"The LORD is with you, mighty warrior," the angel said.

Gideon looked up, searching for evidence of mockery on the stranger's face. But finding none, he decided to probe him: "If the LORD is with us, why do such terrible things happen to us? Where are all the wonders our fathers told us about when they said, 'Did not the LORD bring us up out of Egypt?' Why has the LORD abandoned us and given us over to the hand of Midian?"

Answering none of his questions, the stranger commanded, "Go in the strength you have and save Israel out of Midian's hand. Am I not sending you?"

"Me, save Israel?" protested Gideon. "Don't you know who I am? My clan is the weakest in Manasseh, and I am the least in my family." But the angel simply told Gideon to prepare an offering of meat and bread and place it on a rock. Then, with the tip of the staff that was in his hand, the angel touched the offering, and it burst into flames. For once, Gideon had nothing to say but this: "Ah, Sovereign LORD! I have seen the angel of the LORD face to face!"

"Peace! Do not be afraid. You are not going to die," God assured him. Then Gideon listened carefully as God instructed him to destroy the altar that Joash, his father, had built for Baal. But fearing his family and the other men of the town, Gideon waited until night had fallen to demolish the altar and build another for the Lord.

The next morning, he heard men arguing outside his home, demanding that his father hand him over to be killed for what he had done to Baal. Gideon was relieved to learn that his father's feelings for him ran deeper than his devotion to the Canaanite fertility god, for Joash refused, saying, "Why are you pleading Baal's cause? If he really is a god, he can defend himself when someone breaks down his altar." So the men left Gideon alone.

A short time later, after the Midianites had gathered a large army of raiders in the valley of Jezreel, the Spirit of the Lord came upon Gideon, and he blew a trumpet summoning thousands of men to follow him. Gideon, however, was not yet prepared to rush into battle. Instead, he asked the Lord: "If you will save Israel by my hand as you have promised, please give me a sign. I will place a wool fleece on the threshing floor. If there is dew only on the fleece and all the ground is dry, then I will know that you will save Israel as you said." And that is exactly what happened.

But fear still ruled his heart, and he asked God for yet another sign: "Do not be angry with me. Allow me one more test with the fleece. This time make the fleece dry and cover the ground with dew." And the Lord did as he asked.

Bolstered by miraculous signs and by a fighting force of thirty-two thousand men, Gideon finally felt ready to attack. But there was only one problem. This time God was the one who wasn't ready to rush into battle. The problem concerned the size of the army. The Lord thought Gideon had too many men for the job. But how could a commander have too many soldiers? Still God was adamant: "In order that Israel may not boast that her own strength has saved her, let anyone go home who is afraid." So twenty-two thousand men were subtracted from Gideon's army that day, doing nothing for his morale. Still ten thousand men might prevail if the Lord was with them.

But God hadn't finished remodeling Gideon's army. "You still have too many men," the Lord told him. "Take them down to the water, and I will sift them for you there. Separate those who lap the water with their tongues like a dog from those who kneel down to drink." Seventy-seven hundred men knelt down to drink, while three hundred men lapped with their hands to their mouths. Then the Lord said, "With the three hundred men that lapped I will save you and give your enemies into your hands."

Meanwhile, from their vantage point in the hills, Gideon and his band of warriors could see the Midianites and their allies spread thick as locusts in the valley below—one hundred thousand strong. How could he, an untrained farmer with a few soldiers at his command, ever hope to strike so vast an enemy?

Though the night was warm, Gideon wrapped himself in a blanket, pacing from one end of the camp to the other, as though his restlessness might yield a solution. And as he walked, he heard the Lord say, "If you are afraid to attack, go down to their camp and listen to what they are saying." So Gideon climbed down to the edge of the Midianite camp in time to overhear a man confiding in his friend: "I had a dream. A round loaf of barley bread came tumbling into our camp. It struck the tent with such force that the tent overturned and collapsed."

"This can be nothing other than the sword of Gideon, the Israelite," the other man exclaimed. "God has given us into his hands."

Gideon almost jumped when the man said his name. He was known here. Already God had placed a terror of him in the hearts of his enemies. Feeling suddenly strong, he clambered up the hillside like a young lion. Calling to his army, he commanded: "Get up! The LORD has given the Midianites into your hands." Dividing them into three companies, he handed each man a trumpet and an empty jar with a torch inside. "Follow my lead," he told them. "When I get to the edge of the camp, do exactly as I do. When I blow my trumpet, from all around the camp blow yours and shout, 'A sword for the LORD and for Gideon!'"

Each man held a trumpet in his right hand and a lit torch in his left, the flame hidden by the jar. As soon as his tiny army surrounded the enemy camp, Gideon gave the signal. His soldiers blew their trumpets and smashed the jars, shouting loudly so that the Midianites fell into a panic, certain they were being attacked by a great army. In the midst of the ensuing pandemonium, things became so confused that Israel's enemies began killing each other. Finally, the entire Midianite army fled with Gideon chasing them—a flea after a dog. As soon as the other Israelites heard what had happened, they rallied to Gideon.

That day Gideon and his small band of warriors destroyed an enemy that had oppressed and impoverished the Israelites for seven years running. Hearing their cries for help, God had raised up an unlikely deliverer, a mighty warrior who didn't even know he was one. For the next forty years, Gideon ruled Israel as a judge, and the people prospered in a time of peace.

Tuesday

A LOOK AT THE MAN

Hiding Out

Gideon's story reminds us of the story of another man, centuries earlier, who also felt inadequate for the role God assigned him. His name was Moses, a man who had been hiding out just as Gideon had when God called him. Both Gideon and Moses made excuses, plausible-sounding ones to us though not to God. To both men God simply said, "I am sending you."

When Gideon pleaded that his clan was the weakest in Israel and he the least of his family, he was unwittingly expressing his qualifications for the job. God wasn't looking for a born leader, a man who would be great in the eyes of his own people. He wasn't searching for a self-reliant man who would take credit for every victory. He needed someone whose weakness he could use, a man whose apparent unsuitability would eventually convince his people that their God was still with them, still powerful, still loving.

It's interesting that God called Gideon a mighty warrior precisely at the moment when such a description was hardest to believe. How could Gideon comprehend it when his own idea of himself was so contrary to God's idea? Because of the Lord's remarkable patience, Gideon was eventually able to overcome his doubts and become the man God intended him to be. By believing in God, he lived out his life, not as a timid man, but as a warrior who had won a brilliant victory.

Many of us are like Moses and Gideon were at the moment God first called them. We are hiding out, living our own lives, reluctant to alter the status quo, unable to believe we are capable of any kind of greatness. But God describes his plan for our lives, not in our terms, but in his. And that's how it should be, because he's the only one who knows who we really are and what his power can do within us. If we want to experience God shaping our lives and using us—in our families, our churches, and our communities—we will have to set aside our own vision for ourselves in order to embrace his. Anyone who does that will one day look back, not with regret, but with gratitude, amazed at the great things God has done in a life yielded to him.

Wednesday

HIS LEGACY IN SCRIPTURE

Read Judges 6:7–16.

1. Why do you think the Lord begins (vv. 7–10) by reminding the Israelites of what he has already done for them?
2. Why does the angel of the Lord call Gideon a "mighty warrior," since Gideon was hiding from the Midianites in a winepress?
3. The angel of the Lord told Gideon to "go in the strength you have." When has God said something similar to you? Describe these.
4. The Lord also told Gideon, "I will be with you." But still Gideon asks for a sign. What does this need for a sign reveal about Gideon?

Read Judges 7:1–22.

5. How would you feel if God commanded you to lead an army and then reduced the number of fighting men under your command by 99 percent? How does the divine strategy fit with God's choice of Gideon himself (see Judges 6:15)?
6. What does this part of Gideon's story (vv. 9–22) illustrate about the various ways in which God works out his divine plan?

INTERESTING FACT

Baal, meaning "lord," was the chief Canaanite deity, the god of fertility. Some scholars believe that many of the Israelites may have initially associated Yahweh and his rule only with the wilderness, the place in which he had forged them into a nation. They became vulnerable to Baal worship the moment they began living a more settled, agricultural life in Canaan, where the fertility of land and animals became key to their survival. Baal was often pictured standing on a bull, a figure that emphasized his power and virility. The Israelites' willingness to intermarry with the Canaanites also made them more willing to worship pagan gods.

Thursday

HIS LEGACY OF PROMISE

"But LORD," Gideon asked, "how can I save Israel? My clan is the weakest in Manasseh, and I am the least in my family." Gideon's initial response to God's promised help seems hardly promising itself. Rather than welcoming the words of the angel of the Lord, Gideon questioned him: "If God is with us, why have all these bad things happened to us?" "Who me? Save Israel? You must be kidding!" "Give me a sign that will prove you really are the angel of the Lord." God showed remarkable patience toward his timid servant, calling him not a coward, but a "mighty warrior" and granting him not one but three miraculous signs. Like a man stepping tentatively onto a narrow beam bridging a canyon, Gideon tested the word of the Lord. Would God really hold him up? Was the Lord really speaking to him? Like most of us, Gideon's faith grew as he responded to God's grace and then "used the strength he had" to do what the Lord was calling him to do.

Promises in Scripture

When you and your children return to the LORD your God and obey him with all your heart and with all your soul according to everything I command you today, then the LORD your God will restore your fortunes and have compassion on you. —Deuteronomy 30:2–3

For the foolishness of God is wiser than man's wisdom, and the weakness of God is stronger than man's strength. —1 Corinthians 1:25

My grace is sufficient for you, for my power is made perfect in weakness. —2 Corinthians 12:9

Friday

HIS LEGACY OF PRAYER

Then Gideon said to God, "Do not be angry with me. Let me make just one more request. Allow me one more test with the fleece."

—Judges 6:39

Reflect On: Judges 6:36–40

Praise God: For his patience.

Offer Thanks: For the guidance God gives.

Confess: Any doubts you may have about God's desire to guide you.

Ask God: To help you use "the strength you have" as you seek to do his will.

Though Gideon had his share of fears to contend with, he was anything but timid when it came to asking God for reassurance. Though his request for miraculous signs is not evidence of a mature faith, his story is at least evidence that God was persistently patient with this persistent man. Rather than putting out fleeces (asking God for proof of his guidance) as Gideon did, we can pray persistently for God to help us discern his will for our lives.

Father, I want to do your will. Help me to live so close to you that doing your will becomes like breathing or like eating—something that sustains me every day of my life. When I am afraid, please reassure me of your presence and give me confidence to do what I need to do.

SAMSON

His Name Means "Little Sun"

His Work: To deliver Israel from the Philistines.

His Character: Samson's erotic attachments to foreign women eventually led to his death. A man of mythic strength, he was inwardly weak, given to anger and unfaithful to his Nazirite vows. His prayers as well as his actions against the Philistines seem to have been motivated by the desire for personal vengeance.

His Sorrow: To have been blinded and imprisoned by his lifelong enemies.

His Triumph: To have killed more Philistines by his death than he had while living.

Key Scriptures: Judges 13–16

Monday

HIS STORY

Delilah—her name sounded like *layla,* the Hebrew word for "night," making her seem all the more mysterious, all the more enticing to a man who loved women, especially foreign women. Samson stroked her hair and then cupped her delicate face in his hands, smiling as he peered into eyes as green as the sea and as hard to fathom.

"Tell me, Samson," she said, her voice soft as a dove's cooing, "what is the secret of your great strength and how can you be tied up and subdued?"

Her question surprised him. Why did women always want to know everything about a man? Was she toying with him? Playing a game? Or did she really want to know? Should he tell her about his mother's encounter with the angel who years before had proclaimed her barrenness healed? Who told her to dedicate her son to God as a Nazirite who would never drink wine, never cut his hair, never touch the carcass of man or beast? Would Delilah love him the more for revealing these things to her? Or would she simply remind him of the time he had touched a lion's carcass and then pester him with questions about why he had broken his Nazirite vow? More than that, would she honor the secret once it was confided?

Better to appease her with a lie, he thought, and so he replied, "If anyone ties me with seven fresh thongs that have not been dried, I'll become as weak as any other man."

But Delilah soon found that tying her lover with thongs was like binding a lion with strands of string. Samson merely laughed as he snapped the thongs around his chest and arms, enjoying the game.

Pouting, she scolded him, "Samson, you have made a fool of me; you lied to me. Come now, tell me how you can be tied."

So Samson made up one fanciful tale after another. "If anyone ties me securely with new ropes that have never been used, I'll become as weak as any other man." And then, "If you weave the seven braids of my head into the fabric on the loom and tighten it with the pin, I'll become weak." Each time Delilah fell for the ruse, failing to subdue the man who had proven himself a terror to the Philistines. And each failure increased her impatience for the silver his enemies had promised in return for the secret of her lover's strength.

In addition to beauty, Delilah had a surplus of words as part of her arsenal. She was good at circling back over the same ground, making her point another way, voicing complaints that wore a man down. "How can you say 'I love you' when you won't confide in me? This is the third time you have made a fool of me and haven't told me the secret of your great strength."

Tired to death of her nagging, Samson finally gave in. "No razor has ever been used on my head, because I have been a Nazirite set apart to God since birth. If my head were shaved, my strength would leave me."

Sensing she had heard the truth at last, Delilah waited until Samson fell asleep on her lap. Calling to Philistine conspirators hidden in the room, she signaled a man to shave Samson's hair. Then she woke him, saying, "Samson, the Philistines are upon you!"

Planning to shake off his fetters as before, Samson soon found he lacked the power to resist. The Lord had left him. He was alone now and as weak as other men. Looking around for Delilah, he saw only the open door through which she had fled. Outside was darkness. Then his enemies gouged out his eyes, plunging him into perpetual night, and took him down to Gaza, where they bound him with bronze shackles and imprisoned him.

After a while, Samson's hair began to grow again, though no one seemed to care. What danger could a blind man in chains possibly present? One day he heard jubilant shouting as the people celebrated their victory, praising their god, Dagon:

"Our god has delivered our enemy into our hands,
The one who laid waste our land and multiplied our slain."

While the people were in high spirits, they shouted, "Bring out Samson to entertain us."

As soon as Samson stood among the pillars of the temple, he said to the servant who held his hand, "Put me where I can feel the pillars that support the temple, so that I may lean against them." The temple was filled with men and women, all the rulers of the Philistines were there, and on the roof were about three thousand people.

Then Samson prayed: "O Sovereign LORD, remember me. O God, please strengthen me just once more, and let me with one blow get revenge on the Philistines for my two eyes." Then he reached toward the two central pillars on which the temple stood. Bracing himself against them, his right hand on the one and his left hand on the other, Samson said, "Let me die with the Philistines!" Then he strained against the pillars with all his might, and the temple collapsed. An instant later, Samson was buried under the great heap of rubble that covered his enemies. On the day of his death, Samson killed more Philistines than he had during the twenty-year period he led Israel.

Tuesday

A LOOK AT THE MAN

Squandered Promise

One of the first Bible stories children hear is the story of Samson, the man who defeated his enemies with a superhuman feat of strength. But it is such an unsavory story that we find ourselves leaving out certain details, for example, Samson's boasting, his visits to prostitutes, or his murderous rage. Even the man's prayers were selfish, focused as they were on his own desire for revenge rather than on God's glory.

Why would God, knowing the future, choose such a person to play such a role, even sending an angel to announce his birth? The question is not easily answered. But it is certainly true that Samson would have been a better man had he paid attention to the call God had placed on his life. Instead, he seems to have squandered the promise of his life by living it in a self-centered, self-directed way.

Ironically, the pattern of his life formed a vivid picture of Israel's own unfaithfulness during a period when it seemed incapable of resisting the allurement of foreign gods. And so the people God had set apart and called his own, the nation he intended to build up and make strong, grew progressively weaker in the land he had promised.

Samson's story reminds us of God's faithfulness, of his ability to deliver his people regardless of the circumstances and despite their sins. It also reminds us of what can happen when we allow ourselves to become attached to things and people, however enticing, that might end in our own self-destruction.

Wednesday

HIS LEGACY IN SCRIPTURE

Read Judges 13:1–5.
1. A rhythm runs through the book of Judges. It goes like this: The people turn away from God to false gods; God allows them to fall into the hands of their enemies as punishment; God sees their plight and rescues them. Does this same threefold rhythm—of sin, deliverance into the hand of enemies, and eventual rescue—occur today? If so, give some examples.
2. Like other notable biblical figures—Isaac, Jacob, Samuel, John the Baptist, and Jesus—Samson's mother experienced divine intervention in the birth of her child. What does this signify about God's purpose in his life story?

Read Judges 15:14–19.
3. In this incident, Samson's incredible strength (killing a thousand men) is counterpoised with his human weakness (desperate for a drink of water). What does this contrast reveal about him?

Read Judges 16:15–21.
4. Samson finally gave in to Delilah's insistent demands to know the secret of his strength. What does the story of Samson and Delilah reveal about his priorities?

INTERESTING FACT

The book of Judges tells the stories of twelve tribal heroes who rose to prominence in Israel after the death of Joshua and before the institution of the monarchy in Israel. These judges weren't simply magistrates (some may not have had any judicial function whatever) but charismatic leaders whom God raised up to deliver his people during periods of particular danger. Three of the most famous are Deborah, Gideon, and Samson. Though the Israelites, under the leadership of Joshua, had taken possession of much of Canaan, they still had enemies in the land, the principal of which during Samson's time were the Philistines.

Thursday

HIS LEGACY OF PROMISE

"With a donkey's jawbone I have made donkeys of them. With a donkey's jawbone I have killed a thousand men." With all due respect, it is possible to wonder whether Samson's boast might contain a bit of unintended irony. After all, Samson hardly seems fit for the role of hero—a strong man too weak to control his own passions, his outer strength collapsing because of his inner weakness. And yet he was the rough instrument that God used to deliver his people from an enemy too strong for them. The story of Samson assures us that God can and will do what he intends to do. But how much better would it have been had he been an instrument finely honed and shaped to accomplish the divine intention for his life?

Promises in Scripture

The LORD has heard my cry for mercy;
the LORD accepts my prayer.
All my enemies will be ashamed and dismayed;
they will turn back in sudden disgrace.

—Psalm 6:9–10

Many are the plans in a man's heart,
but it is the LORD's purpose that prevails.

—Proverbs 19:21

Wait for the LORD, and he will deliver you.

—Proverbs 20:22

The LORD Almighty has sworn,
"Surely, as I have planned, so it will be,
and as I have purposed, so it will stand."

—Isaiah 14:24

Friday

HIS LEGACY OF PRAYER

"O Sovereign LORD, remember me. O God, please strengthen me just once more." —Judges 16:28

Reflect On: Judges 16:23–31

Praise God: For his sovereignty.

Offer Thanks: For God's strength working within you.

Confess: Any promises you have made to God and not kept.

Ask God: To make you a person who is strong on the inside.

Punishment has a way of humbling us. Samson must have been a pitiable sight—weak as any other man, blind, reduced to performing menial work normally reserved for women. As he ground the grain day after day, he would certainly have had time in his Philistine captivity to brood over the events of his life. Perhaps his prayer to God, even though centered on a desire to pay back his captors for what they had done to him, shows evidence of repentance, of a readiness to be God's instrument for defeating a people who had so long oppressed his own people. Whatever the case, God heard the last words he spoke and granted his prayer, making him even more effective in death than he had been in life.

Father, I thank you that the plans and purpose of your heart stand firm forever. Help me to be in complete alignment with your plans for my life. If I waver, then bring me back, no matter what it takes. Use the hard things in my life to shape me so that I can be used however and wherever you intend.

BOAZ

His Name May Mean "In Strength"

His Work: He was a wealthy landowner.

His Character: Boaz was a capable and upright man, so touched by the loyalty and generosity of a young widow named Ruth that he responded to her with extraordinary generosity, playing the role of kinsman-redeemer for her and her mother-in-law, Naomi.

His Triumph: To find a well-suited wife who blessed him with a son.

Key Scriptures: Ruth 2–4

Monday

HIS STORY

Ruth woke reluctantly, the gnawing in her stomach prodding her out of bed. Though the famine had ended long ago, there was still precious little bread in Naomi's house. So Ruth spoke with her mother-in-law: "Let me go to the fields and pick up the leftover barley behind anyone in whose eyes I find favor." It mattered little that barley was considered the food of horses and donkeys. She and Naomi had to have something to eat.

Working the fields was hard on a woman. The constant bending and lifting under the sweltering sun made even the young ones look stooped and leathery. But Ruth didn't care. She thought only of the promise she had made to Naomi after both their husbands had died in Moab and Naomi had informed her of her desire to return to her home in Israel: "Where you go I will go, and where you stay I will stay," Ruth had vowed. "Your people will be my people and your God my God. Where you die I will die, and there I will be buried." The young woman's determination had melted the old woman's objections, aware as she was of all that Ruth would leave behind in her homeland in exchange for an uncertain future in Israel. Now that Naomi was back in Bethlehem with no husband or sons to care for her, she needed Ruth more than ever.

So Ruth found work gleaning in a field belonging to a wealthy landowner named Boaz. On the first day, as she stood for a moment and stretched to ease her back, she saw a man looking at her. His face was broad and craggy, sturdy like the land, his hair a thick white, like water foaming in the river. As he turned away to greet the workers in the field and then to speak privately to one of the men, she realized who he was, and then she wondered if he was questioning his foreman about the newly arrived foreigner, the woman gleaning in his fields.

Bending down, Ruth began gathering the copper-colored stalks again, stuffing them into an apronlike sack tied to her waist. Before she could finish the song she was humming, Boaz greeted her, saying, "My daughter, listen to me. Don't go and glean in another field and don't go away from here. Watch the field where the men are harvesting, and follow along after the girls. I have told the men not to touch you. And whenever you are thirsty, go and get a drink from the water jars the men have filled."

Surprised by his generosity, Ruth exclaimed: "Why have I found such favor in your eyes that you notice me—a foreigner?"

"I've been told all about what you have done for your mother-in-law since the death of your husband," Boaz replied, "how you left your father and mother and your homeland and came to live with a people you did not know before. May the LORD repay you for what you have done. May you be richly rewarded by the LORD, the God of Israel, under whose wings you have come to take refuge."

As Ruth worked the fields that morning, she felt Boaz's gaze returning to her. When it came time to eat, he motioned to her, saying, "Take some bread and dip it in the wine vinegar." After he saw she had eaten her fill of bread and roasted grain, she heard him say to the harvesters: "Even if she gathers among the sheaves, don't embarrass her. Instead, pull out some stalks from the bundles and leave them for her to pick up, and don't rebuke her."

That night, when Ruth hauled the day's rich harvest back to town, she was welcomed home by an amazed Naomi: "Where did you glean today? Blessed be the man who took notice of you!" When Naomi learned that Ruth had been working in Boaz's fields, she exclaimed, "The LORD bless him! God has not stopped showing his kindness to the living and the dead. That man is our close relative; he is one of our kinsman-redeemers."

Ruth slept soundly that night, weary from her labors and comforted by the thought of the man's unexpected kindness. It felt good to know that she and Naomi had family connections in Bethlehem. One day Naomi turned to Ruth and said, "My daughter, should I not try to find a home for you, where you will be well provided for? And is not Boaz our kinsman? Tonight he will be winnowing barley on the threshing floor. Wash and perfume yourself, and put on your best clothes. Then go down to the threshing floor, but don't let him know you are there until he has finished eating and drinking. When he lies down, note the place where he is lying. Then go and lie beside him, and he will tell you what to do."

Though women normally stayed clear of the threshing floor during the evening festivities when men celebrated the harvest with too much food and drink, Ruth did as Naomi suggested. Once the revelry had died down, Ruth approached the spot where Boaz was sleeping, uncovered his feet, and lay down. In the middle of the night, he awoke, startled to see a woman lying at his feet.

"Who are you?" he asked.

"I am your servant Ruth," she whispered. "Spread the corner of your garment over me, since you are a kinsman-redeemer." For a moment the man said nothing, and Ruth waited, feeling suddenly exposed, afraid of what she might hear once he found the words to reply.

But the tenderness of his response warmed her: "The LORD bless you, my daughter. This kindness is greater than that which you showed to Naomi. You have not run after the younger men, whether rich or poor. And now, my daughter, don't be afraid. I will do for you all you ask."

Still, there was one problem to be overcome. Boaz explained to Ruth that Naomi had a closer relative than he, a man who had the right to marry Ruth. "Stay here for the night," he instructed her, "and in the morning if he wants to redeem, good; let him redeem. But if he is not willing, as surely as the LORD lives I will do it."

Then Boaz went up to Bethlehem and sat at the town gate until he found the man he was looking for. Cleverly, Boaz began by disclosing only half the bargain he was proposing, telling the man that Naomi had property to sell. "I thought I should bring the matter to your attention," he explained, "and suggest to you that you buy the land. If you will redeem it, do so. But if you will not, tell me. For no one has the right to do it except you, and I am next in line."

"I will redeem it," the man replied, eager to expand his holdings.

Then Boaz revealed the rest of the transaction, saying, "On the day you buy the land from Naomi and from Ruth the Moabitess, you acquire the dead man's widow, in order to maintain the name of the dead with his property."

As though snatching his hand from a hot stove, the man immediately withdrew his offer, saying, "I cannot redeem it because I might endanger my own estate. You redeem it yourself," he said.

So Boaz publicly declared his intention of buying the land and marrying Ruth. And all the elders who were at the city gates concurred, saying, "We are witnesses. May the LORD make the woman who is coming into your home like Rachel and Leah, who together built up the house of Israel. May you have standing in Ephrathah and be famous in Bethlehem. Through the offspring the LORD gives you by this young woman, may your family be like that of Perez, whom Tamar bore to Judah."

So Ruth married Boaz, a man old enough and wise enough to know a good woman when he saw one, a well-established man whose own generosity ended by making him famous in Bethlehem and beyond. For his young wife soon bore him a son they named Obed, and Obed became the father of Jesse, and Jesse became the father of many sons, including the great King David.

Tuesday

A LOOK AT THE MAN

An Unexpected Blessing

Boaz was a good man going about his everyday work when God brought an unexpected blessing into his life. Evidently, he was someone of standing in Bethlehem, a man who may have been content with life the way it was. Nothing in the legal tradition of the time required him to show the degree of kindness he displayed toward Ruth, the young widow from Moab. Boaz went out of his way to act as her protector and provider while she worked in his fields.

But marrying this foreign-born woman was something altogether different, a commitment that would entitle her to a lifetime of his protection and provision. What's more, a firstborn son would not be considered his offspring but that of her first husband's. But when confronted with Ruth's request for marriage, Boaz responded in a way entirely consistent with his character, acting as though she were doing him the favor rather than the other way around.

As a result, Boaz was blessed with a wife who must have been a pleasure to live with and a son who would become the grandfather of King David. Boaz was the living embodiment of the person who heeds the counsel of Philippians 4:8–9: "Whatever is true, whatever is noble, whatever is right, whatever is pure, whatever is lovely, whatever is admirable—if anything is excellent or praiseworthy—think about such things.... And the God of peace will be with you."

The man who sought to be a blessing to a young woman in need is memorialized not only in the book of Ruth but also in the list of ancestors included in the genealogy of Jesus Christ contained in Matthew's gospel.

Wednesday

HIS LEGACY IN SCRIPTURE

Read Ruth 2:1–12.

1. The Law of Moses instructed farmers to tolerate a certain amount of inefficiency at harvest time. Instead of stripping the land bare of its harvest, they were to allow the poor to pick up (glean) whatever the harvesters missed. It seems more than coincidental that Ruth ended up gleaning in Boaz's field. When have you ever experienced a divinely orchestrated "coincidence" in your own life? How did it affect you?

2. What does Boaz's greeting to his workers say about his relationship with them? About the kind of man he was?

3. What does Boaz's interchange with Ruth (vv. 4–12) reveal about both of them?

Read Ruth 3:1–11.

4. Women did not usually spend the night on the threshing floor. Why do you think Naomi asked Ruth to take this unusual, risky step?

5. Earlier in the story (2:12) Boaz prayed that God would bless Ruth: "May you be richly rewarded by the LORD, the God of Israel, under whose wings you have come to take refuge." Later Ruth asked Boaz to "spread the corner of your garment over me." The word translated "the corner of your garment" is also translated as "wings." Comment on the significance of this.

INTERESTING FACT

In ancient Israel the kinsman-redeemer was the male relative in the family responsible for protecting the rights of the family. His role was to avenge family wrongs or, more often, to buy back, or redeem, land that had originally belonged to the family. According to the Law of Moses, the land ultimately belonged to God, not to individuals. Families owned a leasehold on the land, originally given to them by lot, which could be sold during difficult times. But the land was to be returned to the original leaseholder during the jubilee year, which occurred every fifty years. It was the duty of the kinsman-redeemer to buy back, or redeem, the land in the period between the sale of the land and the jubilee year. The practice of levirate marriage, whereby a man's brother married his widow, was different but related to the role of kinsman-redeemer.

Thursday

HIS LEGACY OF PROMISE

Boaz offers us a wonderful portrait of a good man. Quick to admire the virtues of others, he showed extraordinary generosity and kindness to a young widow who came from a land despised by the Israelites. Instead of merely abiding by Mosaic law and allowing Ruth to glean in his fields, he went out of his way to make sure she would be safe and that she would gather a bountiful harvest. Rather than being offended by her unconventional offer of marriage, Boaz considered it more evidence of her kindness. He is the kind of man God promises to bless.

Promises in Scripture

> *Blessed is he who has regard for the weak;*
> *the LORD delivers him in times of trouble.*
> *The LORD will protect him and preserve his life;*
> *he will bless him in the land.*

—Psalm 41:1–2

> *He who finds a wife finds what is good*
> *and receives favor from the LORD.*

—Proverbs 18:22

> *The righteous man leads a blameless life;*
> *blessed are his children after him.*

—Proverbs 20:7

Friday

HIS LEGACY OF PRAYER

"May the LORD repay you for what you have done. May you be richly rewarded by the LORD, the God of Israel, under whose wings you have come to take refuge." —Ruth 2:12

Reflect On: Ruth 2:12–19

Praise God: For rewarding the goodness of those who belong to him.

Offer Thanks: That God has given you the means by which to bless others.

Confess: Any selfishness in the way you approach your belongings.

Ask God: To increase your kindness and sensitivity toward others.

On their first encounter in the fields, Boaz prayed a blessing for Ruth. It must have surprised him later on to realize he had become the answer to his own prayer. For Boaz, it seems, was the Lord's reward for Ruth's demonstrated faith in the God of Israel and for her loyalty to Naomi. In addition to *being* a blessing, Boaz *received* a blessing by marrying a woman whose character matched his own. Together, Ruth and Boaz were additionally blessed by becoming the parents of Obed and the great-grandparents of King David. Both are mentioned in the genealogy of Jesus Christ in Matthew's gospel.

Father, for all the ways you bless me every day I praise you. Help me to be like you by providing for the needs of others and by doing what I can to protect those who are without defenders. Help me to be sensitive to the needs of others so that I can quickly show them your kindness.

SAMUEL

His Name Means "The Name of God"

His Work:	Priest, prophet, and judge, Samuel helped transform Israel from a nation led by charismatic figures called "judges" to one ruled by kings, who were to exercise their authority not as other kings did, but as men who belonged to God. He anointed Israel's first two kings: Saul and David.
His Character:	Samuel was eager to hear God's voice and willing to speak his word, even when doing so meant rebuking a king and risking his life. A spiritual leader who won military victories against the Philistines, he reminded the people of God's faithfulness and of the vital importance of their obedience. Sadly, he failed to pass on these same character traits to his sons, who acted corruptly as judges in his stead.
His Sorrow:	That Saul, Israel's first king, failed to obey God.
His Triumph:	To help shape Israel into a monarchy whose kings were to be God's servants.
Key Scriptures:	1 Samuel 1:1–28; 2:18–26; 3:1–20; 7:2–16; 8:1–10:26; 12:1–25

Monday

HIS STORY

Every time Hannah held her boy in her arms, it was like holding the tangible evidence of God's kindness. For the Lord had heard the prayer she had uttered so fervently at the temple in Shiloh. She had wanted a son and God had given her one. Hannah had promised to dedicate her child to God, not just for a few years, but for the rest of his life. Now that Samuel was three and no longer nursing at her breast, Hannah knew it was time to make the journey up to Shiloh again, this time to entrust her boy to the priest Eli's care.

But Eli wasn't every mother's dream of what a father should be. His own sons, Hophni and Phinehas, were grown men who cared nothing for God, intent as they were on indulging their appetites. As priests, they made it a practice of stealing the best meat from the sacrifices and sleeping with the women who served at the entrance to the Tent of Meeting. But instead of punishing them, the old priest simply looked the other way, too tired, perhaps, to do more than scold them.

True to her promise, Hannah left the child in Eli's hands—and the Lord's. And God watched over Samuel in the temple. Year after year the boy grew in favor with God and people. And each year he received a little robe from his mother, who came up to Shiloh for the annual sacrifice.

In those days the word of the Lord was rarely heard in Israel, and there were not many visions. One night as Samuel was lying down in the temple where the ark of God was, he heard someone calling his name. Running straight to Eli, he said, "Here I am; you called me."

But Eli said, "I did not call; go back and lie down."

Again the boy heard a voice calling, "Samuel!" He got up and went to Eli and said, "Here I am; you called me."

Perplexed, Eli said, "My son, I did not call; go back and lie down."

Then the voice called a third time and Samuel got up and said to Eli, "Here I am; you called me."

Realizing finally that God was calling the boy, Eli advised him, "Go and lie down, and if you hear the voice again, say, 'Speak, LORD, for your servant is listening.'"

When the boy heard the voice calling for the fourth time, "Samuel, Samuel," he responded, "Speak, LORD. Your servant is listening."

The Lord's word was clear. His message to Samuel concerned Eli and his two wicked sons. "See, I am about to do something in Israel that will make the ears of everyone who hears of it tingle. At that time I will carry out against Eli everything I spoke against his family. For I told him I would judge his family forever because of the sin he knew about; his sons made themselves contemptible, and he failed to restrain them."

The next morning Samuel was afraid to tell Eli the vision, but the old man pressed him. After Samuel confided in him, Eli merely responded, "He is the LORD; let him do what is good in his eyes."

One day after the Israelites suffered another defeat at the hand of the Philistines, the elders suggested that the ark of the Lord's covenant be brought from Shiloh and carried into battle "so that it may go well with us and save us from the hand of our enemies." So Hophni and Phinehas brought the ark out, treating it like a charm that would magically insure a victory.

Instead, the ark was quickly captured and thirty thousand Israelites were killed, including Eli's good-for-nothing sons. When the old priest, who had refused to deal with the sin he knew about, heard that the ark had been captured and his sons had perished, he fell out of his chair and broke his neck. The same day Phinehas's wife died while giving birth to a son she named Ichabod, saying, "The glory has departed from Israel, for the ark of God has been captured."

But despite this miserable woman's assessment of the situation, God was still with his people, raising up a leader who would speak his word clearly and faithfully, inciting the Israelites to repentance and obedience. Through the years that followed, God spoke to the man who longed to hear his voice, to the great prophet Samuel, whose ministry began the moment he responded to the Lord with these words: "Speak, LORD, for your servant is listening."

Tuesday

A LOOK AT THE MAN

The King-Maker

Years had passed since the death of Eli and his sons, and Samuel was growing old, his own sons more like Eli's than he cared to admit. He had judged Israel faithfully for many years, but the elders were clamoring for a change, insisting Israel needed a king like the other nations of the world.

This demand for a king seemed to Samuel like more evidence of their waywardness. This stiff-necked people were impossible to lead, always so certain they knew what was best for them. So Samuel railed against the idea until the people became so adamant that he made it a matter for prayer. He heard a surprising answer from the Lord: "Samuel, listen to all that the people are saying to you; it is not you they have rejected, but they have rejected me as their king. As they have done from the day I brought them up out of Egypt until this day, forsaking me and serving other gods, so they are doing to you. Now listen to them; but warn them solemnly and let them know what the king who will reign over them will do."

So Samuel described in frightening detail all the demands a king would place on them—drafting their sons and daughters to work and die for him, devouring the fruits of their labor, requiring so much that they would feel enslaved by him. But the leaders insisted, "We want a king over us. Then we will be like all the other nations with a king to go out before us and fight our battles."

So God gave them a king named Saul, a man who stood a head taller than most other men, yet a man who was no better at following the Lord than they had been. This was the king Samuel had to anoint. The king he had to guide. The king he finally had to pass judgment on, delivering a message any man would fear to render a king—that God intended to tear the crown from him and give it to another man.

Then the Lord told Samuel to fill his horn with oil and go to Jesse of Bethlehem, because one of his sons was to be king. Though Samuel feared Saul's wrath if he were to anoint a new king, he did as the Lord commanded, and as soon as he saw Jesse's eldest son, he was certain he had found Israel's next king.

But the Lord thought otherwise, saying to Samuel, "Do not consider his appearance or his height, for I have rejected him. The LORD does not look at the things man looks at. Man looks at the outward appearance, but the LORD looks at the heart." Six more of Jesse's sons passed before Samuel, but each one was rejected. And then came David, the youngest of Jesse's sons, a shepherd boy, as strong and solid on the inside as he looked on the outside. Samuel took the horn and poured the oil over David's head, anointing him king in the presence of his brothers.

Years passed before David finally ascended to the throne of Israel. By then Samuel was dead. But the man who had been an answer to his mother's prayer and who had been dedicated to God in a special way for the whole of his lifetime had fulfilled God's purpose, helping Israel make the transition from the chaotic period of the judges, when every man did what was right in his own eyes, to the period of the kings of Israel, when the Lord God searched for a ruler who would be a man after his own heart.

Wednesday

HIS LEGACY IN SCRIPTURE

Read 1 Samuel 3:10–21.

1. God's revelation to the boy Samuel took the form of a prophetic judgment of Eli, the priest, regarding his two wicked sons. Why did God hold Eli responsible for their behavior?

Read 1 Samuel 7:1–10.

2. Samuel was Israel's last judge, but he was also a prophet and a priest. How does Samuel show leadership in this passage?

3. What does this incident in Israel's life say about the connection between repentance and deliverance from one's enemies? Do you think this story has parallels in modern life? If possible, give some examples.

Read 1 Samuel 8:1–9, 19–22.

4. Why do you think Samuel objected to the Israelite's demand for a king?

5. Why do you think the people were so insistent about having a king? What is the significance of their desire to "be like all the other nations with a king to lead us"?

INTERESTING FACTS

When the ark of the Lord was captured by the Philistines, the Israelites felt as though God had departed from the midst of his people. The pattern for the ark had originally been revealed to Moses on Mount Sinai. Made of acacia wood, it was a rectangular box, 3¾- feet long and 2¼- feet wide and high. Gold-plated inside and out, it had rings at its four corners into which carrying poles were permanently inserted. A lid of gold was placed over the ark, and two winged cherubim made out of gold were positioned at opposite ends of the lid facing each other. This golden cover became known as "the mercy seat." Inside the ark were the stone tablets containing the Ten Commandments, a gold jar with manna in it, and Aaron's rod—memorials of God's covenant and saving power. The ark became a significant feature in the story of God's people, leading them in their wilderness journeys and also going before them as they crossed the Jordan River at the beginning of Joshua's conquest of Canaan. After a few months it was recovered from the Philistines but remained in relative obscurity during Samuel's tenure in Israel. Many years later King David brought the ark to Jerusalem.

Thursday

HIS LEGACY OF PROMISE

Unlike Samson, who had delivered the Israelites from their Philistine overlords through sheer muscle power, Samuel initiated Israel's deliverance by helping the people face the root cause of their lack of might—their continued disobedience and idolatry. Because Samuel realized God's promised protection depended on their obedience, he led the people through a time of repentance and intercession that restored their relationship with God and called forth his protective care (1 Samuel 7:10).

Promises in Scripture

From the LORD *comes deliverance.*   —Psalm 3:8

In repentance and rest is your salvation.   —Isaiah 30:15

There will be more rejoicing in heaven over one sinner who repents than over ninety-nine righteous persons who do not need to repent.

                                                        —Luke 15:7

Friday

HIS LEGACY OF PRAYER

Then Samuel said, "Speak, for your servant is listening."
　　　　　　　　　　　　　　　　　　　—1 Samuel 3:10

Reflect On:　　1 Samuel 3:1–10

Praise God:　　For speaking to us.

Offer Thanks:　For the way God has revealed himself to you.

Confess:　　　Any failure to listen to what God is saying.

Ask God:　　　To help you listen for his voice.

As soon as Samuel realized (and it took him a while) that God was speaking, he responded by listening carefully to whatever God had to say. Many of us think of prayer not as our time to listen but as our time to talk, telling God about our concerns, begging for his help. We find listening to God a tedious and uncomfortable ordeal. We prefer to cut to the chase, to get God to do things for us right now, this minute. But a life of prayer that is deep and real can develop only by spending time in God's presence, listening as well as talking, allowing him to initiate so that we can respond. Because Samuel was eager to listen to whatever God had to say to him, he was able to fulfill the unique role God intended for him in the life of his people.

Father, sometimes I find it so hard to listen for your voice. I'd much rather do something or say something than make the effort of listening carefully for what you may be trying to say to me. Forgive me for the ways I have failed to listen, and give me a greater desire to hear your voice. Increase my faith that you want to speak to me and that I will be able to hear you.

SAUL

His Name Means "The One Asked For, Requested"

His Work:	As Israel's first king, his role was to unite the tribes of Israel against their enemies and to begin the process of establishing Israel as a monarchy.
His Character:	Though his reign began well, Saul failed to live up to his calling, trusting himself more than he trusted God. Mentally unstable, he became so jealous of David that he tried to murder him. His last battle with the Philistines ended in his suicide and in the death of his eldest son, Jonathan.
His Sorrow:	To become so alienated from God that he could no longer hear the Lord's voice or receive his help; to have the kingdom torn from him and his heirs because of his unfaithfulness.
His Triumph:	His impressive military conquests, including victories over the surrounding Moabites, Ammonites, Philistines, and Amalekites.
Key Scriptures:	1 Samuel 13:5–14; 16:14–23; 18:5–9

Monday

HIS STORY

It was the seventh day, and still there was no sign of Samuel. The prophet's instructions to the new king had seemed simple enough at the time: "Go ahead of me to Gilgal, and I will surely come down to sacrifice burnt offerings and fellowship offerings. Wait seven days until I come to you and tell you what you are to do." But Saul had begun to wonder if Samuel really intended him to wait so long, especially in light of present circumstances. Many of his own troops were beginning to desert him, terrified by the great horde of Philistines gathering at Micmash, just a few miles away. Those who remained were not much better, hiding in caves and thickets among the rocks and in pits and cisterns. How could he rally his men if he could not act? What good was it being king if he couldn't make a move when he needed to?

So Saul made a decision that would destroy the promise his future held. In preparation for battle, he offered the sacrifice with his own hands, foolishly thinking he could win God's favor by disregarding the command of the Lord's prophet.

Just as he finished, Samuel arrived. "What have you done?" the prophet inquired.

Saul tried to excuse himself. "When I saw that the men were scattering, and that you did not come at the set time, and that the Philistines were assembling at Micmash, I thought, 'Now the Philistines will come down against me, and I have not sought the LORD's favor.' So I felt compelled to offer the burnt offering."

"You acted foolishly," Samuel said. "You have not kept the command the LORD your God gave you; if you had, he would have established your kingdom over Israel for all time. But now your kingdom will not endure; the LORD has sought out a man after his own heart and appointed him leader of his people, because you have not kept the LORD's command."

So the Spirit of God departed from Saul, and he fell prey to periods of intense depression brought about by an evil spirit. Eager to relieve his suffering, Saul's attendants advised him to search for a harpist whose music would soothe him. Desperate for any kind of relief, Saul listened carefully as one of the servants told him about a man who could help. "I have seen a son of Jesse of Bethlehem who knows how to play the harp. He is a brave man and a warrior. He speaks well and is a fine-looking man. And the LORD is with him."

So, without knowing it, Saul invited the man who would become his rival for the throne to join his inner circle. From then on, whenever Saul felt tormented, David would take up his harp and play, and relief would come to Saul.

Saul rewarded David by promoting him within the ranks of his army. But the young warrior was so good at fighting that women from all over Israel began greeting Saul's army by dancing and by singing a refrain that angered the king more every time he heard it: "Saul has slain his thousands, and David his tens of thousands."

"They have credited David with tens of thousands, but me with only thousands," Saul thought. "What more can he get but the kingdom?" And from that time on he kept a jealous eye on David.

Tuesday

A LOOK AT THE MAN

A Waste of Talent

A well-known adage indicates how hard it can be to get things right the first time around, reminding us that "the first pickle is always the hardest to get out of the jar." That bit of folk wisdom could certainly apply to Israel's first attempt at transforming itself into a monarchy.

A head taller than other men, Saul must have seemed an excellent choice as a ruler. God, after all, had selected him, the prophet had anointed him, and the people had all shouted, "Long live the king!" But even divine affirmation and popular support were not enough to insure Saul's success. Only Saul could guarantee it by responding faithfully to what God was asking.

But time after time, Saul prevaricated. Told to wait, he took matters into his own hands. Commanded to kill the Amalekites and destroy everything they owned, he spared their king and preserved the best of their livestock. Though fortune-telling was forbidden, he consulted a medium. Whenever he was confronted with his disobedience, he made excuses:

"You didn't come."

"The Philistines were about to destroy us."

"I felt compelled to offer the sacrifice."

"We saved the best of the sheep and cattle to sacrifice to the LORD, but we totally destroyed the rest."

"God won't talk to me, and I need to know what to do."

The excuses kept coming, like one bad penny after another. Centuries later they seem so plausible, so familiar, so understandable—at least to us. But not to the God who reads our hearts by how we act or fail to act.

So Saul's life and his rule as king gradually disintegrated. His mind became poisoned by jealousy and fear. A son and a daughter were estranged from him because of their love for David. Paranoia finally drove him to attempt an impossible task—to kill a man God himself was determined to protect. In the end, he lost more than a kingdom, forfeiting everything that matters in life—his family, his future, his own integrity.

Wednesday

HIS LEGACY IN SCRIPTURE

Read 1 Samuel 13:5–14.

1. Put yourself in Saul's shoes for a moment. Facing a huge force of well-armed Philistines, the Israelites became terrified as they waited day after day for Samuel to show up. How would you have reacted under this pressure?

2. Do you think God still tests us today as he tested Saul and others in biblical times? How has God tested you? Describe the situation and your response.

3. Samuel says that God had rejected Saul and "sought out a man after his own heart" to be leader. What does it mean to be a man or woman after God's own heart? (See Acts 13:22.)

Read 1 Samuel 15:7–22.

4. Why do you think Saul failed to obey the instructions to destroy the Amalekites and all their belongings?

5. Saul was quick to defend his disobedience by rationalizing it (vv. 13–21). What can we learn from Saul's story about our own tendency to rationalize our failures?

GOING DEEPER

Read 1 Samuel 28.

6. Saul's encounter with the medium at Endor is one of the strangest and saddest passages in Scripture because it displays the disintegration of a man whom God had intended for greatness. But Saul's inclination to trust his own instincts rather than to trust the Lord undermined God's plan for his life. Instead of becoming a strong and able leader, Saul became morally and emotionally weak, a man whose judgment consistently failed him and others. What does this story imply about the connection between obedience and our spiritual and emotional health? About our ability to hear God?

Thursday

HIS LEGACY OF PROMISE

Saul offers us a perfect example of how a man can foil God's promises and plans for his life. Chosen to be Israel's first king, he had the opportunity to destroy Israel's enemies completely and secure the kingdom for his heirs. Because of his halfheartedness and his blatant disobedience, his own children (his daughter Michal and his sons Jonathan, Abinadab, Malkishua, Armoni, and Mephibosheth) suffered greatly. Tormented by feelings of depression, anger, jealousy, and fear, he finally killed himself before his enemies could destroy him in battle. When the Philistines found his body, they cut off his head and tacked his corpse onto a city wall as a trophy of victory. Meant to be a great ruler, he instead became a pitiable victim, undermined by his tendency to trust himself more than he trusted God. A life of exceptional promise devolved into a life of great disappointment.

Promises in Scripture

The LORD is my strength and my shield;
my heart trusts in him, and I am helped.

—Psalm 28:7

Your word is a lamp to my feet
and a light for my path.

—Psalm 119:105

Now then, my sons, listen to me;
blessed are those who keep my ways.
Listen to my instruction and be wise;
do not ignore it.
Blessed is the man who listens to me. . . .
For whoever finds me finds life.

—Proverbs 8:32–35

Friday

HIS LEGACY OF PRAYER

"I am in great distress," Saul said. "The Philistines are fighting against me, and God has turned away from me. He no longer answers me, either by prophets or by dreams."

—1 Samuel 28:15

Reflect On: 1 Samuel 28:5–20

Praise God: For his word in Scripture.

Offer Thanks: For all the ways God has spoken during your lifetime.

Confess: Any tendency to disregard God's Word and its authority in your life.

Ask God: To increase your desire to read and pray the Scriptures.

At the end of his life, Saul despaired because he could no longer hear God, which meant that he no longer had access to the divine wisdom for governing his people and defeating his enemies. Saul became so desperate that he broke his own law, consulting a medium in an attempt to know the future. Like the man whose hearing is destroyed by a steady supply of loud music, Saul's spiritual hearing was destroyed by a steady habit of disobedience. Why, after all, should God keep speaking to someone who wouldn't obey the words he had already spoken? Though Saul sets a negative example, it's still a useful one. It tells us that if we are serious about wanting to hear God's voice, we need only obey the word he has already spoken. Trust and obedience will sharpen our spiritual ears so that we will experience the blessing of being connected to the God who loves us and wants to guide us.

Father, thank you for the particular ways you have spoken to me—through your word in Scripture, through other people, and through the circumstances of my life. I ask you to sharpen my spiritual hearing so that I will miss not even one word of what you want to say to me.

DAVID

His Name May Mean "Beloved"

His Work:	A shepherd by trade, David became the second king of Israel.
His Character:	A man of stark contrasts, David was a man who did nothing halfheartedly. Though he sinned terribly, his repentance was deep and lasting. Scripture refers to him as "a man after God's own heart."
His Sorrow:	During his lifetime, David had to come to grips with his own sinfulness and the severity of God's punishment like the death of his sons and his inability to build the temple.
His Triumph:	Under David's leadership, the nation of Israel reached prominence like it had never known before.
Key Scripture:	1 Samuel 17

Monday

HIS STORY

"David."

Jesse's voice echoed off the hillsides until it reached the ears of a shepherd boy watching over his flock in a meadow outside Bethlehem.

"David!"

The young man gathered his things and ran home to meet his father, Jesse, who had an assignment for him. "Take this sack of roasted grain and these ten loaves of bread for your brothers and hurry to their camp. Take along these ten cheeses to the commander of their unit. See how your brothers are and bring back some assurance from them. They are with Saul and all the men of Israel in the valley of Elah, fighting against the Philistines."

The young shepherd eagerly agreed. The battlefront sounded far more exciting than the pasture anyway. So David made arrangements for the care of his sheep and set out to meet his brothers. Though the journey to the front lasted only a single morning, it changed the course of David's life.

He reached camp just as the army was marching to its battle position. Eager to watch his older brothers in action, David ran to the front line. To his surprise, instead of an army of Philistines, he found that the Israelites faced only one man and his shield bearer, standing defiantly before them in the open field. That one man, however, stood over nine feet tall, and his armor weighed as much as a small man. Like a schoolyard bully, the giant drew a line in the sand, challenging the Israelites.

"Choose a man and have him come down to me," he shouted. "If he is able to fight and kill me, we will become your subjects; but if I overcome him and kill him, you will become our subjects and serve us. This day I defy the ranks of Israel! Give me a man, and let us fight each other."

For forty consecutive days, Goliath's words had bellowed throughout the valley of Elah and straight into the hearts (and faltering knees) of the terrified Israelite army. Even Saul, their mighty leader, was afraid.

Winding his way through the ranks of soldiers, David pestered anyone who would pay attention to him, "What will be done for the man who kills this Philistine and removes the disgrace from Israel?"

Seasoned infantrymen looked down to see who was asking this presumptuous question. If it hadn't come from a mere boy, they would have been offended by the insinuation.

Standing in the crowd of soldiers was Eliab, David's oldest brother. *Who is that?* he asked himself. *His voice sounds familiar.* Turning around, he was enraged to see his little brother David. "Why have you come down here?" he barked. "And with whom did you leave those few sheep in the desert?" The older brother's jealousy burst from his lips. "I know how conceited you are and how wicked your heart is. You came down only to watch the battle."

"Now what have I done?" David replied. "Can't I even speak?"

Soon Saul, the king of Israel, heard that there was a youngster in the camp stirring up the ire of his men. "Go get him," Saul ordered one of his lieutenants.

David's first words as he stepped into the presence of the commander in chief of the armies of Israel—a place few soldiers had the right to stand—were these: "Let no one lose heart on account of this Philistine; your servant will go and fight him."

"You are not able to go out against this Philistine and fight him," Saul replied, his heart filled with a mixture of indignation and pity. "Goliath has been a fighting man since his youth."

That was all the boy needed to hear. "I've been a fighting man since my youth, too," David said, as he confidently summarized his experience for the king. "Your servant has killed both the lion and the bear; this uncircumcised Philistine will be like one of them, because he has defied the armies of the living God. The LORD who delivered me from the paw of the lion and the paw of the bear will deliver me from the hand of this Philistine."

Saul had never seen courage like this. *If only my soldiers could say the same,* Saul must have thought. *If only I had this boy's faith,* he might have added.

Moments later a boy holding only a sling and five smooth stones stood before a fully armed giant holding a spear, the point of which weighed fifteen pounds. "Am I a dog?" Goliath shouted. "Come here, and I'll give your flesh to the birds of the air and the beasts of the field."

"You come against me with the sword and spear and javelin, but I come against you in the name of the LORD Almighty, the God of the armies of Israel, whom you have defied," cried David.

An instant later the giant was nothing but a headless carcass, his warm blood soaking into the dry sand of the Valley of Elah.

According to the bargain he had offered, Goliath's defeat was supposed to transform the Philistine soldiers into servants of the Israelites. But in spite of the rules of the game, they fled for their lives like frightened schoolboys. Coming face to face not with a giant but with an eager emissary of the living God had scared the Philistines to death and altered the balance of power once and for all.

Tuesday

A LOOK AT THE MAN

The Boy Who Would Be King

It's the stuff of epic cinematography—hillsides filled with thousands of jostling soldiers, clattering armaments, and everything at stake. But the heart of the story of David and Goliath is real. It's the story of a young man who threw himself at life with great abandonment, confident as he was in the goodness and power of the God of Abraham, Isaac, and Jacob.

There were two defining moments in David's childhood. The first happened when Samuel visited his father's home looking for the man who would someday be king. The youngest son and least likely candidate, David, came in from the pasture to receive the prophet's anointing and then went back to work.

The second defining moment was when he encountered Goliath in a contest that would determine the outcome of a battle. Forerunners of the ancient Greeks, the Philistines were accustomed to deciding battles in an arena rather than between armies. In addition to saving lives, such contests indulged the desire to turn warfare into sport. The Philistine army must have thought they had it made with a warrior like Goliath in their ranks. But they didn't reckon on the young boy who believed that God was capable of anything. Winding his way through the company of Israel's soldiers, David's innocent questions were met with shock and derision. But David was astounded by the Israelites' lack of faith.

Even the king was afraid. "Don't you know who you're fighting for?" David asked Saul. "Where's your trust in him?"

The courage David exhibited as a young man who defended his father's sheep from wild animals and then defended God's people from a godless thug lasted throughout his life. And the same confidence in the God of his fathers marked his life in the years that followed.

Though David wasn't a perfect man, he confessed his sins with the same unfettered confidence in God that had marked his previous dealings. And because he never blamed anyone but himself when he fell, he received God's mercy with no impediments.

Almost five hundred years later the prophet Isaiah would write:

Seek the LORD while he may be found;
   call on him while he is near.
Let the wicked forsake his way
   and the evil man his thoughts.
Let him turn to the LORD, and he will have mercy on him,
   and to our God, for he will freely pardon (Isaiah 55:6–7).

Perhaps Isaiah was remembering David, the man whose courage, confidence, faith, contrition, and trust in God's mercy knew no limits.

David lived without restraint. No giant would deter him. He took the promises of the living God for his own and seized life with the certainty of knowing that God was with him. This was the legacy of the "man after God's own heart."

Wednesday

HIS LEGACY IN SCRIPTURE

Read 1 Samuel 17:1–50.

1. What does the scene in verses 1–11 indicate about the condition of Israel and Saul's faith in the covenant promises of God?

2. As astonishing as David's courage was, it is also astonishing that Saul put him forth as Israel's champion, since the boy's defeat would have meant the defeat of the entire Israelite force. Why do you think he took the risk?

3. Goliath, the giant who looked so impossible to defeat, was quickly dispatched by a boy armed with nothing but a sling, a stone, and unwavering faith, which must have seemed like foolishness to many. When have you needed this kind of faith to defeat an overwhelming obstacle? Describe the circumstances.

Read 1 Samuel 24:1–15.

4. Saul became so jealous of David that David fled to the wilderness for fear of his life. What does this passage tell you about David's character?

GOING DEEPER

5. David was Israel's greatest king. Of course, the prophecies in the Hebrew Scriptures concerning his eternal kingdom were not fulfilled in his lifetime. Instead, they were reserved for the man the Gospels often refer to as the "son of David"—Jesus Christ. Psalm 22 is one of the many psalms attributed to David. Read it through once and think about how it expresses the story of David, particularly during the period when he was fleeing from Saul. Now read it again in light of what you know about the story of Jesus.

Thursday

HIS LEGACY OF PROMISE

The promise God had made hundreds of years earlier to Abraham was brought to a more complete conclusion in the life of David than any other Old Testament figure. Through David, God built his kingdom, shaped his people into a powerful nation, cut off their enemies, and enabled them to live peacefully in the land he had promised to them many years before. In addition to being Israel's greatest king, David was a man who loved music and who loved to worship God through the psalms he wrote. In fact, many of the psalms in the book of Psalms, which is really a book of songs, have traditionally been attributed to him. In David, Israel finally had a king after God's own heart, a man who obeyed the Lord and lived by his promises.

Promises in Scripture

When your days are over and you rest with your fathers, I will raise up your offspring to succeed you, who will come from your own body, and I will establish his kingdom. He is the one who will build a house for my Name, and I will establish the throne of his kingdom forever. I will be his father, and he will be my son.   —2 Samuel 7:12–14

> *Even though I walk*
>   *through the valley of the shadow of death,*
> *I will fear no evil,*
>   *for you are with me;*
> *your rod and your staff,*
>   *they comfort me.*
>
>   —Psalm 23:4

> *Many are the woes of the wicked,*
>   *but the LORD's unfailing love*
> *surrounds the man who trusts in him.*
>
>   —Psalm 32:10

Friday

HIS LEGACY OF PRAYER

"The LORD is my rock, my fortress and my deliverer;
my God is my rock, in whom I take refuge,
my shield and the horn of my salvation.
He is my stronghold, my refuge and my savior."

—2 Samuel 22:2–3

Reflect On: 2 Samuel 22

Praise God: For his promises.

Offer Thanks: For God's faithfulness in keeping his covenants.

Confess: The unconfessed sin that keeps you from serving God wholeheartedly.

Ask God: For a renewed willingness to follow him.

David's great song of praise gives credit where credit is due. It is a song that recounts God's faithful love in glorious detail, specifying all that God has done for him—saving him from violent men, drawing him out of deep waters, rescuing him from powerful enemies, and stooping down to make him great. It is the prayer of a man intimately familiar with the character of God. David knew what the Lord was willing to do for the person who trusted in him. But instead of asking God to do something for you today, pray David's prayer of praise as though it is your own. Praise God in glorious detail for everything he has already done.

Lord, I will praise you for all the good you have done for me. For hearing my prayer and rescuing me. For lifting me up when I was in trouble. For blessing me in ways I could not have imagined. For defeating my enemies. For being my refuge and my shield. The Lord lives! Praise be to my Rock! Exalted be God, the Rock, my Savior!

JONATHAN

His Name Means "Yahweh Has Given"

His Work: The firstborn son of King Saul, Jonathan was a capable warrior and military strategist.

His Character: Jonathan demonstrated remarkable capabilities for friendship, selflessness, and loyalty.

His Sorrow: Although the rightful heir to the throne of Israel, Jonathan never became king. He also had to deal with the mental and emotional pathology of his father, King Saul.

Key Scriptures: 1 Samuel 14; 19; 20

Monday

HIS STORY

Their first meeting was in the Valley of Elah as the entire Israelite army watched the Philistines run for their lives. It was a historic moment and had the potential trappings of a celebrity encounter for both David and Jonathan. But as they continued to see each other, the camaraderie, the jostling, the laughter, the banter, and the serious conversation confirmed to both men that this was a great friendship—a once-in-a-lifetime alliance.

But the friendship between Jonathan and David was about to encounter unfathomable odds.

One day Saul, the king of Israel, gathered his personal staff—his attendants and his son, Jonathan—together. He gave them an order that stunned Jonathan. "I want you to kill David," Saul told them, his furrowed brow betraying his jealousy of David and confirming his anger and resolve.

"Father," Jonathan called, taking Saul aside, not wanting to embarrass the king in front of his men, "let not the king do wrong to his servant David; he has not wronged you." Jonathan's heart was pounding, yet he courageously spoke the truth. Son or no son, Saul could have Jonathan executed for this.

But Jonathan forged ahead. "You know how terrified we were in the Valley of Elah—you, me, and our entire army. And you saw with your own eyes what David did to the giant." Jonathan's intensity drew him closer to his father. "What David did out there made *you* the victor. Why then would you do wrong to an innocent man like David by killing him for no reason?"

Moved by his son's candor and conviction, Saul swore an oath. "David is safe," he said. "As surely as the LORD lives, David will not be put to death."

Jonathan hurried to tell his friend that the king had sworn a lifelong armistice. "Come quickly," he said to David. "My father has something to say to you." The men ran to the palace to hear Saul's promise again. "I will never harm you," Saul repeated. "God is my witness. I will not harm you."

"Thank you, my friend," David said to Jonathan as they walked away, his arm wrapped tightly across Jonathan's broad shoulders.

Soon the Philistines moved against the Israelites again. David was called into battle. And as he had done before, "he struck them with such force that they fled before him."

David's triumph reignited Saul's jealousy. Saul sent him a summons, and David appeared.

"You have need of me, my king?"

Saul turned and grabbed a spear from one of his soldiers at the ready. "No longer," he said, thrusting the spear toward the younger man. David dodged the weapon and fled the palace.

Saul was furious that David had escaped. So, ignoring his oath before his son, Saul called his men together once more with a directive to kill David. Jonathan was not present. Saul knew better than to invite him this time.

Before Saul's men arrived at David's home with their orders to murder him, David's wife, Michal, arranged for his escape through a window. Once free, David ran straight to his closest friend, Jonathan.

"I don't understand!" David cried, pacing the secluded hall. "Your father's hatred is unjustified! I want nothing more than to serve him!"

"What has happened?" Jonathan exclaimed, taking him by the arms to stop his friend's nervous pacing.

David looked him in the eye. "Your father tried to *kill* me. He threw his spear at me, and I barely escaped." Then David wept, utterly miserable, inconsolable. "What have I done?" he muttered through his tears, sinking to his knees. "What is my crime, Jonathan?" he pled. "How have I so wronged your father that he is trying to kill me?"

Jonathan's heart was torn. *Father swore to me he wouldn't . . . but David would not lie!* "Look," Jonathan finally said, his voice filled with as much confidence as he could muster, "my father doesn't do anything, great or small, without confiding in me. Why would he hide this from me? It's not so."

David lifted his eyes to meet Jonathan's gaze. "Forgive me, friend, this painful truth. Your father has gone against his oath to you and me."

But Jonathan wanted to know the truth for himself. "I will surely sound out my father by this time the day after tomorrow!" he told David. "If Saul is favorably disposed toward you, will I not send you word and let you know? But if my father is inclined to harm you, may the LORD deal with me, be it ever so severely, if I do not let you know and send you away safely."

Jonathan was his father's firstborn son and the king's loyal military leader. But if the evil in Saul's heart was going to put his friend in danger, then he had no choice but to protect him, risking his own life in the process. He gripped David's shoulder once more. How could his father be trying to kill such a man? "Listen to me, David. Do not appear at the feast table. I will see how my father reacts to your absence. And I will send you word."

The following day began a two-day celebration of the new moon. Saul expected David to be present, and Jonathan paid close attention to his father's reaction to David's absence.

On the first day, Saul paid little attention to the empty chair. But on the second day, he asked Jonathan, "Why hasn't the son of Jesse come to the meal, either yesterday or today?"

"David earnestly asked me for permission to go to Bethlehem," Jonathan lied.

Saul was furious. Not only had David missed the celebration, but he had received permission from his own son to miss the occasion. "You son of a rebellious woman!" he shouted. "Don't I know that you have sided with the son of Jesse to your own shame and to the shame of your mother who bore you?"

And then, in an attempt to push Jonathan, the heir to the throne, into the same raging jealousy that haunted him, he added, "As long as the son of Jesse lives on this earth, neither you nor your kingdom will be established. Now bring him to me, for he must die!"

But Saul's wicked attempt to drive a wedge between Jonathan and David failed. Jonathan stormed out of the room, and he refused to eat all that day, because he was crushed by his father's shameful behavior toward David. The thought of any harm coming to his friend nauseated him.

Jonathan ran to tell David what had just happened. "My father is going to kill you," he gasped, still out of breath. "You must run for your life."

And then, realizing that this meant that they would never see each other again, Jonathan and David kissed each other and wept. But David wept the most.

Tuesday

A LOOK AT THE MAN

Closer Than a Brother

By his own foolishness, Saul put his children in impossible situations.

His youngest daughter, Michal, was married to David, a man Saul openly hated. And his son, Jonathan, was David's closest friend.

Because of her father's unrestrained jealousy, Michal was forced to lower David from an open window to protect him from Saul. And Saul's irrational rage against David forced Jonathan to take sides against his father, the king of Israel.

As their friendship unfolded, we can assume that David confided in Jonathan about his anointing to be the next king of Israel. He would have told Jonathan about the prophet Samuel's visit to his father's home in search of Saul's replacement. Imagine the two-pronged disappointment that would have devastated a smaller man than Jonathan. First, he would have been greatly displeased with the news of the Lord's message to Samuel about his father. "I have rejected Saul as king over Israel." Second, it would mean that he, the oldest son of the king, was not going to be the successor to the throne.

There is no record of Jonathan being devastated with this news. Because he trusted God, he knew that Samuel never would have anointed David as the heir to his father's throne if he hadn't been divinely appointed.

The account of Jonathan is the story of loyalty at many levels. First, he was loyal to his father. At no point did Jonathan complain to David that his father was a deranged madman. In the midst of terrible conflict, Jonathan was steadfast in his respect for his father, even dying with him in battle.

Second, Jonathan was loyal to David. He had legitimate reasons to envy the successor to his father's throne, but he loved him instead. Like David, he was a capable leader and victorious warrior. But he refused to set himself against David, even though his father did everything he could to push him in that direction.

Finally, Jonathan was loyal to the living God. Even though he could have complained that his father's actions spoiled his own future, he trusted God's sovereignty. Whether through verbal confrontations with his father or delivering bad news to his friend, Jonathan was a man of impeccable integrity.

Some people imagine David's friend Jonathan as a milquetoast wimp looking to find esteem through his friendship with a man much greater than he. Nothing could be further from the truth. Jonathan was a strong man, a mighty soldier, and a successful leader. And it is from this position of influence that Jonathan introduces us to the greater power of loyalty.

Wednesday

HIS LEGACY IN SCRIPTURE

Read 1 Samuel 14:6–15, 20–23.

1. Because the Philistines held a monopoly over the production of iron, no one in Saul's army but himself and his son Jonathan possessed a sword or a spear. What does Jonathan's action say about his character and his faith?

2. What does this story say about God's ability to fight on behalf of his people? Have you ever experienced God fighting on your behalf? Describe the circumstances.

Read 1 Samuel 20:24–42.

3. Contrast Jonathan's attitude toward David with that of his father's. Note that both men knew they would lose the throne to David. What accounts for their different reactions?

Read 2 Samuel 1:25–27.

4. Some readers may wonder whether David's remarks about Jonathan carry sexual overtones. But to read them as such would be to interpret his words in light of our own culture rather than his. Instead, David's heartfelt lament illustrates the depth of his friendship with a man who "loved him as himself " (1 Samuel 18:3). What kind of character traits did Jonathan and David share? Have you ever had the kind of friend that Proverbs describes as one who "sticks closer than a brother" (Proverbs 18:24)? Describe this relationship.

GOING DEEPER
Read 1 Samuel 31.

5. Jonathan must have watched the steady disintegration of his father's personality as he tried to oppose God by fighting against the man who was to be his successor. Though Jonathan already knew who the clear winner would be, he still did not abandon Saul but stood with him in their last battle. What does this reveal about the kind of man Jonathan was?

Thursday

HIS LEGACY OF PROMISE

Jonathan is one of the few men in the Bible who seemed to be without character flaws. While Saul's jealousy toward David eventually drove him insane, Jonathan peacefully accepted God's choice of David as the next king, even though it meant giving up his own right to the throne. While Saul failed to believe in God's power on numerous occasions, Jonathan consistently believed, saying, "Nothing can hinder the LORD from saving, whether by many or by few" (1 Samuel 14:6). While Saul was disloyal, attempting to kill even his own son (1 Samuel 20:33), Jonathan was the soul of loyalty—to his father, to David, and ultimately to God. He was a man of integrity, courage, humility, and loyalty. A capable man, he was secure enough to let someone else be first. He possessed the confidence and generosity of heart to befriend a man others would have considered his arch rival.

Promises in Scripture

Let love and faithfulness never leave you;
bind them around your neck,
write them on the tablet of your heart.
Then you will win favor and a good name
in the sight of God and man.

—Proverbs 3:3

The memory of the righteous will be a blessing,
but the name of the wicked will rot.

—Proverbs 10:7

He who fears the LORD has a secure fortress,
and for his children it will be a refuge.

—Proverbs 14:26

Friday

HIS LEGACY OF PRAYER

"Show me unfailing kindness like that of the LORD as long as I live, so that I may not be killed, and do not ever cut off your kindness from my family—not even when the LORD has cut off every one of David's enemies from the face of the earth."   —1 Samuel 20:14–15

Reflect On: 1 Samuel 20:11–17

Praise God: For blessing our loved ones through us.

Offer Thanks: For God's faithfulness from generation to generation.

Confess: Any failure to believe that God intends to use you to extend his blessings to the next generation.

Ask God: To make you the kind of person whose righteousness blesses others.

When a new king wanted to secure his dynasty, he commonly destroyed any and all rivals to the throne. Jonathan called on his friend David not to act like other kings but instead to deal kindly with him and his family. Because of Jonathan's loyalty, his son's life was spared when David came to power. We too can bless our children and our families by the kind of lives we lead, by the loyalty we show to God. As Scripture says, the children of the righteous will be blessed (Proverbs 20:7). Ask God for the grace to lead a life so pleasing to him that his blessings are reflected in the lives of your children and grandchildren.

Lord, watch over my family and protect us always. I ask you to show us your unfailing kindness. Be our refuge when life is difficult, our strength in time of trouble. Help my children to love you all the days of their lives and to pass on their faith to the children you give them.

MEPHIBOSHETH

His Name Means "From the Mouth of the Shameful Thing"

His Work:	Nothing is said about his occupation; because he lived his life without the use of his legs, Mephibosheth must have lived on the charity of others.
His Character:	Although he had good reason for self-pity, he was deeply grateful for David's kindness and was very loyal to him.
His Sorrow:	He was disabled, unable to walk.
His Triumph:	Because of David's generosity, Mephibosheth received land and servants and was welcomed at the king's table.
Key Scriptures:	2 Samuel 4:4; 9:6–13; 16:1–4; 19:24–30

Monday

HIS STORY

Saul and his son Jonathan were dead, killed in the same disastrous battle with the Philistines. When news came of their defeat, a nurse serving in Jonathan's household attempted to hide his son Mephibosheth, fearing for his life. But instead of saving him, she dropped the five-year-old, rendering him a lifelong cripple.

Despite the loss of Saul and Jonathan, Israel was not entirely defeated by the Philistines. Soon Ish-Bosheth, the boy's uncle and Saul's son, was proclaimed king. But one of Israel's tribes refused to follow him. Judah had already crowned David as king.

Finally, after two years of political chaos, assassins stole into Ish-Bosheth's chambers while he was napping and stabbed him to death.

When they cut off his head and carried it proudly to David, thinking they had done him a great favor, he had them executed for their wickedness.

With his father and grandfather gone and his uncle now dead, the crippled Mephibosheth had no choice but to live on the charity of others. Once the child of a prince, this tragic man could not earn a living for himself.

Many years later, when his monarchy was flourishing, David recalled a promise he had made to his dearest friend, Jonathan. That promise was to care for Jonathan and his family. David called for Ziba, one of Saul's former servants. "Is there no one still left of the house of Saul to whom I can show God's kindness?"

"Yes," Ziba answered. "There is still a son of Jonathan; he is crippled in both legs."

David sent an order that Mephibosheth be brought into his presence. This man who would have been considered David's natural enemy bowed down, paying David honor. "Mephibosheth," David said, his voice revealing his feelings for his old friend Jonathan.

"Your servant," Mephibosheth replied.

"Do not be afraid," David answered.

Mephibosheth looked into the face of the king, as though finding it difficult to comprehend the kindness he saw there. "What is your servant," he sighed, "that you should notice a dead dog like me?"

"For the sake of your father Jonathan," David continued, "I will surely restore to you all the land that belonged to your grandfather Saul."

Mephibosheth was stunned by David's generosity.

But the king was not finished. "And you will always eat at my table."

Mephibosheth had never known such mercy, such grace.

David summoned Ziba to return to his chambers, repeating the promise he had made to Mephibosheth. Then the king ordered Ziba and his sons and servants to farm the land he had just given to Mephibosheth, to use the harvest to provide for his needs, and to act as the disabled man's personal servants.

After several years, Absalom, one of David's sons, led a rebellion against him. As David fled Jerusalem, he was surprised to see Ziba approaching on horseback. Following him were "a string of donkeys, saddled and loaded with two hundred loaves of bread, a hundred cakes of raisins, a hundred cakes of figs and a skin of wine."

Surprised by the offering, David asked Ziba about his master. "Where's Mephibosheth?"

"He's back in Jerusalem," Ziba reported, "waiting for your kingdom to fall and for Absalom to come to power. Mephibosheth believes that today the house of Israel will give him back his grandfather's kingdom."

"However, *I'm* still loyal to you," Ziba could have added. Now his gift seemed more like a bribe.

David was furious at the news of how Mephibosheth had repaid his kindness. "All that belonged to Mephibosheth is now yours," he told Ziba.

"I humbly bow," Ziba said. "May I find favor in your eyes, my lord the king."

After a while, David's men defeated Absalom and the king returned to the city. This time he was met by Mephibosheth. David hardly recognized the disheveled man who stood before him.

Mephibosheth pleaded with David, telling him that his servant Ziba had lied about his betraying the king. Surely his appearance was proof of his loyalty. For he had been so disturbed by David's absence during Absalom's revolt that he expressed his grief by refusing to bathe, cut his hair, or trim his nails. He begged David to believe the evidence of his own eyes.

Not knowing whom to believe, David recanted his earlier decision to strip Mephibosheth of his land and ordered Mephibosheth and Ziba to "divide the fields" equally.

"Let Ziba take everything," Mephibosheth protested, "now that my lord the king has arrived home safely."

But, as David had ordered, the land was divided between Ziba and Mephibosheth.

Making good one final time on his promise to "show kindness to Jonathan's family," David spared Mephibosheth's life and gave him more than he deserved.

Tuesday

A LOOK AT THE MAN

A Pledge of Allegiance

Mephibosheth was a broken man. When he was only five years old, his father and grandfather were killed in battle. That day the heir-apparent prince was stripped of his royalty. And, if that were not tragic enough, a fall from his nurse's arms permanently disabled him.

Some men are victims of their own poor judgment. But others suffer at the hands of others. This was the lot of Mephibosheth.

We can only imagine what life was like for him. Growing up, he must have heard stories of his grandfather Saul, Israel's first king and mighty warrior. His family would have told him that his father, Jonathan, should have been the rightful heir to the throne. And he certainly heard stories of David, the man who now reigned as the king of Israel.

But instead of growing up in luxury, prestige, health, and favor, Mephibosheth was forced to deal with life's "if onlys."

If only my grandfather had been faithful. If only my father had lived. If only I could walk. If only someone would remember me.

So Mephibosheth lived in obscurity in the home of a man named Makir on the opposite side of the Jordan River from Jerusalem. And then one day a message was delivered to Mephibosheth: "King David has called for you. You are hereby summoned to the palace."

We can only imagine how fearful Mephibosheth must have been to have an audience with the king. Sitting on the ground was a familiar posture for Mephibosheth, but even from that position, he bowed down when he was brought into the presence of the king.

David could have thanked this humble man for his respectful gesture. He could have reminded him that he was simply carrying out an old commitment made to his father. Or David could have told him of his plan to grant him his grandfather's land and give him servants and a home in the palace. Actually, he eventually did all these things, but his first words to this man were the most exquisite and comforting he could have spoken.

"Mephibosheth," David said, "do not be afraid."

And then David lavished Mephibosheth with more than he ever could have dreamed: land, servants, and access to the king's table. Mephibosheth had not deserved the misfortune that had marked his life. But neither did he earn the good fortune that suddenly befell him. Mephibosheth must have been overwhelmed by it all.

In the years that followed, it would have been understandable if Mephibosheth would have gotten accustomed to the lavish treatment—his initial humility eventually turning to pride. But this did not happen.

When his caretaker committed treachery and set David against him, Mephibosheth did not retaliate. Instead, he mourned the loss of the king's trust. And when David came to his senses and restored Mephibosheth's estate, Mephibosheth humbly refused the king's generosity.

Mephibosheth's gratitude for what the king had done for him was unshakable. His loyalty to David stood firm.

Wednesday

HIS LEGACY IN SCRIPTURE

Read 2 Samuel 9.

1. Imagine for a moment that you are King Saul's grandson. Your Uncle Ish-Bosheth, Saul's successor, was murdered by two of his own men. You yourself have been unable to walk since the age of five. Now David has established his rule in Jerusalem. The last thing you want is to be noticed by the new king. But he calls you to meet him at court. What are your thoughts? How do you react when you discover his true intentions toward you?

2. Have you experienced "God's kindness" (v. 3) in your own life? How has it affected you? Read 2 Samuel 19:24–30.

3. Now imagine that you are King David, displaced from Jerusalem because of the revolt of one of your sons. As you flee the city, Ziba meets you with provisions for your journey and tells you that Mephibosheth has betrayed you. But on your triumphant return, Mephibosheth greets you and swears his loyalty. Which man would you believe and why?

INTERESTING FACT

Many people hide their grief behind a façade of normalcy. As we pass them in grocery stores and office buildings, we have little idea of the internal anguish they may be experiencing. But Mephibosheth mourned openly for the tragic rift between David and his son Absalom by his refusal to maintain personal hygiene. Odd as the practice seems to us, such ancient mourning customs served a significant purpose by expressing visibly what a person was experiencing internally. Though David would have found it difficult to corroborate either Ziba's or Mephibosheth's story, the latter's appearance would certainly have shed doubt on Ziba's claim that Mephibosheth had been disloyal to David.

Thursday

HIS LEGACY OF PROMISE

In the world of power politics, Mephibosheth was a man without a future. As Jonathan's son and Saul's grandson, he could well have been killed by the new king seeking to establish the legitimacy of his own dynasty. When the king summoned him to court, he may have feared the worst. But that wasn't how David, "a man after God's own heart," intended to build his kingdom. As Mephibosheth bowed low before David, he must have been astonished to learn of the king's plans not to destroy him, but to bless him. Fearing judgment, he received mercy and blessing. Through David's kindness, God showed Mephibosheth his own great mercy.

Promises in Scripture

> *But you, O LORD, are a compassionate and gracious God,*
> *slow to anger, abounding in love and faithfulness.*
> *Turn to me and have mercy on me.*
>
> —Psalm 86:15–16

> *See, the Sovereign LORD comes with power,*
> *and his arm rules for him.*
> *See, his reward is with him,*
> *and his recompense accompanies him.*
> *He tends his flock like a shepherd:*
> *He gathers the lambs in his arms*
> *and carries them close to his heart;*
> *he gently leads those that have young.*
>
> —Isaiah 40:10–11

> *"For I know the plans I have for you," declares the LORD, "plans to prosper you and not to harm you, plans to give you hope and a future."*
>
> —Jeremiah 29:11

Friday

HIS LEGACY OF PRAYER

"Is there anyone still left of the house of Saul to whom I can show kindness for Jonathan's sake?" —2 Samuel 9:1

Reflect On: 2 Samuel 9

Praise God: Because he is still looking for people to show kindness to.

Offer Thanks: For the way God has expressed his mercy to you.

Confess: Any tendency to take God's mercy for granted, as though it is something you deserve.

Ask God: To help you reveal his kindness to others.

In many ways, Mephibosheth is such a pitiful figure—fatherless from an early age, crippled and unable to provide for himself, his future in jeopardy because of his familial ties. And yet he experienced a profound reversal of fortune because of one man's mercy. Though none of us like to admit it, we are not so different from this unfortunate man. Crippled by sin, cut off from the family of God, at one time our future was even bleaker than his. But if we now belong to God, we too have experienced the profound reversal that has resulted from one man's mercy—Jesus Christ, the great king who continues to surprise us by building his kingdom through the power of his mercy.

Lord, you tell us that mercy triumphs over judgment. I know this is true in my own life. Thank you for the tremendous mercy you have already shown to me. Never let me take your kindness for granted. Instead, help me to look for ways to be merciful to others.

NATHAN

His Name Means "He [God] Has Given"

His Work:	He was a prophet in Israel during the reign of King David and the early years of King Solomon.
His Character:	Nathan was a fearless man whose obedience to God's voice put him nose to nose with the most powerful person in the land, first announcing that King David would not have the honor of building the temple and later declaring his immorality and his severe punishment for it.
His Sorrow:	With great hopes for Israel's success under the monarchy, Nathan was an eyewitness to sin, corruption, and mutiny that tore the nation apart.
His Triumph:	Because of his own faithfulness, Nathan was given the privilege of being God's mouthpiece to an entire nation.
Key Scriptures:	2 Samuel 7; 12

Monday

HIS STORY

King David and Nathan the prophet were friends.

One day during a time of relative peace while David was relaxing in his home, he said to Nathan, "Here I am, living in a palace of cedar, while the ark of God remains in a tent." Always the irrepressible visionary, David dreamed about a permanent place to house the ark. For too many generations this most precious relic had boarded in temporary quarters. It was time to build a temple.

Nathan's response was immediate. "Whatever you have in mind, go ahead and do it." Then as if to convince himself, "For the LORD is with you."

Maybe he was afraid to challenge the king's dream of building a temple, but Nathan's promise of God's blessing wasn't true. In fact, David's vision was not the Lord's vision, and that night the Lord paid a visit to Nathan, challenging his presumptive remark to the king. "Go and tell my servant David," God said, "*this* is what the LORD says." The message that followed was very different from David's vision to build a temple himself.

There must have been a lag in Nathan's step as he went to see the king the following morning with news he'd rather not deliver. But Nathan knew that it was his job to convey God's message to all the people—whole and uncut—including the king, so he went to the palace.

David listened carefully as Nathan repeated God's words: "Who does the king think he is? Does he presume to tell me when my house is to be built? Am I not capable of taking care of the ark myself?"

The prophet continued, reminding David that his life had been in God's hands since his days as a shepherd, but David would not live to see the temple. God had said, "I will be his father and he will be my son. When he does wrong I will punish him, . . . but my love will never be taken away. His house and his kingdom will endure forever before me; his throne will be established forever." Nathan finished, daring to look up again at his king.

David stood and walked away from Nathan's presence. If Nathan had been apprehensive to this point, David's immediate exit must have terrorized him.

But Nathan had nothing to worry about. David's reverence for God and his word was nonnegotiable. In his private chamber, David cried out to the Lord, "Who am I, O Sovereign LORD, and what is my family, that you have brought me this far? And if this were not enough in your sight, O Sovereign LORD, you have also spoken about the future of the house of your servant."

Nathan's uncalculated response to David's temple dream had been corrected by the Almighty, and David's response was flawless—humble, God-centered, obedient.

Time passed as David's reign successfully unfolded. His military victories were innumerable. And in the spring, kings traditionally went off to war. This had also been David's habit. But that spring was different. A strange twinge of lethargy swept through his soul. As the trees budded and blossomed, David decided to stay in the palace, sending Joab in his stead.

But neglecting his responsibilities as king filled his nights with fitfulness. Restful sleep, while his lieutenants and troops were engaged in battle, was not to be. On one of those sleepless nights, while the king scanned the city from his rooftop, he saw something mesmerizing. In the dim light, he saw a woman stepping from her ceremonial bath and quickly wrapping herself against the cool night air.

David's innocent glance became a gaze, then a fantasy, an idea, a plan—and at last an obsession.

"Find out about that woman," David told a servant the following morning. "What is her name?"

"Bathsheba," the man replied later. "Daughter of Eliam and the wife of Uriah the Hittite, one of your soldiers."

Although it probably would have been preferable if the woman had not been married, this news made no difference. David knew what he wanted, and as the king, nothing would stop him. David sent messengers to summon the woman. The news that the king wanted to see her must have been met with mixed emotions. Who wouldn't be genuinely flattered? But she was a married woman.

Very little is written about the amount of time David and Bathsheba spent together. All we know for sure was that before "she went back home," she spent enough time with the king for her to conceive.

The next time David heard from Bathsheba her message was crisp and clear. "I am pregnant."

Confronted by his sins in such a tangible way, David's emotions must have nearly spun out of control, yet he chose to entrench himself further rather than confess and return to the ways of God. *If I can get Uriah home soon enough to sleep with his wife,* David schemed, *then no one will know the baby is mine.*

So David brought Uriah home from the front lines, but on the first night he refused to sleep with Bathsheba. On the second night, David wined and dined Uriah, hoping to dull his loyalty to his comrades on the front lines. But, once again, drunk or not, Uriah would not sleep with his wife.

As Uriah returned to the battlefield, David issued an order to Joab, his commanding officer. "Put Uriah in the front where the fighting is fiercest." What may have looked like a vote of confidence in the brave soldier, in another circumstance, was really a death sentence. Within days the man was dead.

God told Nathan all about it. And then the Lord issued an order to Nathan to confront the king with his sin. If Nathan trembled at the assignment of telling David that he would not be the one to build the temple, one can only imagine what incredible dread this mission must have brought to Nathan's heart.

But Nathan's job was not to be liked; it was to be obedient. And so Nathan approached the king once more.

Tuesday

A LOOK AT THE MAN

Speaking the Truth

Nathan loved David, the king of Israel.

The proof of this love was in Nathan's allegiance to the monarch and his sincere attempts to encourage the king, even to the point of affirming his ideas of a grand temple when God had not blessed the venture.

But the acid test of the prophet's affection was not in supportive or affirming words, but in truthful confrontation—the kind of confrontation that could cost the prophet his friendship with the king, not to mention his life.

Nathan was clever and creative. His involvement in the selection of worship music in the sanctuary (2 Chronicles 29:25) tells us of his sensitivity. His personal involvement in the naming of the baby Solomon hints to us of Nathan's tenderness (2 Samuel 12:25).

But Nathan had been given a terrifying assignment fit for the bravest warrior. And, if the nature of the commission wasn't tough enough, it had come as a directive of the living God.

Friendships are often put to the test over long hours of work or waiting. Friends pay a price by listening or issuing words of love and encouragement. But friendship knows no bravery like the bravery of brutal, truthful confrontation.

Those who have named this clash of emotions "tough love" have named it well. It *is* tough, but it is *also* the deepest form of love.

Although it was not Nathan's only challenge during David's reign, the confrontation following the king's adulterous affair with Bathsheba and murderous attempt to cover it up was his most grueling.

But instead of going nose to nose with David—a strategy that could have gotten Nathan in serious trouble—the prophet told a story. Drawing out the compassionate shepherd in the king, Nathan told him a story of a poor man's family, their only possession a ewe. Much more than simply an animal on the man's farm, this lamb was in every way a household pet. It "shared the man's food, drank from his cup, and even slept in his arms." The lamb was "like a daughter to the man."

Nathan must have known, as he watched the king's face, that David was captivated by the tale.

"In the same town was a rich man," Nathan continued. "Now a traveler came to the rich man, but the rich man refrained from taking one of his own sheep or cattle to prepare a meal. . . . Instead, he took the ewe lamb that belonged to the poor man and prepared it."

David was blind with rage. "The man who did this deserves to die!"

Nathan must have taken a deep breath, knowing he had the king exactly where God wanted him to be. "You are the man," Nathan said in measured tones. "You are the man."

The great challenge in truth telling, even with a close friend, is to keep the focus on the deed and the guilty party, not on the confronter's need to be right. In this, Nathan was brilliant. In Nathan's message, David clearly heard God's voice. Years later David would write: "Against you [the LORD], you only, have I sinned and done what is evil in your sight" (Psalm 51:4).

Nathan dared to prove his love for his friend by telling him the truth in loving confrontation. And so skillful was the prophet at dealing with the king that when the third child was born to David and Bathsheba, they named him Nathan after the man who risked it all.

Wednesday

HIS LEGACY IN SCRIPTURE

Read 2 Samuel 7:1–17.

1. Why do you think the prophet Nathan was so quick to assure David that his plan met with God's approval?
2. Have you ever made the same mistake, assuming your plans were from the Lord only to discover they weren't? What did your mistake teach you about discerning God's will?
3. Do you think God still uses prophets today? Why or why not?

Read 2 Samuel 12:1–14.

4. Why do you think there were such serious consequences to David's sins even though God had forgiven him?

GOING DEEPER

5. Nathan indicated that David would suffer multiple punishments for the sins of adultery and murder. To see how Nathan's prophetic word played out in David's family, read the following passages:

- "Now, therefore, the sword will never depart from your house, because you despised me and took the wife of Uriah the Hittite to be your own."   —2 Samuel 12:10

2 Samuel 13:28–29	(Absalom's revenge murder of his half brother Amnon for the rape of Tamar. Both Absalom and Amnon were David's sons, and Tamar was his daughter.)
2 Samuel 18:14	(Absalom is killed by Joab, the commander of David's army.)
1 Kings 2:23–25	(Solomon kills his half brother Adonijah for trying to usurp the throne. Both are David's sons.)

- "Out of your own household I am going to bring calamity upon you."   —2 Samuel 12:11

2 Samuel 15:1–15	(Absalom attempts to take over David's kingdom.)

• "Before your very eyes I will take your wives and give them to one who is close to you, and he will lie with your wives in broad daylight. You did it in secret, but I will do this thing in broad daylight before all Israel."   —2 Samuel 12:11–12

2 Samuel 16:22   (Absalom pitched a tent on the roof of the palace and slept with his father's concubines, thereby declaring himself the new king.)

Thursday

HIS LEGACY OF PROMISE

Nathan was a man with an unenviable task—to speak the painful truth to the most powerful man in Israel regardless of the consequences. By doing so, he wasn't just risking his influence with the king or putting his job on the line. No, it was much worse than that. Nathan could have lost his life, because the king had absolute power over his subjects, a power David had already abused. Fortunately for Nathan and the rest of Israel, David recognized himself in Nathan's parable and immediately repented. Because Nathan was more intent on pleasing God than pleasing men, David had the opportunity to do what Saul never did, though he too had the opportunity—to turn back to the Lord by humbly asking his forgiveness. And though he and all of Israel suffered for his sins, David still experienced the blessing of belonging to the one who had never ceased to be his refuge and his strength.

Promises in Scripture

> *Truthful lips endure forever.*
>
> —Proverbs 12:19

> *Fear of man will prove to be a snare,*
> *but whoever trusts in the LORD is kept safe.*
>
> —Proverbs 29:25

> *Anyone who receives a prophet because he is a prophet will receive a prophet's reward.*   —Matthew 10:41

Friday

HIS LEGACY OF PRAYER

Have mercy on me, O God,
according to your unfailing love;
according to your great compassion
blot out my transgressions.
Wash away all my iniquity
and cleanse me from my sin.

—Psalm 51:1–2

Reflect On: Psalm 51
Praise God: Because he is quick to forgive.
Offer Thanks: That God does not hold our sins against us as long as we repent.
Confess: Any sin you have tried to hide from yourself and from God.
Ask God: To purify your heart, making it "whiter than snow."

Nathan's name is included in the heading of this well-known psalm, because David is thought to have written it in response to the prophet's parable exposing his sin. Despite his greatness, David never reached a point in his life when he was invulnerable to sin's destructive power. And neither do we. Like David, we may even be more vulnerable to temptation when things are going well. And one of the worst things about giving into one temptation is that it is quickly followed by another and then another. Nathan offered David a chance to stop the corruption that was quickly settling into his soul by applying the only cure that works—the one that comes through repentance and forgiveness. By humbling himself before the Lord and openly repenting of his sin, David was spared the kind of corruption that overtook his predecessor Saul.

Lord, my sin is always before me. There's no hiding from it, no denying it. I know that you desire truth in my inmost heart. Therefore, I ask you to show me the truth about myself in light of the truth about your love. Cleanse me, and I will be clean; wash me, and I will be whiter than snow.

ABSALOM

His Name Means "Father Is Peace"

His Work:	David's third son, Absalom, was a brilliant military and political strategist.
His Character:	Absalom's remarkable assets of good looks and diplomacy became great liabilities, leading to his untimely death.
His Sorrow:	When Absalom's sister was raped by his oldest half brother, Absalom began a life of anger, rebellion, and revenge.
His Triumph:	For a time, Absalom was successful in gathering support against his father's reign.
Key Scriptures:	2 Samuel 13–15

Monday

HIS STORY

"Honor your father and your mother, so that you may live long in the land the LORD your God is giving you."

As little boys, the sons of the reigning king of Israel repeated these words—and the rest of the commandments—until they were accurately memorized. It was an important part of growing up as a Hebrew. But it was *essential* for the king's children to know the Law.

Absalom learned this commandment along with the others. But they were only empty words. This boy had other plans that would, in the end, cost him both land and life.

Absalom had the makings of a king—the looks, the passion, and the charm. "What a handsome prince you are," folks would say to him. "Perhaps you'll be a great king someday."

I'll be the king all right, Absalom might have mused. *And it'll be sooner than they think.* His plan began with regular contact with commoners. Not shy about using his father's influence, Absalom often picked out the finest chariot and summoned fifty men to run ahead of him. Early in the morning, he would venture outside the gates and stand by the side of one of the roads leading to the city.

There he warmly greeted the people and then asked if they had any complaints. Many openly expressed their concerns to David's son. *What a wonderful king we have,* they must have thought, *that he would send his son to hear our concerns.*

Absalom's reason for collecting the news, however, was not to help his father toward a more effective monarchy but to gather information and support against him.

"What town are you from?" Absalom asked.

"Mizpah," said one. "Joppa," said another. One after another they'd arrive, from Beth Shemesh and Hebron, among others. He talked with them all, listening to their cries and complaints against their king.

"I am no different from you," Absalom responded. "I am from one of the twelve tribes of Israel. So I feel your pain."

Then Absalom began to distance himself from his father, David, in the eyes of the people. "Look, your claims are valid and proper, but there is no representative of the king to hear you."

"You're right," they said. "Where *is* our king? Why does he not listen to us?"

"If only I were appointed judge in the land!" Absalom lamented. "Then everyone who has a complaint or case could come to me, and I would see that he gets justice." He knew how to get to the thorn in every heel, and his arrogance knew no bounds.

But the people lacked discernment. They saw Absalom's caring actions and words as genuine rather than treasonous. A son against his father. A subject against his lord. Day after day for four years, Absalom commiserated with the people. "He stole the hearts of the men of Israel." They loved him. Absalom's scheme was right on schedule.

Absalom's first strategy was to obtain public favor. His second appeared to be pious, but his intent was to reach the people of the kingdom and gain their favor. David knew none of this.

"Let me go to Hebron and fulfill a vow I made to the LORD," Absalom lied to David.

"Go in peace," David blessed his son.

Two hundred men accompanied Absalom from Jerusalem. They had been invited as guests and went with him, knowing nothing about the matter. In Hebron, Absalom sustained the charade by offering sacrifices.

Absalom's final strategy was political. He sent secret messengers throughout the tribes of Israel to say, "As soon as you hear the sound of the trumpets, then say, 'Absalom is king in Hebron.'" He also sent for Ahithophel, one of his father's counselors from Giloh—no doubt someone Absalom believed would support his coup d'etat. He guessed well.

Absalom's following grew.

Then one day a messenger came to David in Jerusalem with the awful news. "The hearts of the men of Israel are with Absalom," he reported to the king. David's heart was both ravaged and terrified, for news of this betrayal was nothing short of a declaration of war.

And David, the man who had not fled from the mouth of the lion or the paw of the bear, the one who had slain the giant in the Valley of Elah, ran for his life from his own son like a desperately frightened little boy. "Come! We must flee, or none of us will escape from Absalom. We must leave immediately, or he will move quickly to overtake us and bring ruin upon us and put the city to the sword."

"The king set out, with his entire household . . . and all the people . . . following him." This included not only David's family, but his counselors and the priests, carrying the ark. The whole countryside wept aloud as all the people passed by.

Once outside the city, the entire entourage stopped and the high priest offered sacrifices to the Lord. Then David ordered the Levites to return the ark to Jerusalem. "If I find favor in the LORD's eyes," he told them, "he will bring me back and let me see it and his dwelling place again. But if he says, 'I am not pleased with you,' then I am ready; let him do to me whatever seems good to him."

David and his people walked on toward the Mount of Olives. As David walked, he wept, his heart deeply broken. On his way, he received word that his old friend and adviser Ahithophel had joined Absalom's band. "O LORD," David prayed, "turn Ahithophel's counsel into foolishness."

As a seasoned leader, David knew the power of a king's counselors. To shore up his strategy, David sent his friend Hushai as a secret agent to Absalom. "I will be your servant, O king," David instructed Hushai to say to Absalom. "I was your father's servant in the past, but now I will be your servant."

So Hushai traveled to Jerusalem and met Absalom and his men just as they were entering the city. "Long live the king!" Hushai said as he greeted Absalom. "Long live the king!"

Recognizing his father's ally, Absalom challenged Hushai. "Is this the love you show your friend? Why didn't you go with your friend?"

"No," Hushai responded, tickling Absalom's ego. "The one chosen by the LORD, by these people, and by all the men in Israel—his I will be, and I will remain with him."

Because of Hushai's flattery, Absalom bought his story, and David's spy entered Absalom's ranks.

On Ahithophel's advice, in his first act as the self-declared king of Israel, Absalom pitched a tent on the roof of the palace. There in utter defiance of David and David's God, he took his father's concubines and had an orgy in the sight of all Israel.

Then, on Hushai's spurious recommendation, Absalom gathered troops from across Israel and marched against his father. When the news that Absalom was coming in battle reached him, David gathered his army, selecting three commanders to lead them. Then, just before they went into battle, David pulled in front of his commanders on his mount and looked at each of them. "Be gentle with the young man Absalom for my sake," he said.

Joab, Abishai, and Ittai were shocked at what they heard. *Gentle?* these commanders thought to themselves. *After what Absalom has done to you?* But they remained silent.

The armies of Absalom and David clashed in the forest of Ephraim. Twenty thousand men perished that day, and David's army emerged victorious. As the battle was winding down, some of David's men came upon Absalom. He had ridden his mule under a sprawling oak tree, and his hair had gotten caught in its low-hanging branches. The men quickly rode to their commander, Joab, with the news.

"Why didn't you strike him to the ground right there?" Joab shouted.

"In our hearing," the men protested, "the king commanded . . . 'protect the young man Absalom for my sake.'"

Ignoring their words—and David's request of him—Joab took three javelins and rushed to the place where Absalom was tangled in the oak tree and plunged the spears into the prince's heart. At the news of his death, Absalom's troops fled to their homes.

A messenger hurried to David to tell him that his army had prevailed. Ignoring the news, David asked one thing. "Is the young man Absalom safe?"

Tuesday

A LOOK AT THE MAN

Some Call It Treason

Absalom was a very special young man. Brimming with gifts and natural abilities, he was a natural-born leader. People were drawn toward him.

But Absalom was also a vicious conniver. Throughout his life, his bitter heart became a caldron of hatred and death.

Growing up in the palace of the king of Israel may not have been as delight as some in the kingdom may have envisioned. Absalom's father's sinfulness and the confusion of living in a home with David's multiple wives and a houseful of half siblings would likely have created untold chaos. Imagine this . . .

Absalom had a sister, Tamar, by his mother, Maacah. His half brother and David's oldest son, Amnon, was in love with her and tried to seduce her. Because she resisted, he set a trap for her. Pretending to be sick, Amnon asked David to order Tamar to tend to her half brother, which he did. But when Tamar brought food to Amnon, he pled with her to sleep with him. When she resisted, he raped her.

When word came to Absalom that his sister had been violated, he hated Amnon but said nothing to him. For two years Absalom seethed, plotting his revenge against his half brother. When the trap was set, Absalom had Amnon murdered.

Absalom did not see his father for three years. And instead of seeking out Absalom and confronting him with his treachery, David "longed to go to Absalom." What Absalom needed was a father who loved him enough to deal strictly with his violence. What Absalom got was a tentative father who was unwilling to jeopardize his son's affection. And what David got in exchange for his fear was a son who hated him for his powerlessness—a son who secretly resolved to overthrow him.

Suffering from the guilt of his own sinfulness, David was unwilling to hand Absalom any semblance of justice. For three years Absalom plotted his father's demise. And like an unsheltered man unwilling to acknowledge a gathering storm, David refused to see the dark clouds in his son's eyes.

Absalom was a man overflowing with potential. If only he had channeled those talents wisely! If only his father had helped him. But because he had neither the self-control nor the parental control to reign in his resentment and acrimony, Absalom died violently.

And David was forced to spend the rest of his life dealing with the agonizing "if onlys." *If only I had not sinned with Bathsheba, bringing all of this treachery to my family. If only I had loved my children enough to discipline them.*

When the Cushite reported to David that Absalom was dead, he was shaken. "O my son Absalom! My son Absalom!"

The tragic story of Absalom ends with one final "if only" from the king. "If only I had died instead of you," David wailed uncontrollably. "O Absalom, my son, my son!"

Wednesday

HIS LEGACY IN SCRIPTURE

Read 2 Samuel 13:19–29.

1. Sometime after David's affair with Bathsheba, his first son, Amnon, raped his half sister Tamar. Tamar's brother Absalom (David's third son) hated Amnon for what he had done. Why do you think the story of this family tragedy immediately follows the story of Nathan's rebuke of David?

2. Exodus 34:6–7 indicates that though God is merciful and compassionate, he punishes the guilty, even punishing children for the sins of their fathers. How is this revealed in the story of David's sons? Do you think God still punishes children for the sins of their fathers and mothers? Why or why not?

3. King David was furious (v. 14) when he heard what Amnon had done to Tamar, and yet he did nothing. Why do you think he failed to punish Amnon? How did David's failure to act justly contribute to the fulfillment of Nathan's prophecy?

Read 2 Samuel 18:9–18.

4. After Absalom's attempted revolt, he was hunted down and killed by Joab, the commander of David's army. Ironically, the mound under which he was buried seems a more fitting monument than the one he erected to memorialize himself (vv. 17–18). And the head that was so handsome (2 Samuel 14:25–26) proved to be his undoing, ensnaring him in an oak tree, where he became an easy target for Joab and his men. How did Absalom's character flaws lead to his downfall?

GOING DEEPER

Read 1 Samuel 16:15–23 and 17:1–16.

5. Ahithophel, the counselor who betrayed David, may have been the grandfather of Bathsheba. Some commentators believe he may have aligned himself with Absalom to pay David back for how he had treated Bathsheba and Uriah. Why do you think Absalom listened to his father's spy, Hushai, rather than to the wise counsel of Ahithophel?

Thursday

HIS LEGACY OF PROMISE

Scripture says that children are a reward from the Lord (Psalm 127:3). Yet children can also provoke our greatest worry and our deepest grief. On the outside, Absalom looked like a son any man or woman might desire—handsome, intelligent, well-spoken—a man to be admired, a man to follow. And yet Absalom's future was destroyed by his foolish pursuit of revenge and power. Instead of succeeding his father as king, he suffered the fate of a fool, hanging by his head from a tree. And David, the father who loved him but could not save him, cried out in grief, "O my son Absalom! O Absalom, my son, my son!" Like David, many of us have watched our own children with growing concern because they seem intent on pursuing a path that will lead them far from God. Though we may feel helpless to save them, there is still something we can do for them. We can choose to keep following the Lord faithfully, to listen to his voice and hold fast to him, remembering that the Lord is able to reach our children, even to the point of making us a channel of his blessing.

Promises in Scripture

With pain you will give birth to children.   —Genesis 3:16

Honor your father and your mother, as the LORD your God has commanded you, so that you may live long and that it may go well with you in the land the LORD your God is giving you.
                                                —Deuteronomy 5:16

Now choose life, so that you and your children may live and that you may love the LORD your God, listen to his voice, and hold fast to him. For the LORD is your life.   —Deuteronomy 30:19–20

Friday

HIS LEGACY OF PRAYER

"This is what the LORD says: 'Out of your own household I am going to bring calamity upon you.'"   —2 Samuel 12:11

Reflect On: 2 Samuel 15:1–12

Praise God: For acting with both justice and mercy.

Offer Thanks: For the ways God has disciplined you.

Confess: Any tendency to blame others for problems and difficulties you have brought on yourself.

Ask God: To treat you not as your sins deserve but according to his mercy.

Many of us fail to realize that evil is often the direct result of sin. We suffer and the world suffers because sin is rampant. Through no fault of her own, the baby of a crack cocaine addict is born with an addiction. The child of an abusive father becomes the school bully. The teenage daughter of an alcoholic parent develops a drinking problem. Even though sin winds its way through families and communities, generation after generation, grace winds its way as well, untangling the strands of sin so that fathers and sons, mothers and daughters cannot only be at peace with one another but at peace with God and with the world around them. Today, take time to pray for God's grace to be at work in your own family. If you need to, ask forgiveness for any way you have allowed God's law to slip from your heart. Ask him to repair the effects of your sin on others so that you and your children might enjoy a life that is blessed with his presence.

Father, I ask you to forgive me for my sins. I want to rededicate my life to you today. Please heal the effect of my sins on those closest to me. As I grow and mature as your child, help my own children to grow in their love for you and your ways.

SOLOMON

His Name Means "Peaceable"

His Work: The son of King David and Bathsheba, Solomon was the third king of Israel.

His Character: Known until this day as the wisest man who ever lived.

His Sorrow: Although he was an extremely intelligent man, later in his life he became disobedient to God and sacrificed everything on the altar of sexual excess. His inability to lead his own children led to the kingdom's division and ultimate fall.

His Triumph: Solomon built the kingdom of Israel to its greatest level in material wealth and land.

Key Scriptures: 1 Kings 2–5

Monday

HIS STORY

Early in his reign as king, Solomon visited the city of Gibeon, not far from Jerusalem, to offer a sacrifice to the Lord. That night in a dream, God paid Solomon a visit of his own, and his invitation was stunning: "Ask for whatever you want me to give you."

Solomon stepped back in surprise. *Just think of the possibilities,* he thought to himself.

"You have shown great kindness to your servant, my father David," Solomon began thoughtfully, "because he was faithful to you and righteous and upright in heart. You have continued this great kindness to him and have given him a son to sit on his throne this very day. . . . But I am only a child and do not know how to carry out my duties. . . . So give your servant a discerning heart to govern your people and to distinguish between right and wrong. For who is able to govern this great people of yours?"

"I will give you a wise and discerning heart," the Lord responded, "so that there will never have been anyone like you, nor will there ever be. Moreover, I will give you what you have not asked for—both riches and honor—so that in your lifetime you will have no equal among kings."

Solomon's eyes widened as his pulse quickened with wonder. Wisdom, riches, and honor—what else could a man hope for?

But then God added a sobering stipulation: "If you walk in my ways and obey my statutes and commands as David your father did, I will give you a long life." Solomon's face flushed in shame. He had already been disobedient. His first act as the king had been to take the daughter of the pharaoh of Egypt as his wife. But Solomon was moved by God's promise through his dream. When he returned to Jerusalem, he stood before the ark of the covenant and vowed his allegiance and obedience to the God of his father.

Soon God's provision of a wise and discerning heart was put to the test.

One day, two women stood before Solomon. "The living child is mine," one woman pled. Pointing to the other woman, she said, "It was she who rolled over in the night and smothered her child to death. Then, before I awoke, she gave me her dead child and took mine as her own"

"No, the living child is mine," the other woman demanded. "It was she who smothered her child."

"Bring me a sword," King Solomon commanded of his servants. "Now cut the living child in two and give half to one and half to the other."

The women—and all who were there—were shocked by the king's heartless plan.

"Please, my lord," cried one of the women. "Give her the living baby. Don't kill him!"

And with that, the king declared, "Give the living baby to the first woman. Do not kill him; she is his mother."

Even world-renowned dignitaries paid visits to Solomon. They came to see what he had accomplished and to test his wisdom with "hard questions." Such was the visit to Jerusalem by the queen of Sheba—a trip of almost twelve hundred miles. She arrived with a very great caravan—with camels carrying spices, large quantities of gold, and precious stones. The queen also came with all her questions. And, to her amazement, nothing was too hard for the king to explain to her.

Solomon accomplished many good things as Israel's third king. He orchestrated the building of a palace and the temple, a permanent house of worship and an apt dwelling place for the ark of the covenant. Built to elegant specifications, this holy building mirrored Solomon's love for God and his eye for beauty and attention to the smallest detail.

Politically, he organized the kingdom into twelve districts and appointed governors over each one. Educationally, Solomon held clinics and "described plant life, from the cedar of Lebanon to the hyssop that grew out of the walls. He taught the people about animals and birds, reptiles and fish." A lover of the arts, Solomon spoke three thousand proverbs and his songs numbered a thousand and five.

But Solomon was a failure. His great accomplishments did not compensate for his unwillingness to "keep God's statutes." Solomon loved foreign women and had an insatiable appetite for them. In spite of God's specific instructions, the king married not one, but multiple women from neighboring countries. His rationale was that he was building coalitions with these nations. How could the Moabites, the Ammonites, the Edomites, the Hittites, and the Sidonians attack the Israelites when the population included their own daughters and grandchildren?

However, God's laws were clear. As a nation, Israel was young and vulnerable. Intermarrying with foreigners meant the unavoidable blending of their infant faith with pagan beliefs. God knew that his people—including someone as strong and wise as Solomon—would have a difficult time standing against these extraneous persuasions. He was right. And not only was Solomon to blame for not stopping this cancer, he was guilty of encouraging it.

Like Saul and David before him, God had recruited Israel's king from the ranks of mortal, sinful men. Saul's transgressions led to his destruction; David's led to contrition and repentance. With no legitimate excuse, Solomon did not follow David's example. Instead, like

Saul, his flagrant disregard of God's laws led to his own spiritual destitution and death.

God's promise was clear: *Obey me and live a long life. Disobey me and die.*

In the end, Solomon's wisdom could not save him.

Tuesday

A LOOK AT THE MAN

The Legacy That Could Have Been

It's one of the most incredible moments in all of Scripture. The Lord of Israel, the Creator of the universe, makes an offer to a mortal man—Solomon, the son of David and the newly anointed king of Israel. Like the archetypal genie in the bottle, God asks Solomon to make a wish. But Solomon's historic opportunity becomes his greatest tragedy.

This may be the saddest story in the Bible.

It's the account of a man who literally had *everything*. The only thing more difficult to comprehend than his great mind, his enormous wealth, and his enormous power were the prospects of what he could have done with these things. Solomon had the incredible capability to change his world.

But in spite of doing many good things during his lifetime, he actually squandered this potential. Of course he built a name for himself. Go ahead and ask anyone to finish this sentence: "That guy over there has the wisdom of _____."

What happened to Solomon? The reason for his pathetic failure is actually quite clear. He broke this commandment: "You shall not make for yourself an idol in the form of anything in heaven above or on the earth beneath or in the waters below. You shall not bow down to them or worship them; for I, the LORD your God, am a jealous God" (Exodus 20:4–5).

Solomon should have known better. In fact, he *did* know better. As his father, David, was dying, Solomon heard these words. "Observe what the LORD your God requires: Walk in his ways, and keep his decrees and commands, his laws and requirements, as written in the Law of Moses, so that you may prosper in all you do and wherever you go."

But somehow Solomon believed he could be the exception to the rule, the one man who could break God's law without suffering the consequences. But God was not going to ignore all the idols and altars he had set up to please his foreign wives, accustomed as they were to worshiping various idols. Because of his infidelity, the kingdom of Israel split apart after his death, with Judah and its capital, Jerusalem, in the south and Israel and its capital, Samaria, in the north.

It was too late for Solomon to discover that a man before God's throne is judged by what is in his heart. "Set your affection on things above, not on things on the earth" (Colossians 3:2 KJV).

Instead of leaving a world-changing legacy, Solomon left us with a graphic lesson in eternal fruitlessness—with no excuses.

Wednesday

HIS LEGACY IN SCRIPTURE

Read 1 Kings 3:5–15.
1. God appeared to Solomon and invited him to ask for anything he wanted. What did the new king's response reveal about his character? What did the Lord's response reveal about God?
2. If God made the same invitation to you, what would you ask for?

Read 1 Kings 8:10–11, 27–30.
3. Why was it so important for Solomon to build a temple?
4. Why do you think Solomon acknowledged that God cannot be contained in a place despite clear evidence that God was dwelling in the temple he had built?

Read 1 Kings 11:1–13.
5. Even though he experienced a life of tremendous blessing, Solomon strayed from God and fell into the sin of idolatry. How did the condition of his heart deteriorate over time?
6. How can prosperity be dangerous to your spiritual health?

INTERESTING FACT

God inspired King David with the pattern for the temple, which he passed on to Solomon. Because the entire building and everything in it was ordained by God, no detail of its construction was considered insignificant. For instance, 1 Kings 6 describes carvings of cherubim and beautiful trees and flowers on the doors leading to the inner sanctuary. These were to remind the Israelites of the Garden of Eden, the paradise from which Adam and Eve were ejected because of their sin. The carved, olive wood doors symbolized the way back to paradise through the atonement for sin made in the sanctuary of the temple.

Thursday

HIS LEGACY OF PROMISE

Solomon and his kingdom represent the flowering of God's promises made many centuries earlier to Abraham. It's as though God had been trying through all the long years to lead his people back to paradise, blessing them despite their stubbornness, making them "as numerous as the sand on the seashore," giving them rest from their enemies, establishing them in a promised land of peace and prosperity where he would dwell among them. Yet the glory of Solomon's kingdom was as fragile as the king's heart. Fortunately, a far better king than Solomon has come to take his place. His name is Jesus, Immanuel, the new and greatest King who will lead us to paradise and establish God's reign forever.

Promises in Scripture

Your house and your kingdom will endure forever before me; your throne will be established forever.   —2 Samuel 7:16

Praise be to the LORD, who has given rest to his people Israel just as he promised. Not one word has failed of all the good promises he gave.
                                                         —1 Kings 8:56

> *For to us a child is born,*
> *to us a son is given,*
> *and the government will be on his shoulders.*
> *And he will be called*
> *Wonderful Counselor, Mighty God,*
> *Everlasting Father, Prince of Peace.*
> *Of the increase of his government and peace*
> *there will be no end.*

                                                         —Isaiah 9:6–7

Friday

HIS LEGACY OF PRAYER

"Your hearts must be fully committed to the LORD our God, to live by his decrees and obey his commands."   —1 Kings 8:61

Reflect On: 1 Kings 8:56–61; 11:9–13
Praise God: For his constancy. He is the same yesterday, today, and forever.
Offer Thanks: That God's words are consistent with his character.
Confess: Any wavering in your devotion to God.
Ask God: To help you maintain a course that will daily bring you closer to him.

It's called *drift*. Strong currents pull you west when you intend to go east or north when you want to head south. It happens when you either fail to notice or fail to make timely course corrections to maintain your heading. Remember the old saying, "The road to hell is paved with good intentions"? That's exactly what can happen to a person whose heart has drifted away from God. Perhaps the person started with the best of intentions. But intentions are so easy, so pleasant to entertain. Good ones make us feel good about ourselves. The hard part is staying the course, resisting the temptation to let personal desires or circumstances push you off course. Drift is what happened to Solomon. His heart drifted from complete devotion to God to a halfhearted devotion. He wanted God, but he wanted other things as well—powerful alliances, beautiful women, other gods. And so his kingdom drifted away from God. Today, pray for the grace to recognize whatever drift has occurred in your own life. Ask God to anchor you more completely in him. If you need to change course, ask for the wisdom and courage to do whatever it takes to get back on track with him.

Father in heaven, Solomon warned the people to "fully commit" their hearts to you. And then he failed to take his own advice. Help me to recognize any drift that's occurred in my life. Restore the deepest desires of my heart, the ones you have put there. Bring me back to you and give me a stronger resolve to do whatever it takes to remain faithful. In Jesus' name. Amen.

ELIJAH

His Name Means "Yahweh Is My God"

His Work:	Elijah was a prophet active in Israel in the middle of the ninth century B.C. His primary work was to combat Baal worship and restore the worship of the true God of Israel.
His Character:	Like Moses, who stood against the false gods of Egypt and the oppression of Pharaoh, Elijah was a prophet who stood against the worship of Baal at great risk to himself. To do so meant defying Ahab and Jezebel, Israel's royal couple, and trusting God to take care of him when his life was threatened by famine and violence.
His Sorrow:	Though Elijah was not the only true prophet left in Israel, he appears to have thought he was, perhaps because the rest of the prophets were silent and in hiding. Exhausted after his battle with the false prophets of Baal and his narrow escape from Queen Jezebel, he became so despondent that he prayed God would take his life. Instead, the Lord sent an angel to strengthen him.
His Triumph:	Elijah was a miracle-working prophet, whose powerful prayer life and whose persistence in speaking God's word helped preserve the faith of God's people during a time of religious persecution.
Key Scriptures:	1 Kings 17–19

Monday

HIS STORY

After the death of King Solomon, Israel split into two kingdoms—Judah in the south and Israel in the north. Though the northern kingdom suffered through a succession of kings "who did evil in the eyes of the LORD," the seventh king of Israel seems to have been the worst of the lot. Under the influence of his Phoenician wife, Jezebel, King Ahab imported Baal worship into Israel, even building a temple to this pagan god in the capital city of Samaria. His wife was even more zealous, doing her best to kill off every prophet of God she could lay her hands on and replacing him with her own.

Only one man, Elijah the Tishbite, was bold enough to challenge Ahab. One day the prophet confronted the king, predicting a prolonged drought as a result of the king's sinfulness. Month after month passed without a drop of rain. Then, in the third year of the drought, when Israel was suffering a severe famine, Elijah contacted Ahab again, this time to challenge him to a lopsided spiritual contest: "You have abandoned the LORD's commands and have followed the Baals. Now summon the people to meet me on Mount Carmel. And bring the four hundred and fifty prophets of Baal and the four hundred prophets of Asherah who eat at Jezebel's table."

Once everyone had gathered on Mount Carmel, eager for the spectacle to come, Elijah questioned the people: "How long will you waver between two opinions? If the LORD is God, follow him; but if Baal is God, follow him."

Elijah continued: "I am the only one of the LORD's prophets left, but Baal has four hundred and fifty prophets. Get two bulls for us. Let them choose one for themselves, and let them cut it into pieces and put it on the wood but not set fire to it. I will prepare the other bull and put it on the wood but not set fire to it. Then you call on the name of your god, and I will call on the name of the LORD. The god who answers by fire—he is God."

Soon Baal's prophets began shouting and dancing around their sacrifice, whipping themselves into a frenzy, calling on their god to send down his fire. But nothing happened. The scene, in fact, was so comical that Elijah couldn't resist a few well-aimed barbs: "Shout louder.

Perhaps your god is deep in thought, or busy, or traveling. Maybe he is sleeping and must be awakened." Missing the irony of his remarks, Baal's prophets shouted all the louder, slashing themselves with swords and spears until their blood flowed, as was their custom. But still there was no response, no one answered, no one paid the least attention.

When it was Elijah's turn, he began by repairing the altar of the Lord, which had been in ruins. Digging a trench around it, he arranged the wood, cut the bull into pieces, and then laid it carefully on the wood. Then, to make things a little more interesting, he told the people to fill four large jars with water and pour it on the offering and on the wood.

"Do it again," he told them, and they did it again.

"Do it a third time," he instructed. By then the water had soaked the sacrifice and filled up the trench around the altar. Then Elijah stepped forward and uttered a simple prayer:

> O LORD, God of Abraham, Isaac and Israel, let it be known today that you are God in Israel and that I am your servant and have done all these things at your command. Answer me, O LORD, answer me, so these people will know that you, O LORD, are God and that you are turning their hearts back again.

There was no begging, no shouting. Elijah didn't dance around like a crazy man or cut himself from head to toe. He merely prayed, and immediately fire came down and consumed the sacrifice, the wood, the stones, and even the water pooling in the trench around the altar.

The contest on Mount Carmel had indeed been one of the most lopsided ever recorded in the Bible. One man standing against 450 prophets of Baal. But despite appearances, the advantage had always belonged to Elijah. For he had the God of the universe on his side—the Lord of the fire, the Creator of heaven and earth, the all-powerful one who was determined to turn the hearts of his people back to himself. With so great a love and so great a power behind him, Elijah knew he could not possibly lose.

Tuesday

A LOOK AT THE MAN

Wavering

"How long will you waver between two opinions? If the LORD is God, follow him; but if Baal is God, follow him." Elijah's no-nonsense challenge seems all the more powerful, all the more compelling nearly three thousand years later because of the witness of his life.

Persecuted for speaking the truth, hunted by powerful enemies, he was a man with the unenviable task of speaking truth to those who held the truth in contempt. His enemies had not only embraced a lie but were forcing it on others. At times the task seemed too heavy to bear. But just when he thought he could not possibly go on, God supplied whatever he needed—rest, food, strength, hope. Elijah never lacked the grace to remain faithful to God. His dedication was unwavering.

It's tempting to think of the prophets as superhuman figures, fanatics who relished delivering one thundering pronouncement after another. But preserving the truth in a time of darkness is the costliest of ventures. It would have taken tremendous moral, emotional, and physical strength to stand against the king and queen, their prophets, and all the rank and file who had embraced their false gods. But strength wouldn't have been enough. Such a task also would have required love—love for God and for the people who had strayed so far from him. Love is what must have kept Elijah on the path God had chosen for him.

Elijah's strong words still strike a chord today. They remind us to stop wavering between two opinions, to stop hedging our bets and straddling the line when it comes to living out our faith in a world that is so often hostile to faith. They remind us that if the Lord truly is God, then we must follow him. And following him means loving him with all our hearts.

Wednesday

HIS LEGACY IN SCRIPTURE

Read 1 Kings 18:15–46.

1. How do Ahab's accusation and Elijah's rebuttal (vv. 17–18) reflect the common tendency to blame God for the troubles we bring on ourselves?

2. What are the consequences of wavering between two opinions (v. 21) when it comes to God? Why do you think God is so adamant that we are to worship him alone?

3. Elijah proclaimed an end to the drought before there was even a wisp of a cloud in the sky. How has God required you to have faith for things you believe he will do but cannot yet see?

4. What is the connection between having faith for something you can't see and then praying for its fulfillment?

Read 1 Kings 19:1–9.

5. Why do you think Elijah was so dejected after he had just performed several miracles and witnessed the incredible power of God on his behalf? How has your own experience paralleled his?

INTERESTING FACTS

- When Elijah predicted a drought, he was not only announcing God's judgment on Israel for its apostasy; he was also saying that God would utterly humiliate the pagan god Baal, because the so-called god of fertility and the supposed lord of the rain would not be able to produce even a single drop of rain for three years running.

- Elijah is a lonely figure with a lonely task. Hailing from Gilead, a land east of the Jordan, he probably would have been considered something of a yokel and ill-mannered fanatic in the developed cities of the northern kingdom. His loneliness is further revealed in the contest between him and the prophets of Baal on Mount Carmel and by his flight to Mount Horeb, where he complained (inaccurately) that he was the only prophet who hadn't been put to death by King Ahab and his wife, Jezebel (see 1 Kings 19).

Thursday

HIS LEGACY OF PROMISE

Early in Elijah's story God sent him to a non-Israelite widow in the town of Zarephath, between Tyre and Sidon. The location is significant because Zarephath was right in the middle of a region riddled with the kind of Baal worship that had been so aggressively exported to Israel (1 Kings 17:8–24). There, in the midst of enemy territory, God provided miraculously for Elijah, the widow, and her son. Later, when the widow's son died, God used Elijah to perform a miracle that had never before been recorded in the Bible—to raise the dead to life. Of all the miracles of God, this was the most spectacular. And it was given to someone who wasn't even part of God's people, as though God were trying to make his people jealous by showing them all that they were missing because of their apostasy and failure to believe.

Promises in Scripture

The LORD brings death and makes alive;
  he brings down to the grave and raises up.

—1 Samuel 2:6

Therefore my heart is glad and my tongue rejoices;
  my body also will rest secure,
because you will not abandon me to the grave,
  nor will you let your Holy One see decay.

—Psalm 16:9–10

On this mountain he will destroy
  the shroud that enfolds all peoples,
the sheet that covers all nations;
  he will swallow up death forever.

—Isaiah 25:7–8

Friday

HIS LEGACY OF PRAYER

The prayer of a righteous man is powerful and effective.

Elijah was a man just like us. He prayed earnestly that it would not rain, and it did not rain on the land for three and a half years. Again he prayed, and the heavens gave rain, and the earth produced its crops.

—James 5:16–18

Reflect On: 1 Kings 18:41–46; 19:1–8
Praise God: For hearing our prayers.
Offer Thanks: For the way God has answered your prayers in the past.
Confess: Any tendency to believe your prayers won't make a difference.
Ask God: To show you how to pray for the things he has promised.

Elijah was a prophet, a man who heard God's word and proclaimed it despite considerable threats to his own life. A bold man with enormous faith, yet he experienced a depression so profound that he wanted to die. He complained to God about how hard it was to speak a word that nobody would listen to, that made people want to kill him. Nevertheless, he kept on speaking, because God strengthened him and enabled him to remain faithful. In addition to speaking the word that God had given him, he prayed for its fulfillment. Eventually everything happened just as God had said it would. God heard Elijah's prayer not because he was a superhuman prophet, but because, as James said, he was a righteous man. That knowledge alone should sustain us when God entrusts us with a promise that seems impossible to fulfill. Like Elijah, we can believe God's Word and then express our faith through prayer.

Father, open my heart to your Word and help me to live by it no matter how the world around me is living. Give me the faith to pray consistently for the promises you have made, that your will and your purpose will be accomplished regardless of who or what stands against them. Amen.

ELISHA

His Name Means "My God Saves"

His Work:	Elisha was Elijah's successor. A prophet and miracle worker active in the northern kingdom from 850–800 B.C., his ministry involved rebuking Israel's unfaithful kings, inaugurating a new royal line, and helping to sustain the faith of all those in Israel who believed in God.
His Character:	Elisha renounced the life he could have had as the son of a wealthy man to live as a prophet. His single-hearted devotion to the Lord made him a spiritual leader whose integrity, vision, and courage helped sustain the people's faith in God.
His Sorrow:	He wept when given a vision of how much Israel would suffer at the hands of the king of Syria.
His Triumph:	Elisha asked to inherit a double portion of Elijah's spirit, the portion reserved for the eldest son, and received it.
Key Scriptures:	1 Kings 19:19–21; 2 Kings 2:1–14; 4:1–7; 6:8–23; 13:21

Monday

HIS STORY

Elisha was plowing the fields when it happened, supervising a team of eleven men, each driving a pair of oxen across the rough ground. Holding the plow steady as he urged the animals forward, he noticed a stranger approaching. The man moved quickly, seemingly propelled by the wind, his cloak swirling frantically behind him as though trying

221

to keep pace. Though Elisha couldn't make out his features, there was no mistaking him. It was Elijah, the prophet whose reputation as a miracle worker had made him famous throughout Israel.

Elisha called out a greeting, but the prophet was silent. Advancing toward Elisha, he simply threw his cloak around him and then turned and walked away. The younger man stood where he was. For a moment he heard nothing, felt nothing—not the wind on his skin or the smell of the draft animals or the curious stares of the workers now idled in the field. He was only aware of the future calling him across its threshold. He had to decide. He could stay where he was, enjoying the benefits that belonged to the son of a wealthy family, or he could follow Elijah into a future that was ill-defined, perhaps perilous, yet a place where a man might know God in a way few other men ever had.

Throwing down the plow, the younger man ran after Elijah, saying, "Let me kiss my father and mother good-bye, and then I will come with you." With that he slaughtered his oxen, burning the plowing equipment to cook the meat, which he then gave to the people to eat. After that he set out to follow Elijah, becoming his attendant.

Many years passed, and Elijah was gone now, taken up to heaven in a whirlwind, transported by fiery chariots and horses. Elisha had watched the spectacle with wonder, picking up the cloak that had fallen from the prophet's shoulders as Elijah disappeared into the sky. It was Elisha's turn now to carry on the work the older man had begun.

Sometime later the king of Aram (Syria) began attacking Israel along its northern borders, probing for weaknesses, hoping to wear down Israel's defenses. But each time he planned a surprise assault, the king of Israel eluded him, as though hearing of his plans in advance.

Certain there was a traitor in his camp, the enraged king summoned his officers, demanding to know the truth: "Which one of you is on the side of the king of Israel?"

But there were no admissions of guilt. Instead, one of his officers spoke up: "None of us have betrayed you. It is Elisha the prophet who tells the king of Israel the very words you speak in your bedroom."

"Then find him and capture him," the king commanded. Discovering that Elisha was in Dothan, just a few miles north of Israel's capital city, Samaria, the king sent a large contingent of men and chariots to surround the city by night.

As soon as he learned of their predicament, Elisha's terrified servant pleaded with the prophet, "Oh, my lord, what shall we do?"

But Elisha merely replied, "Don't be afraid. Those who are with us are more than those who are with them." Then he prayed, "O LORD, open his eyes so he may see." At once the Lord opened the servant's eyes, and he looked and saw the hills full of horses and chariots of fire all around Elisha.

As the enemy advanced, Elisha prayed again, "LORD, strike them with blindness." And God did.

Taking advantage of their confusion, Elisha approached the army, saying, "This is not the road and this is not the city. Follow me, and I will lead you to the man you are looking for." And he led them straight to Samaria.

After they entered the city, Elisha said, "LORD, open the eyes of these men so they can see." Looking around, they suddenly realized they were captives in Samaria.

When the king of Israel saw them, he was astonished and even questioned Elisha about what he should do with them. "Shall I kill them, my father. Shall I kill them?"

"No, do not kill them," the prophet replied. "Set food and water before them so that they may eat and drink and then go back to their master."

So the king of Israel prepared a great feast for them and then sent them back to their master. After that, Aram stopped raiding Israel's territory.

After many years, Elisha, the man who had left his home to follow Elijah into an uncertain future, died and was buried. But even in death he continued to display God's power. His last miracle happened in the spring of the year when a group of Israelites were burying a man. Interrupted in their task by Moabite raiders, they quickly tossed the dead man into Elisha's tomb. As soon as the body touched Elisha's bones, the man sprang back to life, standing on his feet. Scripture doesn't say what happened next, but it isn't hard to imagine the Moabite raiders making a quick about-face, running as fast and far away as possible from this strange land, a place abounding in miracles, a place where God worked wonders on behalf of his people through his servants, the prophets.

Tuesday

A LOOK AT THE MAN

Seeing

Elisha was a man who was never deceived by appearances. Perhaps this is what it means to be a prophet—to have a vision that extends beyond what is merely apparent, to be able to penetrate a set of circumstances to perceive what is really going on. Because of his relationship with God, Elisha was able to live with a keen awareness of both the natural and supernatural aspects of life. He understood that what happens in heaven affects life on earth and that what we do on earth has ramifications in heaven.

When Elisha learned that his city was surrounded, he showed no sign of terror as an ordinary man might have. Instead, he looked up and saw the hills covered with horses and chariots of fire; the army of heaven stood ready to protect him. In the midst of what looked like certain defeat, his ability to perceive reality enabled him to remain calm and confident. Rather than cowering or despairing, he was able to encourage his servant with the truth, saying, "Don't be afraid. Those who are with us are more than those who are with them."

Elisha's enemies, on the other hand, were at a keen disadvantage. Blinded by an act of God, they became fools—prisoners of the man they had meant to take captive. The truth about their ridiculous predicament only became apparent once Elisha asked God to open their eyes again.

Seeing and not seeing—believing and not believing—these are the connections that determine our understanding of the world around us. As we wait for understanding concerning our own difficulties or for the grace to endure without fully understanding them, we can recall Elisha's words: "Don't be afraid. Those who are with us are more than those who are with them."

Wednesday

HIS LEGACY IN SCRIPTURE

Read 2 Kings 4:1–7.

1. How did the widow's faith affect the miracle Elisha performed?
2. Consider times in your life when you felt especially vulnerable and in need of help. How strong was your faith? How did you experience God's provision?
3. Why do you think Elisha asked the widow to tell him what she had in her house?

Read 2 Kings 6:8–23.

4. Elisha appears to have had supernatural knowledge of the location of Israel's enemies, enabling him numerous times to warn the king of their presence. How do the themes of "sight" and "blindness" play themselves out in the story?
5. How did Elisha's awareness of the supernatural world affect his ministry? How has your awareness of the supernatural world affected your perception of the world you can see, touch, and hear?

INTERESTING FACT

In ancient Israel oil was a symbol of plenty. To possess it was a sign of God's blessing. To lack it was a sign that you had incurred God's displeasure. Olive oil was used for various purposes—for lighting, nutrition, medicine, cosmetics, and for religious use. It was so valuable that it was kept in royal storehouses along with gold, silver, and spices.

Thursday

HIS LEGACY OF PROMISE

As Elijah's successor, Elisha exercised a power far superior to that of Israel's corrupt kings. As such, he became part of a line of prophets that God raised up to call his people back to himself. His numerous miracles, one even performed after his death (2 Kings 13:21), encouraged the faithful remnant (who suffered by virtue of the fact that they belonged to a faithless nation) by assuring them that God was still present, still powerful, and still merciful toward those who kept his commandments and followed his ways.

Promises in Scripture

> For out of Jerusalem will come a remnant,
>> and out of Mount Zion a band of survivors.
>>> —2 Kings 19:31

> Have faith in the LORD your God and you will be upheld; have faith in his prophets and you will be successful.   —2 Chronicles 20:20

> My eyes will be on the faithful in the land.   —Psalm 101:6

> As the mountains surround Jerusalem,
>> so the LORD surrounds his people
>> both now and forevermore.
>>> —Psalm 125:2

Friday

HIS LEGACY OF PRAYER

When they had crossed [the Jordan River], Elijah said to Elisha, "Tell me, what can I do for you before I am taken from you?"

"Let me inherit a double portion of your spirit," Elisha replied.

—2 Kings 2:9

Reflect On:	2 Kings 2:5–15
Praise God:	For speaking to us through his prophets.
Offer Thanks:	For the ways God has challenged you through others.
Confess:	Any failure to respond to God's corrective word.
Ask God:	For a greater sense of what it means to live every day for his kingdom.

Elisha watched as his mentor, Elijah, was whisked up to heaven in a chariot of fire. Such an experience of the supernatural power of God must have shaped his perception that life is lived on more than one plane at once. During the fifty-year period of his prophetic ministry, he must have had a keen sense that what happened in the unseen world profoundly affected what happened in the natural world and vice versa. His zeal for God was evident when he asked Elijah for "a double portion of your spirit." In biblical times this didn't mean he was asking for a ministry twice as spectacular as Elijah's. Instead, he was asking for the portion of the inheritance normally reserved for the firstborn son. None of us are likely to have the kind of visions Elisha had, but we can ask God to give us a greater awareness of our inheritance as his sons and daughters and a greater zeal for building up his kingdom, a kingdom that will endure long after the world we know with our five senses has passed away.

Father, it's so easy to think that this world is what really matters. Remind me that it's passing away, and give me a greater appetite for the world that is to come. Help me right now to start living in a way that will prepare me to live forever in your kingdom.

NAAMAN

His Name Means "Pleasantness"

His Work:	Naaman was the commander of Syria's army.
His Character:	A brave man lauded for his military victories, his position would have guaranteed considerable respect in both Syria (known as Aram) and Israel. He would have been accustomed to getting his way, especially with social inferiors, which is what he may have considered Elisha and most everyone else in Israel. His no-nonsense approach made it difficult for him to follow Elisha's instructions.
His Sorrow:	Naaman suffered from leprosy, not the illness we call Hansen's Disease, but a skin disorder so serious that he left his country to seek healing in Israel.
His Triumph:	To have received not only the healing he asked for, but a relationship with the one true God.
Key Scriptures:	2 Kings 5; Luke 4:27

Monday

HIS STORY

Naaman had won victories that not even he could explain. Surely, he thought, the gods were with him as they had been with few other men. Ben-Hadad, the great king of Syria, had spoken so well of him publicly that he felt his success even more keenly. But if the gods favored him so, why did he suffer day after day with a disgusting disease—his skin raw from scratching the sores that no potion or priest could heal? Even his wife's servant girl had noticed, suggesting he consult a prophet from her homeland, a man who lived in Samaria well to the south.

So Naaman went to the king and told him what the girl from Israel had said. "By all means go," the king of Syria replied. "I will send a letter to the king of Israel." The letter said this: "With this letter I am sending my servant Naaman to you so that you may cure him of his leprosy." So Naaman left, taking with him ten talents of silver, six thousand shekels of gold, and ten sets of clothing as payment for the healing he sought.

But when Naaman reached the king of Israel and submitted the royal letter, Joram surprised him by tearing his robes and complaining: "Am I God? Can I kill and bring back to life? What man can cure leprosy? Surely the king of Syria is trying to pick a quarrel with me!"

But soon Naaman was directed to the house of the prophet Elisha. When he reached the house with his retinue of horses and chariots, he was surprised to be met by a messenger rather than the prophet himself. "Go," the man told him, "wash yourself seven times in the Jordan, and your flesh will be restored and you will be cleansed."

"Why doesn't the prophet come out to me himself," Naaman raged, "and call on the name of the LORD his God? He need only wave his hand to cure me of my leprosy. Why should I wash in a dirty river in Israel when we have much better rivers in Damascus?"

But as Naaman turned to leave, one of his servants spoke up, "My father, if the prophet had told you to do some great thing, would you not have done it? How much more, then, when he tells you, 'Wash and be cleansed'!"

Even though Naaman had been angered by the prophet's ridiculous instructions, he had to agree with his servant. He had already gone to great expense and trouble to seek a cure. He would do anything, pay any price, if only he could be healed. So what if he seemed the fool wading into the Jordan's muddy waters.

Naaman set aside his natural repulsion and washed himself in the river not once but seven times. And the longer he was in the river, the more he felt strange sensations spreading across his body as the cool water eased the itching and took away the pain. But there was more to it than that. Rubbing his hands across arms and legs, over torso and face, he felt all the crusty sores falling away. No longer did his skin feel like the bark of a sycamore. Now it felt as smooth and soft as a young boy's.

Then Naaman went back and stood before Elisha. "Now I know," he exulted, "that there is no God in all the world except in Israel. Please accept a gift from your servant."

But Elisha refused to put a price on the gift of God and said, "As surely as the LORD lives, whom I serve, I will not accept a thing." Despite Naaman's repeated urging, the man of God refused any payment.

"Go in peace," Elisha said.

And Naaman did.

Tuesday

A LOOK AT THE MAN

A Stunning Reversal

Naaman, a man whose success as a military commander placed him close to the king of Syria, was faced with a choice. Listen to his wife's servant girl, to the lowly messenger of a prophet, and to one of his own servants, and obey. Or return home with his dignity intact but without the healing he longed for. It wasn't an easy choice for a proud man to make. Give up your sense of how things should go, of how people should treat you, of how you should conduct yourself for the chance—not the certainty—of being healed.

Naaman nearly made the mistake of cherishing his pride at the cost of the miracle he desired. Yet something inside him asserted itself, some hope that perhaps the prophet's crazy instructions were not as crazy as they seemed. So he took a chance, deciding to let go of his own ideas of how his healing should be accomplished, deciding to let go of his own perceptions of how the universe should be ordered.

Naaman's obedience would have felt uncomfortable. How much easier it would have been to play it safe and do what came naturally—to nurse his anger and preserve his dignity. Instead, Naaman did exactly as he was told, and his obedience opened his heart to a greater miracle than the one for which he longed. Instead of a proud man, he became a humble one. Instead of a man incapable of knowing God, he became a man who knew and celebrated the fact that in all the earth there is only one God, the God who loved him and made him whole.

Wednesday

HIS LEGACY IN SCRIPTURE

Read 2 Kings 5:1–19.

1. Joram, the king of Israel, believed the king of Syria's letter was merely an attempt to start a fight because he knew it was humanly impossible to cure Naaman's skin disease. What does Joram's response indicate about the condition of his faith?
2. Where in the story do you see evidence that God was humbling Naaman?
3. Why do you think Elisha refused to meet Naaman when he showed up at his door and instead sent a messenger to greet him?
4. Naaman expected to be healed but on his terms. How have your own expectations of how God should act in your life and in the lives of those you love been changed and challenged over time?
5. How was Naaman's healing and transformation a sign to disobedient Israel?

Read 2 Kings 5:20–27.

6. Gehazi had been Elisha's servant for many years. But instead of learning from the prophet's example and instead of standing in awe of the miracles he had witnessed, he thought only of personal gain. How does his attempt to profit from God's gift of grace act as a warning to believers today?

INTERESTING FACT

Gehazi faced a powerful temptation when Naaman showed up at Elisha's door offering five times the amount of silver a former king of Israel had paid for the hills of Samaria just a few decades earlier. He may have rationalized his action by asking for two talents rather than all ten the wealthy Naaman had been prepared to pay.

Thursday

HIS LEGACY OF PROMISE

Naaman's pride was defeated by God's gracious response to his obedience. But the situation could have turned out differently and almost did. Why hadn't Elisha had the courtesy to speak directly to him rather than sending a messenger, especially after he had made the long journey from his home in Syria? Why hadn't the prophet merely waved his hand and healed him? Why should he, the commander of an army, be himself commanded to wash not once but seven times in a little river in Israel? It made no sense. But despite his anger, in the face of his bewilderment, Naaman did exactly as the prophet instructed. He dipped himself into the water and was amazed when he began to feel his body changing as the crusty sores on his skin fell away and his flesh became clear again. The man who almost forfeited a miracle because of his pride humbled himself to receive the promise God had made to him through the prophet Elisha.

Promises in Scripture

For I am the LORD, *who heals you.* —Exodus 15:26

> *Heal me, O* LORD, *and I will be healed;*
> *save me and I will be saved,*
> *for you are the one I praise.*
>
> —Jeremiah 17:14

A man with leprosy came and knelt before him and said, "Lord, if you are willing, you can make me clean."

Jesus reached out his hand and touched the man. "I am willing," he said. "Be clean!" Immediately he was cured of his leprosy.

—Matthew 8:2–3

Friday

HIS LEGACY OF PRAYER

"Now I know that there is no God in all the world except in Israel."
—2 Kings 5:15

Reflect On: 2 Kings 5:15–17
Praise God: For offering salvation as a free gift to all.
Offer Thanks: For God's gift of salvation to you.
Confess: Any tendency you may have to think that God can-
                 not or will not work in the lives of certain individu-
                 als, groups, or nations.
Ask God: To give you a heart as loving as his for those who are
                 far from him.

Naaman must have created quite a stir in Israel. After all, he was considered a great man in his own country. Furthermore, he was the victorious commander of the army of Syria, a country generally
unfriendly toward Israel. So the people of Israel must have been astonished when he came bearing gifts and more astonished yet when they
learned of his healing in their own Jordan River. Word of his great
proclamation of faith, "Now I know that there is no God in all the
world except in Israel," would have spread throughout the country,
challenging God's people for their weak faith and their foolish pursuit of false gods. Naaman's story reminds us of what Jesus said to the
Pharisees who criticized his disciples for praising him on his triumphal
entry into Jerusalem prior to his death: "I tell you, if they keep quiet,
the stones will cry out." In this case, Naaman was like these stones, a
man who did not belong to the chosen people, whom God raised up
to praise his name.

---

*Father, there are no boundaries to your grace, no limits to your mercy. Thank
you for calling people to yourself from every tribe and nation. Lord, you heal
all our afflictions, you forgive all our sins, you draw us to yourself with cords
of mercy. Indeed, you are the God of the whole world. May the whole world
acclaim you.*

HEZEKIAH

His Name Means "Yahweh Has Strengthened"

His Work:	He became coregent of Judah with his father, Ahaz, in 729 B.C., six years before the fall of Samaria to the Assyrians. He reigned on his own for twenty-nine years, during which time he reopened the temple and restored Jerusalem as the center of worship, destroying the pagan altars and high places his father had built.
His Character:	Hezekiah is one of only four kings that the Bible compares favorably with King David, saying, "Hezekiah trusted in the LORD, the God of Israel. There was no one like him among all the kings of Judah. . . . He held fast to the LORD and did not cease to follow him; he kept the commands the LORD had given Moses. And the LORD was with him; he was successful in whatever he undertook."
His Sorrow:	That Judah and Israel had fallen away from the Lord, worshiping the gods of the nations around them.
His Triumph:	Hezekiah reformed the religious practices of Judah and with the Lord's help withstood the Assyrian invaders.
Key Scriptures:	2 Kings 18–19; 2 Chronicles 28:19–25; 29:1–10

Monday

HIS STORY

"If you do not stand firm in your faith, you will not stand at all." Isaiah's words fell like drops of rain on a slab of granite, unable to penetrate the hardness of the king's heart. Now Ahaz, the twelfth king of Judah, lay cold as stone on his bier. His determined reliance on Assyria and its pantheon of gods had brought him not the help he sought, but the trouble he feared.

In his effort to curry favor, Ahaz had shut the doors of the temple and set up altars on every street corner in Jerusalem. He had built up high places throughout Judah, shrines where the gods of other nations could be conveniently worshiped. But rather than building up his nation, his efforts had reduced Judah to a vassal state of Assyria, one of many nations forced to pay an annual tribute of silver and gold.

After Ahaz's death, his son Hezekiah mourned not for his father but for his father's appalling unfaithfulness to the Lord. He began his reign, not by building up the walls of Jerusalem, but by ridding the city of its idolatrous practices. In the first month of his reign, he reopened the temple in Jerusalem and then quickly restored its worship. After that he pulled down the high places, inviting the people of both Judah and Israel to worship the Lord at the temple.

Then, in preparation for an Assyrian assault, he built up the city walls and began stockpiling weapons and shields. In the fourteenth year of Hezekiah's reign, Sennacherib, the king of Assyria, attacked and captured all the fortified cities of Judah. Though fear was rampant, Hezekiah urged his people: "Be strong and courageous. Do not be afraid or discouraged because of the king of Assyria and the vast army with him, for there is a greater power with us than with him. With him is only the arm of flesh, but with us is the LORD our God to help us and to fight our battles."

Sometime later Sennacherib, who was camped several miles southwest of Jerusalem, sent his officers and an army ahead of him with a message calculated to terrify Hezekiah and his people. Meeting with Hezekiah's officials, the field commander boasted: "This is what the great king, the king of Assyria, says: 'What are you basing your confidence on? You say you have strategy and military strength—but your words are empty. Who are you depending on, that you rebel against me? Look now, you are depending on Egypt, that splintered reed of a staff, which pierces a man's hand and wounds him if he leans on it! Such is Pharaoh king of Egypt to all who depend on him. And if you say to me, "We are depending on the LORD our God"—isn't he the one whose high places and altars Hezekiah removed, saying to Judah and Jerusalem, "You must worship before this altar in Jerusalem"? Come now, make a bargain with my master, the king of Assyria.'"

Hezekiah's officials tried hushing the man, saying, "Please speak to your servants in Aramaic, since we understand it. Don't speak to us in Hebrew in the hearing of the people on the wall."

But instead of complying, the man kept hammering them: "Why should the men sitting on the wall not hear my words? They will have to eat their own filth and drink their own urine just like you if we place Jerusalem under a siege."

Then he called out loudly in Hebrew: "This is what the king of Assyria says: 'Don't let Hezekiah deceive you. He can't possibly deliver you from my hand. Don't let him persuade you to trust in the LORD. Make peace and surrender. Come out from behind your walls. Then you and your families will eat from your own vine and fig tree and drink water from your own well until I come and take you to a land like your own, a land of grain, new wine, bread and honey. Choose life and not death! Has the god of any nation ever delivered his land from the king of Assyria? How then can your god deliver Jerusalem from my hand?'"

Hezekiah shook when he heard of Sennacherib's boast. It wasn't from fear—not of men anyway—but from his certainty that the man had crossed a line no man should ever cross, not even a king. Then he tore his clothes and put on sackcloth. Entering the temple he fell on his face and prayed:

"O LORD, God of Israel, enthroned between the cherubim, you alone are God over all the kingdoms of the earth. You made heaven and earth. Give ear, O LORD, and hear; open your eyes, O LORD, and see; listen to the words Sennacherib has spoken to insult the living God.

"You know, O LORD, that the Assyrian kings have crushed many nations, destroying their gods. But these were not gods at all, only pieces of wood and stone fashioned by men's hands. Now, O LORD our God, deliver us from his hand, so that all kingdoms on earth may know that you alone, O LORD, are God."

The answer to Hezekiah's prayer came swiftly, delivered to him by the prophet Isaiah:

"This is what the LORD, the God of Israel says: I have heard your prayer concerning Sennacherib king of Assyria. This is the word that the LORD has spoken against him:

"The Virgin Daughter of Zion
   despises you and mocks you.
The Daughter of Jerusalem
   tosses her head as you flee.
Who is it you have insulted and blasphemed?
   Against whom have you raised your voice
and lifted your eyes in pride?
   Against the Holy One of Israel!
By your messengers
   you have heaped insults on the Lord.
And you have said,
   'With my many chariots
I have ascended the heights of the mountains . . .'

"But I know where you stay
   and when you come and go
   and how you rage against me.
Because you rage against me
   and your insolence has reached my ears,
I will put my hook in your nose
   and my bit in your mouth,
and I will make you return
   by the way you came."
   (2 Kings 19:20–23, 27–28)

That night, as Hezekiah lay sleeping on his bed safe behind Jerusalem's high walls, 185,000 men perished suddenly and mysteriously in the Assyrian camp. Finding his army decimated, Sennacherib returned to Nineveh.

Many years later, the king of Assyria went into the temple in Nineveh to worship his god, Nisroch. As he bowed down, two of his sons slaughtered him. The great Sennacherib, the king who had boasted of his invincible power, lay still as a stone in the temple of his god.

Tuesday

A LOOK AT THE MAN

Holding Fast to God

Hezekiah's character stands in sharp contrast to the character of the other two kings who appear in the story. His father, Ahaz, trusted not in the God of Israel, but in the gods of other nations, particularly Assyria, believing them to be the source of its great power. By currying favor with idols, he must have hoped to increase his own power. But the reverse happened, and Judah grew weaker, not stronger.

Sennacherib was like him, trusting the power of his empire and then attempting to undermine Judah's trust in God. Three times his spokesman advised the people, "Don't trust Hezekiah when he tells you your god will save you. It's a fantasy! Your god is no different than the gods of all the other nations, none of whom have been able to resist us." Then, to entice them further, he promised to take them to a land of ease, a place with olive trees and honey, admonishing them to "choose life and not death."

It's no accident that Sennacherib's words directly contradict the counsel of Moses just before the Israelites entered the Promised Land, a land filled with milk and honey. At the end of his ministry, Moses warned them: "This day I call heaven and earth as witnesses against you that I have set before you life and death, blessings and curses. Now choose life, so that you and your children may live and that you may love the LORD your God, listen to his voice, and hold fast to him. For the LORD is your life, and he will give you many years in the land he swore to give to your fathers, Abraham, Isaac and Jacob" (Deuteronomy 30:19–20).

By attempting to persuade the people of Judah that everything good in life comes from trusting in the power of human beings, Sennacherib urged them toward the path of least resistance. Fortunately for Judah, Hezekiah recognized the lie and continued to trust in the Lord, thus inviting God's help and assuring Judah's survival.

Though the details of our stories differ vastly from the story of this ancient king, the principles are identical. We are still assailed by voices assuring us that the good life consists of amassing wealth, accumulating personal power, achieving success, and forging the kind of relationships we desire. But to mistake earthly blessings for the life that only God can give is to place our future in jeopardy. The choice is ours to make—today, tomorrow, and the day after that. The joy we seek lies in loving the Lord our God, listening to his voice, and holding fast to him.

Wednesday

HIS LEGACY IN SCRIPTURE

Read 2 Chronicles 28:19–27 and 29:1–20.

1. Idolatry was a strong and recurrent temptation for kings and people alike. Why do you think the Israelites were so vulnerable to this temptation? Why was it so offensive to the Lord?

2. How are modern people still vulnerable to idolatry? What forms does it take in our world?

3. Why do you think Hezekiah began his reign by reopening the temple and restoring Jerusalem as the center of worship for God's people?

Read 2 Kings 18:17–36.

4. Imagine yourself standing on the walls of Jerusalem, listening to Assyria's challenge. How would you have responded?

5. How do you respond today when people or circumstances attempt to undermine your trust in God? Give some examples.

Read 2 Kings 19:9–28.

6. What can we learn about prayer from the way this king of Judah prayed?

GOING DEEPER

Read 2 Kings 20:1–7.

7. This story about the power of prayer to change the present and the future underlines the vital importance of prayer. What kind of results have you experienced in prayer?

Thursday

HIS LEGACY OF PROMISE

Hezekiah began his reign by taking a stand that demanded a great deal of courage. It would have been far easier to simply maintain the status quo, to continue to forge foreign alliances and tolerate religious syncretism as the cost of doing business in a world where politics and religion were inextricably linked. But Hezekiah wasn't a political pragmatist. He was a king after God's own heart, like David had been before him. Through his leadership the southern tribes were, at least for a time, spared the fate that had overtaken their neighbor to the north.

Promises in Scripture

He answered their prayers, because they trusted in him.

—1 Chronicles 5:20

Trust in the LORD with all your heart
and lean not on your own understanding;
in all your ways acknowledge him,
and he will make your paths straight.

—Proverbs 3:5

In quietness and trust is your strength.　　　　—Isaiah 30:15

Do not set your heart on what you will eat or drink; do not worry about it. For the pagan world runs after all such things, and your Father knows that you need them. But seek his kingdom, and these things will be given to you as well.　　　　—Luke 12:29–31

Friday

HIS LEGACY OF PRAYER

"O LORD, God of Israel, enthroned between the cherubim, you alone are God over all the kingdoms of the earth. You have made heaven and earth. Give ear, O LORD, and hear; open your eyes, O LORD, and see; listen to the words Sennacherib has sent to insult the living God."

—2 Kings 19:15–16

Reflect On:	2 Kings 19:15–28
Praise God:	Because he is the Lord of heaven and earth.
Offer Thanks:	That no human being can ever overrule his sovereign power.
Confess:	Any unbelief that makes you doubt God's willingness to exercise his power on your behalf.
Ask God:	To give you a greater desire to live for his glory and his glory alone.

Hezekiah trusted in the Lord. But what does trust look like on an everyday basis? Trusting God means failing to believe evil reports about his character. Instead of listening to lies that are sometimes suggested to our minds implying that God is weak, unfaithful, or uninterested, we choose to believe in his goodness, his power, and his love. We cling to the truth about him regardless of the problems we face. Trust also involves running to the Lord in prayer as Hezekiah did, pouring out our hearts before him, and then listening carefully to what he says. Ultimately, trust is about obedience, about doing what God wants regardless of how we feel. As our trust in God grows, so will our knowledge of him; and as our knowledge grows, so will our trust.

Father, I admit that I often find it easier to trust in myself than to trust in you. Forgive me. Help me to realize that the peace and confidence I crave come not from self-reliance but from developing the kind of trust that is rooted and grounded in your character. Give me an opportunity to trust you today, and as I do, lift up your name so that others may recognize your work in my life.

JOSIAH

His Name Means "Yahweh Supports Him"

His Work:	Josiah was the last good king of Judah, reigning from about 640–609 B.C. Like his great-grandfather Hezekiah, he instituted sweeping religious reforms in Judah. Because of his faithfulness, the prophetess Huldah assured him he would not see the destruction that would one day overtake Jerusalem and Judah.
His Character:	Though Josiah became king when he was only a boy, he became one of Judah's strongest spiritual leaders, a man whose devotion, obedience, humility, and repentance on behalf of the people helped for a time to restore Judah's fractured relationship with the Lord.
His Sorrow:	That his reforms, which were not supported by those who succeeded him, occurred too late to avert judgment on Judah.
His Triumph:	So strong was Josiah's influence that it extended beyond Judah to embrace the northern tribes as well.
Key Scriptures:	1 Kings 12:25–33; 13:2–3; 2 Kings 22–23; 2 Chronicles 34–35

Monday

HIS STORY

The king stood still, arms folded, head cocked slightly, as though listening for the land to speak to him. In the predawn shadows, he closed his eyes, remembering that this had once been sacred ground for

Abraham and for Jacob, a place where even the ark had rested for a time. Though the ground was silent now, he could feel its trouble, as though ancient powers still struggled beneath his feet.

This was Bethel, where Jeroboam had enticed the northern tribes to worship the Lord, hoping to keep them from returning to the temple in Jerusalem. But idols had been worshiped here instead, and God had been dishonored year after year, century after century. Josiah remembered the words of a prophecy spoken three hundred years earlier, when Bethel had first emerged as Jerusalem's rival: "O altar, altar! This is what the LORD says: 'A son named Josiah will be born to the house of David. On you he will sacrifice the priests of the high places who now make offerings here, and human bones will be burned on you.'"

The king's men held torches aloft as Josiah surveyed the scene. Tombs pocked the hillside, holding the remains of the priests who had once offered the sacrifices. Seeing them, Josiah ordered his men to plunder the graves, burning their bones on the altar. Having thus defiled the altar, he then demolished it and the high place, grinding them to powder.

Mission completed, the king turned to leave. Then the sun rose a fiery red against the horizon, spreading its crimson rays over the spot where the altar had once stood.

Since childhood, Josiah's mind had been filled with thoughts that should not concern a boy. He knew the reputation of his grandfather Manassah, a king who had practiced the darkest of arts—worshiping the stars, delighting in sorcery, consulting spiritists, and feeding the god Molech with the bodies of his own children. What's more, he knew that his father, Amnon, had been no better, a man murdered by assassins after reigning for only two years. Though Josiah was only eight years old, he knew too that the time had come for him to wear Judah's crown.

Josiah was determined to be as different from his father and grandfather as one man could be from another, his boy's heart vowing to stamp out the idolatry that once again threatened Judah. His ambitions were fed by stories he had heard of the great King David and of his own great-grandfather Hezekiah, a reforming king whose devotion to the Lord had helped save his people from an Assyrian invasion.

When Josiah was sixteen, he began purging Judah and Jerusalem of all the high places, of carved idols and cast images that had spread like scabs across the countryside. Baal, Ashtoreth, Chemosh, Molech—these foreign gods along with their vile practices were no longer welcome in Judah. Gone too were the spiritists, shrine prostitutes, and mediums that had held sway for nearly sixty years.

When Josiah was twenty-six, he hired carpenters, builders, and stonemasons to begin restoring the temple, which had been desecrated by Manassah. In the process, Hilkiah the high priest discovered a lost book. It was the Book of the Law, whose strong words made Josiah tremble with fear: "You have made God jealous with your foreign gods and angered him with your detestable idols. You have sacrificed to demons, which are not God—gods you have not known, gods that recently appeared, gods your fathers did not fear. You deserted the Rock who fathered you; you forgot the God who gave you birth. The LORD saw this and rejected you because he was angered by his sons and daughters."

Josiah tore at his robes and covered his eyes, weeping. Then he consulted a prophetess named Huldah, who spoke words both frightening and reassuring: "This is what the LORD, the God of Israel, says: Tell the man who sent you to me, 'This is what the LORD says: I am going to bring disaster on this place and its people, according to everything written in the book the king of Judah has read. Because they have forsaken me and burned incense to other gods and provoked me to anger by all the idols their hands have made, my anger will burn against this place and will not be quenched.' Tell the king of Judah, who sent you to inquire of the LORD, 'This is what the LORD, the God of Israel, says concerning the words you heard: Because your heart was responsive and you humbled yourself before the LORD when you heard what I have spoken against this place and its people . . . and because you tore your robes and wept in my presence, I have heard you, declares the LORD. Therefore I will gather you to your fathers, and you will be buried in peace. Your eyes will not see all the disaster I am going to bring on this place.'"

Then Josiah read the words of the Book of the Law to all the people and celebrated the Passover feast for the first time in many years. After a long and fruitful reign, at the age of thirty-nine, Josiah died in battle. Twenty-four years later, his kingdom was destroyed, and many of Judah's inhabitants were led in chains to Babylon.

Tuesday

A LOOK AT THE MAN

Faithfulness, Not Success

Josiah was one of twenty kings who ruled Judah during the period of the divided kingdom. Many of the kings who preceded him had little regard for preserving the spiritual vitality of Judah, absorbed as they were in the struggle to secure their own power. And even though his reign was one of the best and brightest, Josiah was incapable of reversing Judah's steady slide toward paganism. Sadly, his reforms perished with him, and a few years later Judah suffered the punishment long prophesied.

Like few leaders in the history of the world, Josiah knew the outcome of his story in advance. God had told him, through the prophetess Huldah, that Judah would eventually suffer disaster because of its sins. Such knowledge could have prompted him to give up, to conclude that he was wasting precious time and energy on a lost cause. But instead of abandoning his reforms, Josiah stepped up his efforts. Refusing to be deflected from his life's purpose, he continued clearing away the detritus of paganism in hopes of bringing Judah back to God.

The young king must have understood a principle we often lose sight of, namely, that faithfulness is more important than success. That doing what's right, regardless of the odds, is crucial. Josiah must have known that spiritual greatness is measured not by victory but by our determination to use the power God gives us, however great or small, to further his purposes. Because of his faithfulness, the Lord spared him the pain and grief of witnessing the disaster that eventually overtook the land he loved.

Like Josiah, we sometimes face situations that seem impossible: a difficult marriage, a challenging job, a divided church, or life in a world that sometimes despises the things we cherish most. We wonder how anything good can result from the current course of affairs. Unlike Josiah, we don't know the outcome in advance. None of us can preclude the possibility that our circumstances will radically change for the better. But like him, we can remember that God never requires us to be successful, only faithful.

Wednesday

HIS LEGACY IN SCRIPTURE

Read 1 Kings 12:25–33; 13:2–3.
1. Why was it problematic to set up altars and high places rather than limiting worship to the temple in Jerusalem? How is it possible today to worship God in ways that are displeasing to him?

Read 2 Kings 22.
2. Contrast Josiah's attitude toward the first years of his reign with Jeroboam's attitude during the first years of his reign (see 1 Kings 12:25–33).
3. What does it mean to have a heart that is responsive to God (v. 19)? Describe a time in your life when your own heart was not as responsive as it should have been. Describe another incident when you were responsive.

INTERESTING FACT

Jerusalem was destroyed by King Nebuchadnezzar of Babylon in 586 B.C. At that time, many of the Jews who lived in the southern kingdom were transported to Babylon, a city fifty miles south of Baghdad, the capital of modern-day Iraq. Though God allowed his people to be forcibly expelled from their land as punishment for their idolatry, he continued to be with them during the exile. Fifty years later, when they were finally allowed to return to Jerusalem, they had become strict monotheists, people who believed in the one true God of Israel.

Thursday

HIS LEGACY OF PROMISE

Josiah had the worst of examples to follow. His grandfather murdered his own children, and his father "did evil in the eyes of the LORD." So how did a boy with such poor role models turn out so well? Scripture doesn't supply the details. Perhaps his mother made the crucial difference, imparting a vision for the kind of leader he could become. Or maybe his imagination was fired by stories he heard about his great-grandfather Hezekiah's reforms. Whatever happened, the story of the young boy who grew up to be a great king is evidence that grace inhabits the worst of families. Because of God's love, evil is never inevitable. To hearts that are open to God, anything is possible.

Promises in Scripture

If my people, who are called by my name, will humble themselves and pray and seek my face and turn from their wicked ways, then will I hear from heaven and will forgive their sin and will heal their land.

—2 Chronicles 7:14

To the faithful you show yourself faithful,
*   to the blameless you show yourself blameless,*
to the pure you show yourself pure,
*   but to the crooked you show yourself shrewd.*

—Psalm 18:25–26

With your help I can advance against a troop;
*   with my God I can scale a wall.*

—Psalm 18:29

Friday

HIS LEGACY OF PRAYER

"Because your heart was responsive and you humbled yourself before the
LORD *when you heard what I have spoken against this place and its*
people, that they would become accursed and laid waste, and because you
tore your robes and wept in my presence, I have heard you, declares the
LORD." —2 Kings 22:19

Reflect On:	2 Kings 22:3–20
Praise God:	For hearing the prayers of the humble.
Offer Thanks:	For the freedom we have to worship him.
Confess:	Any self-righteousness that keeps you from identifying with the sins and failures of God's people.
Ask God:	To renew the church, so that all of his people may worship him in spirit and truth.

It doesn't take a genius to realize that many of our churches desperately need renewal. One has merely to read the morning newspaper to learn of the latest scandal—a minister or priest who looked good on the outside but who was actually rotting on the inside, under the grip of sin. We are disgusted and embarrassed by each new revelation. We want to distance ourselves from that person or that denomination, as though such a thing could never happen in *our* church. But instead of merely expressing our revulsion, we would do well to fall on our faces before God, begging his forgiveness for the coldness we find in our own hearts as a result of sin. Instead of distancing ourselves from brothers and sisters whose sin has been so publicly exposed, we need to pray for them. We need to plead for God to change his people, pouring his life into us so that together we can be the church, the body of Christ on earth.

Father, forgive me. My heart has grown cold and weary over time. I have
wanted you, but I have wanted so many other things as well. Help me to set
aside everything else so that I may love you more than I love myself, my
spouse, my children, my job, my comforts, or my financial security. Give me,
Lord, a deeper vision of who you are. Purify my heart and restore my faith.
Put a fire in my soul that will set others on fire with love for you.

EZRA

His Name Probably Means "Helps"

His Work: A priest living in exile in Babylon.

His Character: Courageous to face any foe, diligent in his study of the law, skilled in leadership, and humble before the Lord.

His Sorrow: His own sinfulness and need of forgiveness and the sinfulness and disobedience of his people.

His Triumph: Being the catalyst for genuine repentance among those Hebrews who returned from exile to their homeland.

Key Scriptures: The book of Ezra

Monday

HIS STORY

As a boy, Ezra had heard stories of his own land—stories of God's provision, of military conquests under King David's leadership, and of worship in the great temple. But these were only stories, fascinating details about somewhere he had never been but longed to go—a place his fellow Hebrews called home.

Along with other exiled Jews, Ezra lived in Babylon, a land east of Canaan. A priest who enjoyed some standing in the court of Artaxerxes, king of Persia, Ezra approached him one day requesting permission to lead a contingent of Jews back to Judah. Eighty years earlier Cyrus the Great had given more than forty-two thousand Jews permission to return to Jerusalem to rebuild the city and the temple. But though the work on the temple had been completed, the Israelites were not yet following the Law of Moses, the law Ezra loved.

251

It took courage to approach an absolute monarch with so bold a plan. But remarkably Artaxerxes seemed touched by Ezra's devotion. Instead of raising objections to so many of his subjects journeying west to Judah, the pagan ruler of the vast Persian empire issued a written decree: "Now I decree that any of the Israelites in my kingdom, including priests and Levites, who wish to go to Jerusalem with you, may go. You are sent by the king and his seven advisers to inquire about Judah and Jerusalem with regard to the Law of your God, which is in your hand."

Perhaps thinking Ezra capable of restoring this province to its former greatness, thus enhancing his empire, Artaxerxes even offered to fund the expedition.

Once the decree had been distributed among the Israelites, over seven thousand people responded, including women and children. But as he pored over the list of volunteers, Ezra became troubled. "There are no Levites among the people," he said. Without a team designated to assist the priests in spiritual leadership, returning to Jerusalem would be a waste of time. Ezra was intent not just on moving a crowd of people back to Judah, but on restoring their hearts before God.

So Ezra sent out an invitation, and 38 Levites, along with 220 temple servants, chose to join him. Once everyone was assembled, Ezra stood before the people. "I am declaring a fast," he told them. "We must humble ourselves before our God and ask him for a safe journey for ourselves and our children, with all our possessions. Because of the generosity of the king, we have plenty of provisions and money." Looking around at the vast congregation of willing travelers, he added, "And there are plenty of people to join in this journey."

After several months of traveling over treacherous terrain and fending off marauding bandits, the Jews arrived safely in Jerusalem. Following three days of rest, the exiles gathered at the rebuilt temple, offering sacrifices, not just for themselves but "for all Israel."

Then a handful of Jewish leaders brought a troubling report to Ezra. "The people of Israel, including the priests and the Levites, have not kept themselves separate from the neighboring peoples and their detestable practices," they said. Sinfulness was going unchallenged.

The news broke Ezra's heart. Tearing his tunic, he collapsed to his knees. "O my God," Ezra prayed, "I am too ashamed and disgraced to lift up my face to you, because our sins are higher than our heads and our guilt has reached to the heavens. From the days of our forefathers until now, our guilt has been great. Because of our sins, we and our kings and our priests have been subjected to the sword and captivity, to pillage and humiliation at the hand of foreign kings, as it is today. But now, for a brief moment, the LORD our God has been gracious in leaving us a remnant and giving us a firm place in his sanctuary."

While Ezra was praying and weeping in the house of God, a large crowd of Israelites—men, women, and children—gathered around him, as though his tears were a magnet too strong to resist. They too wept bitterly.

At long last, after years of exile and hardship, God's people were once again bowing their hearts before him. Ezra had begun a task more difficult even than rebuilding a city or a temple, a task that involved restoring the hearts of God's people, turning them back to the law of Moses, a law whose purpose it was to make them a special people, holy to the Lord and safe in his keeping.

Tuesday

A LOOK AT THE MAN

Revive Our Hearts

Ezra was a student and a teacher of Scripture. His dedication to learning made him well versed in the substance and nuances of the law. He had a commanding knowledge of its truth. Is it any wonder why God selected him to initiate revival among the Hebrews?

Not much is said of Ezra's conversation with Artaxerxes that day, but God empowered Ezra and softened the king in a remarkable way. Of course, Artaxerxes was impressed with Ezra's understanding of his own religion and thoughtful preparation for this return to the homeland.

And although he would have been hard-pressed to explain it, the king knew that there was something else going on with this humble man who stood in his presence. Scripture tells us that "the hand of the LORD his God was on Ezra." God revealed himself through Ezra and moved the heart of a pagan monarch.

The king also must have observed Ezra's leadership skills. He knew that the task of moving thousands of Jews back to their homeland would need to be shouldered by a group of men who shared Ezra's vision and were loyal to him. In his letter, the king directs Ezra and his "brother Jews" to "do whatever seems best" with the vast provisions he sends along. This was not going to be a solo operation, and Artaxerxes was impressed with Ezra's ability to find other leaders to assist him.

Ezra was a man of vision demonstrated by his calling of the Levites to join the caravan to Jerusalem. He made it clear that this voyage was not simply a sightseeing tour of the rebuilt temple, but a spiritual pilgrimage.

Ezra's close relationship to the God of Abraham, Isaac, and Jacob is undeniable. Ezra "was well versed in the law" and had devoted himself to studying and keeping the law, as well as teaching its commands.

But it was Ezra's humility before God that is the most telling part of the story. Nowhere was this more clearly demonstrated than when the report of Israel's sinfulness was brought to his attention.

You would think, after seeing how Ezra had prepared for this trip and how he had demonstrated his fidelity to God and his leadership skills, that Ezra would be outraged by the report. "Who do these Jews think they are?" Ezra could have thundered. "God will surely judge them for their sin."

Instead, Ezra fell on his knees lamenting the sins of God's people. Soon others gathered around the weeping priest, pouring out their own sins before the throne of God. What an amazing sight that must have been. Then Ezra, empowered by the Holy Spirit, made a declaration before the people that Israel's unfaithfulness had manifested itself in the Jewish men marrying foreign women. He told them to confess their sin and make a covenant to send away these wives and their children. "You are right!" the people responded. "We must do as you say."

Often the fires of revival are kindled in the souls of people like Ezra who come before the Lord on behalf of God's people.

Wednesday

HIS LEGACY IN SCRIPTURE

Read Ezra 9:5–15.

1. Ezra had caught his people red-handed. They had broken God's laws regarding intermarriage. What did this bad news cause Ezra to do?

2. What was his attitude toward these sinful people? What might you have done?

3. Many religious leaders act like Lone Rangers. What are the lessons we can learn from Ezra's life about leadership?

4. Ezra does not close his prayer with a review of his own sinfulness but a declaration of God's righteousness. Why does he do this?

GOING DEEPER

5. In Ezra 7, Ezra went before King Artaxerxes to make his appeal. How long did it take for Ezra to get ready for this meeting? What did he do to prepare?

6. What big thing are you planning to do? How should you get ready?

Thursday

HIS LEGACY OF PROMISE

Ezra didn't have a corner on challenging situations. Hardly a day goes by that you and I are not confronted with a tough one. But Ezra was blessed with the discipline of study, the skills of leadership, the courage to face whatever obstacles lay in front of him, and a passionate love for God. Once Ezra had received permission to lead an expedition back to Canaan, he then had to find the people willing to make the dangerous trek. Then, back in Jerusalem, Ezra had to deal with the people's sinfulness head-on.

Come to think of it, each of the qualities that Ezra demonstrated were learned skills. It's no good wishing we had the same natural gifts as Ezra, as though these alone enabled him to spark a revival in Judah. If we want God to use us, we will need to actively practice the discipline of study, seek the help of others, and boldly do what God asks us to do. That's how faith is built. That's how God's work is accomplished. That's how we respond to his grace.

Promises in Scripture

> *He is the Rock, his works are perfect,*
> *and all his ways are just.*
>
> —Deuteronomy 32:4

> *Plans fail for lack of counsel,*
> *but with many advisers they succeed.*
>
> —Proverbs 15:22

> *Do your best to present yourself to God as one approved, a workman who does not need to be ashamed and who correctly handles the word of truth.*
> —2 Timothy 2:15

> *Confess your sins to each other and pray for each other so that you may be healed. The prayer of a righteous man is powerful and effective.*
> —James 5:16

Friday

HIS LEGACY OF PRAYER

"O my God, I am too ashamed and disgraced to lift up my face to you, my God, because our sins are higher than our heads and our guilt has reached to the heavens. . . .

"But now, for a brief moment, the LORD our God has been gracious in leaving us a remnant and giving us a firm place in his sanctuary, and so our God gives light to our eyes and a little relief in our bondage."

—Ezra 9:6, 8

Reflect On:	Ezra 10:1
Praise God:	For his faithfulness in Ezra's life and his promise to be faithful in yours.
Offer Thanks:	For the insurmountable challenges that force you into his presence.
Confess:	Any propensity to be critical of others' sins without confessing the gravity of your own.
Ask God:	To fill you with his presence, to give you dreams and plans that honor him, and grant you wisdom.

Ezra's successes could have lured him into believing he was something special on his own. But God kept his heart right and, regardless of these temporal victories—a favorable response from the king, safe travel to Jerusalem, and purging sin from the land—Ezra remained humble before the Lord.

Treat those things that God has blessed you with in the same way that Ezra treated the animals at the evening sacrifice—be willing to watch them go up in smoke in surrender to something greater—a deeper walk with God.

Father, thank you for the life and example of Ezra, for his obedience, leadership, and love. Mostly, thank you for Ezra's humility. Please teach me to admit my own sinfulness and need of your grace before I criticize others. Help me gain the discipline to work on areas of my life that need the most growth rather than being satisfied to linger where I feel the most accomplished. I willingly submit to your leadership in my life. I pray this in Jesus' name. Amen.

NEHEMIAH

His Name Means "God Is Consolation"

His Work:	Nehemiah was a Jew living in Babylon. He and his people had been defeated by the Assyrians and taken as slaves to a foreign land. The Persians had conquered the Assyrians and were now in power. Nehemiah served Artaxerxes, the king of Persia, as his personal adviser and escort, or cupbearer. Surrounded by the opulence of a palace, Nehemiah had an eye for building and construction.
His Character:	Nehemiah was a tenderhearted man who loved God's people. He honored the living God and was also a man of courage and vision.
His Sorrow:	Living as an exile deeply troubled Nehemiah. He longed for "home" even though he had never lived there.
His Triumph:	Unlike his forefathers who had been defeated by the size of the task, Nehemiah's dream was to rebuild the wall surrounding Jerusalem.
Key Scriptures:	Nehemiah 1–4

Monday

HIS STORY

It was a quiet night on the road to Jerusalem. The sky was crystal clear with only a sliver of a moon for light. Except for the crickets, the only noise was the sound of horses slowly clomping along the road. The hoofbeats were haphazard, not ordered or rhythmic. The men on horseback included a man named Nehemiah. He and his companions were not in a hurry.

In the faint light the men saw something disturbing. Unwilling to believe it true, they drew a little closer. Nehemiah let out an audible gasp and pulled back on the reins. The messengers had spoken the truth.

Lying before them were the shattered pieces of the wall that once surrounded the city. For centuries this vast structure had protected God's people. Now it lay in ruins. Nehemiah remained still, taking it all in. He had heard about the devastation, but seeing it for himself was another matter entirely. His eyes welled with tears.

Nehemiah slackened the reins and gave his horse a gentle kick. The mare moved forward, stepping carefully through the rubble. Occasionally Nehemiah would stop again and weep, his heart broken like a clay pot carelessly tossed to the ground.

Three days later, after more carefully inspecting the ruined walls, Nehemiah's heart filled with resolve. He gathered together from the surrounding areas a group of Jewish leaders—priests, nobles, and other leaders—remnants of God's people. He told them what he had seen the night before, and, for the first time, he disclosed the purpose of his journey from Babylon to Jerusalem.

"We're going to rebuild the wall," Nehemiah announced, his voice rising with passion.

The people had been waiting for this day. "Yes," they shouted. "Let us start rebuilding."

Several months earlier Nehemiah had been next to the power of Persia. As King Artaxerxes' servant and personal cupbearer, he was known throughout the country as a man in the monarch's inner circle. And even though he was a captive in a foreign land surrounded by people who did not fear the Lord, Nehemiah loved and served God.

One day a man named Hanani came to Nehemiah with some news. Hanani was a brother Israelite and had just been to Judah. Nehemiah was eager to hear how his people were doing, since Zerubbabel, the governor of the region, had taken more than forty thousand Jews back to Jerusalem to rebuild the temple.

"Those who are in Judah are in great trouble and disgrace," Hanani reported. "The wall of Jerusalem is broken down, and its gates have been burned with fire."

Nehemiah let the words sink in. From the time he was a small boy, he had heard of the walled city of Jerusalem—the city on a hill especially set aside for God's chosen ones. Old men had told of the bustling commerce within the security of the walls. Elderly women had described the joy of being surrounded by family and fellow Jews. Everyone had told of the great temple in the city's center. Nehemiah had always tried to picture what the city would have looked like. Now, although he had never been there, he could envision the walls and gates in ruins and feel the devastation like a tangible shame and vulnerability upon his people.

Nehemiah broke down and wept. For several days he mourned and fasted and prayed before the God of heaven. He repented of his own sinfulness, interceded before God's throne on behalf of his people, and pled with the Lord to grant him favor with Artaxerxes the king, to whom he was about to make a bold request.

Some time later Nehemiah was serving the king. As he handed the king a goblet of wine, the sovereign stopped him in his tracks with a surprising question. "What's the matter, Nehemiah?" the king asked. "You're not sick, so why do you look so sad? Something is troubling you."

Nehemiah was stunned by the king's directness. And he was filled with fear at the thought of telling the king why he was upset.

Nehemiah took a deep breath. "Long live the king!" he said, wanting to reassure the man of his loyalty. Then he ventured forward by saying, "The city where my fathers are buried is in ruins. Its walls have been destroyed, and its gates have been burned to the ground."

The king listened carefully, visibly moved by the story. As he watched the king's expression, Nehemiah knew that God had answered his prayer.

"What do you want me to do?" Artaxerxes asked.

The question stunned the cupbearer. The king of Persia was asking Nehemiah what he could do for *him!*

But this was the moment Nehemiah had beseeched the Lord to give him, and he was not going to squander it. *O God,* he silently prayed, *please grant me courage and wisdom.*

"If it pleases the king, and if I have found favor in your eyes," Nehemiah began, "please send me to Jerusalem." He paused. "I want to rebuild the wall."

The king considered this bold endeavor, chin in hand. "How long will it take and when will you return?" he asked at last.

The relief and joy in Nehemiah's heart was undeniable. He had long been ready for such a question, having planned out the expedition a thousand times. Heads together, king and servant conferred for long hours.

Artaxerxes appointed Nehemiah governor of Judea and supplied him with official letters to grant him safe passage between Babylon and Judah. And he summoned army officers and mounted soldiers to escort him safely back to Jerusalem.

As Nehemiah and his friends slowly circled the city that night, he knew that God had assigned him to be the one to rebuild the wall. He was overwhelmed by the magnitude of the task and the grace of the one who had called him. And as he stood before the people to announce the purpose of his return to Jerusalem, his heart overflowed with gratitude.

Tuesday

A LOOK AT THE MAN

A Dream Fulfilled

It's hard to imagine living your life in captivity. Rights that free men take for granted—where to live, where to work, where to go—may be denied someone living in exile. This was the lot of Nehemiah. His beloved nation had been conquered, his people driven to a foreign land where they lived as captives. But Nehemiah was not going to let external circumstances control his character. Instead, he resolved to live with integrity and in reverence before God, regardless of his locale.

Nehemiah had a dream that would not be denied by his circumstances. Like so many of the "ordinary" men of the Bible, Nehemiah believed that God was with him and would call him someday to a great task.

One day that mission presented itself to Nehemiah in the form of a fellow Hebrew named Hanani. The man reported to Nehemiah that the wall surrounding Jerusalem lay in ruin. Many years before, conquering nations had decimated it, tearing the stones to the ground and burning the great wooden gates.

In his mind, lying in bed at night, Nehemiah could see the walls of Jerusalem shining in the noonday sun, standing strong as a testament to God's presence therein. A skeptic could have argued that the odds were stacked against him, and everything told him it was impossible. *How will you quit your job? The king will never let you go. How will you get back to Jerusalem? The journey is long and dangerous. Who will pay for this project? The cost in human labor and materials is well beyond your reach. You're a slave, Nehemiah. You're hundreds of miles from home, Nehemiah. You don't have a shekel to your name, Nehemiah.*

But Nehemiah was not to be denied. The story of his successful campaign—the fulfillment of his dream—is the stuff of folklore and legend.

Ironically, as the story of the rebuilding of the wall unfolded, Nehemiah's greatest foes were not those tactical challenges—travel, safety, funding—but the emotional ones. Nehemiah and those who were working with him were forced to face the greatest test of all—discouragement.

In his sovereignty, God allowed two men, Sanballat and Tobiah, to attempt to interfere with Nehemiah's work. At first their taunts were verbal: "What are those feeble Jews doing? If even a fox climbed up on it, he would break down their wall of stones." But when their words didn't stop the men's efforts, their mocking words turned to threats of sabotage.

So Nehemiah stationed half of the workers as sentries with swords, spears, and bows to guard the walls. The rest of the workers—even those who were carrying the building materials—kept their weapons close by. Because of his steadfastness and confidence in God, these attempts to thwart Nehemiah's dream were crushed. And he knew where his protection was coming from. "Our God will fight for us," he told the people.

Wednesday

HIS LEGACY IN SCRIPTURE

Read Nehemiah 2:1–18.

1. Nehemiah had never been to Jerusalem before, yet the thought of the destroyed wall broke his heart. What does this say about Nehemiah?
2. Nehemiah's countenance exposed his brokenness about the wall. King Artaxerxes had never seen this kind of sadness in his cupbearer. What does this tell us about Nehemiah's usual daily attitude despite his lowly career? What can we learn from this?
3. Nehemiah was afraid to tell the king about his plan. Was this apprehension a good thing or a bad thing? Why?
4. Kids sometimes chant, "Sticks and stones may break my bones, but words will never hurt me." Sanballat and Tobiah turned this old saying into a lie. How?

GOING DEEPER

5. The sheer work of finishing the wall was not Nehemiah's biggest challenge. Nehemiah 4, verse 14 gives us a look at his strategy to face this greater foe. What did he do?
6. Soldiers used to say, "Trust God and keep your powder dry." Explain what such a strategy might look like in your own life.

INTERESTING FACT

In the Bible a wall can represent more than a physical structure. It is a metaphor for salvation: "We have a strong city; God makes salvation its walls and ramparts" (Isaiah 26:1); God's protection: "'I myself will be a wall of fire around it,' declares the LORD, 'and I will be its glory within'" (Zechariah 2:5); and a symbol of those who provided security: "Night and day they were a wall around us all the time we were herding our sheep near them" (1 Samuel 25:16). Is it any wonder that Nehemiah was so determined to rebuild Jerusalem's wall? It meant even more to him—and his people—than shattered masonry and broken gates.

Thursday

HIS LEGACY OF PROMISE

The dreams of ordinary men and women have changed the world. When Nehemiah heard the news that the wall surrounding Jerusalem had been destroyed, that news planted a seed in his soul. That seed grew to become a dream, then almost an obsession. In spite of incredible odds, Nehemiah and his people rebuilt the wall.

But the story of this rebuilding is not primarily the story of one man's dream and hard work to bring it to fulfillment. This is the account of a man who humbled himself before the living God and then, by his Holy Spirit, shaped the hearts of others to complete his will.

Promises in Scripture

> He whose walk is blameless
>   and who does what is righteous,
> who speaks the truth from his heart
>   and has no slander on his tongue,
> who does his neighbor no wrong
>   and casts no slur on his fellowman . . .
> He who does these things
>   will never be shaken.
>
> —Psalm 15:2–3, 5

> In his heart a man plans his course,
>   but the LORD determines his steps.
>
> —Proverbs 16:9

> Whoever humbles himself . . . is the greatest in the kingdom of heaven.
>
> —Matthew 18:4

Friday

HIS LEGACY OF PRAYER

"O LORD, God of heaven, the great and awesome God, who keeps his covenant of love with those who love him and obey his commands, let your ear be attentive and your eyes open to hear the prayer your servant is praying before you day and night. . . . I confess the sins we Israelites, including myself and my father's house, have committed against you."

—Nehemiah 1:5–6

Reflect On:	Nehemiah 6:15–16
Praise God:	For empowering his faithful servants to do great things.
Offer Thanks:	For granting us minds to dream and courage to tackle those dreams.
Confess:	The temptation to take a dream that only serves our purposes and ask God to bless it, rather than to listen first to his voice.
Ask God:	To give you joy in your work—to see it as the place where God wants you to be to accomplish his purposes.

It's remarkable, considering Nehemiah's exile, to hear the boldness and confidence in his voice. However, it's clear that God empowered him to do these things because Nehemiah first humbled himself before the Lord and confessed his own sin.

God gave Nehemiah a tender heart. His compassion for his own people and concern for their protection drove him to undertake a daunting task.

Father, thank you for the life and example of Nehemiah. Thank you for the endurance of a man who did not allow his life as an exile to tarnish his dream of leadership. And thank you for his tender heart toward others who were suffering and his willingness to challenge those who would discourage him from his obedience to you. Please grant me the courage of my convictions, give me sensitivity to my own need for confession, and tune my heart to the hurts of other. I willingly submit to your direction in my life. I pray this in Jesus' name. Amen.

JOB

His Work:	Job was a wealthy farmer, herdsman, and landowner.
His Character:	Next to Jesus Christ, no one in the Bible carries a more remarkable résumé. "This man was blameless and upright; he feared God and shunned evil. . . . He was the greatest man among all the peoples of the East."
His Sorrow:	Except for his own life and the life of his spouse, Job lost everything: cattle, camels, sheep, buildings, servants, and ten children. No one in all of Scripture— except Jesus—suffered more than he. Then to add to the physical devastation, Job had to endure the cross-examination and derision of three friends who clearly did not know what they were talking about.
His Triumph:	In the end, Job was vindicated by the Lord, and God blessed him with more wealth than he had before. The Lord also gave him ten more children.
Key Scriptures:	Job 1; 2; 40

Monday

HIS STORY

"Master, Master, Master . . . something terrible has happened!"

The young messenger had never been so brazen. Ignoring protocol, he pushed back the servants and burst through the door into Job's private dining chamber.

Job stood and walked toward the panicked messenger. Grasping the young man's forearms with his hands, he tried to bring calm. But the man was inconsolable.

"The Sabeans . . . they came to our fields . . . they stole our live-stock—the oxen, the donkeys . . . and . . . and they killed all the servants." Between gulps of air, the man told Job that he was the only one to survive. With these words, he collapsed against Job's chest and wept like a child.

Job held the messenger close, but his mind was in a whirl. *The Sabeans? I have no enemies among the Sabeans! What has provoked this attack? I must go and. . . .* Before Job was able to finish the thought, another messenger came rushing into the room. His face and hands were black with soot, his clothes seared and reeking of smoke.

"Fire!" he shouted. "Fire has come from the heavens . . . fire as I have never seen . . . the skies opened and flames poured out onto our fields!"

"Tell me what you saw," Job commanded, his eyes fixed on the frantic man's face. "Tell me everything."

"Your sheep were grazing in the fields, my lord. There was a sound, like thunder . . . but there were no clouds." The young man searched for words.

"Go on. Go on!" Job ordered, his voice rising to an uncommon level.

"Fire descended from heaven and destroyed the sheep, my lord. And the servants. . . ." He paused as he realized what he was about to say. "Except for me, all the servants are dead." He began to cry. His body shook with sobs. Job drew the messenger to himself as the tears flowed.

Fire? Job's mind rifled through the possibilities. *Fire from the skies? How could this—*

Yet another messenger came running into his chambers, interrupting his thought. He told Job of the Chaldeans—some on foot, some on horseback, but all with weapons. "Three hordes of them descended on your fields, my lord. They slew all your camels and the servants that attended to them. I was the only one to escape."

"The Chaldeans?" Job bellowed. "What have I done to the Chal—"

Another messenger stormed into the room then, eyes glassy and face ashen. His lips were moving, but he made no sound. *Surely there cannot be more bad news,* Job thought. He stepped toward the panic-stricken man and grasped his shoulders, steeling himself for the worst.

"What is it?" Job asked the messenger, his voice hinting of a resigned calm. Inside, he already knew what was coming.

As if in a trance, the fourth messenger spoke evenly. "Your sons and daughters are dead." Job's hands fell from the man's shoulders. He did not speak. "A mighty wind came sweeping in from the desert," the messenger said. "The house collapsed on your children. They were crushed under the weight of the walls and the roof. No one survived. Only I was able to escape."

Job stood motionless. A grinding nausea formed in his stomach. His eyes were open, but nothing came into focus. Grasping his robe in both hands, he ripped the garment from top to bottom. He showed no anger. No rage. Only sorrow and unspeakable grief. And then suddenly Job's heart was filled with a strange sense of awe.

He called for his servants and ordered them to shave his head. Then, clearing the room, he fell to the ground in worship.

> "Naked I came from my mother's womb,
>   and naked I will depart.
> The LORD gave and the LORD has taken away;
>   may the name of the LORD be praised."

Tuesday

A LOOK AT THE MAN

The Contest

It all seems so unfair. God and Satan climbed into opposing grandstands and thrust the unsuspecting Job into the arena.

"There is no one on earth like him," God asserted. "He is blameless and upright, a man who fears God and shuns evil."

"Of course he's faithful," Satan sneered. "Job's no fool. Look at what you've given him. Who wouldn't be upright with all that prosperity? He's got a good thing going." God knew exactly where this conversation was headed. He wrote the script before the earth was formed. "But open your hand and let me strike everything he has," Satan scoffed. "If I do this, he will curse you to your face. Destroy his things, and then we'll see how upright he is."

"Very well," God replied. "His possessions are all yours."

In that moment Job walked into the arena alone. And in less than a single day, he lost everything—five hundred yoke of oxen and five hundred donkeys, seven thousand sheep, and three thousand camels. In just a few hours, nearly all of Job's servants were dead, and then, in a final devastating blow, his seven sons and three daughters were destroyed in a tornado.

Job was broken yet steadfast.

But Satan was not ready to concede. "Open your hand and let me strike his body," Satan chortled to God. "No one can deal with that kind of pain. He will surely curse you to your face."

"Very well," God repeated. "His body is yours, but you may not kill him."

Then, just as Job was burying his last child, painful sores broke out over his entire body. From the top of his head to the bottom of his feet, he was covered with horrible wounds.

His wife had seen enough. "Are you still holding on to your God? What's the use?" she mocked. "Curse him and die!"

But Job refused. "Should we accept good from God and not trouble?"

Then three of Job's friends appeared. For one week they sat quietly with their suffering friend. Not a single word was spoken. At first their kindness opened Job's heart. Then it opened his mouth. He began the slow and downward spiral of asking "why?" "Why?" he asked one friend, shaking his head in disbelief. "Why?" he asked another, clinging to his hands. "Why?" he screamed at the sky. He cursed the day of his birth and expressed his longing to die.

Then Job and his three friends entered into a dialogue that lasted for many days. The conversation was deeply philosophical, tedious, and depressing. The words of Job's friends were neither comforting nor helpful.

"How long will you torment me and crush me with your words?" Job finally lamented.

Then God spoke to Job. "Brace yourself like a man," the Almighty began. "I will question you, and you shall answer me."

Job had never heard anything like this.

"Where were you when I laid the earth's foundations?" the sovereign God asked. "Tell me, if you understand, who marked off its dimensions? Surely you know!"

God's soliloquy continued uninterrupted. He exposed the greatness of his creation and the mystery and power of his being.

Job was stunned by God's words and overwhelmed by God's very presence amid his pain. "My ears had heard of you," Job finally said. "But now my eyes have seen you."

Wednesday

HIS LEGACY IN SCRIPTURE

Read Job 23.
1. What is the world's view of suffering? What reasons do people give for suffering?
2. Find the words in this passage that underscore Job's deep loneliness. Tell about a time when you have had similar feelings.
3. Find the words in this passage that describe his ongoing love for God. How can suffering enhance our devotion to the Lord?

GOING DEEPER

Read Job 38:1–2.
4. Job was enrolled in graduate school. His loss and pain were the tuition fees, and the conversations between himself, his friends, and God were his course work. These are the opening words of God's commencement address. What do you think they mean?

Read Job 42:1–3.
5. These words represent Job's diploma. What do you think they mean?
6. What does Job's experience say to us today about suffering?

Thursday

HIS LEGACY OF PROMISE

Some wish this story could be stricken from the Bible. Over the centuries it has raised more puzzling questions than it has answered.

How could a loving God allow a man who had been so upright, so faithful to suffer? Was his life merely a cosmic game of tug of war?

The account of this God-fearing and righteous man facing the loss of everything precious to him is one of the most powerful reminders of God's sovereignty in all of Scripture. Of course, suffering may be a consequence of our disobedience, even God's punishment for it. Our Father has the right to do this.

But God may allow suffering in order to draw his presence into sharp relief, shading out what we thought was so important and giving us a greater appreciation for his perfect love and grace. How else could believers—in the Bible and through the centuries—express faith in God despite their pain?

Promises in Scripture

Trouble and distress have come upon me,
but your commands are my delight.

—Psalm 119:143

Whoever trusts in his riches will fall,
but the righteous will thrive like a green leaf.

—Proverbs 11:28

Be joyful always; pray continually; give thanks in all circumstances, for this is God's will for you in Christ Jesus.   —1 Thessalonians 5:16–18

Friday

HIS LEGACY OF PRAYER

*"Naked I came from my mother's womb,
   and naked I will depart.
The LORD gave and the LORD has taken away;
   may the name of the LORD be praised."*

—Job 1:21

*"My ears had heard of you
   but now my eyes have seen you."*

—Job 42:5

Reflect On: Job 40:1–7

Praise God: For this lesson graphically illustrated by his faithful servant.

Offer Thanks: For allowing us to draw closer to him no matter how painful our circumstances.

Confess: Our propensity to accuse God of unfairness when he allows suffering to come our way.

Ask God: To show you his perspective on your pain and your doubts and to grant you his peace—the peace that transcends understanding.

The two prayers above form bookends on Job's life. Job offers the first prayer soon after we meet him and the last near the end of the book. Like a boy maturing to manhood, Job's love for God grows from simple praise—a very good thing—to intimacy—something even better.

Father, thank you for the life and example of Job. I praise you for his faithfulness in the face of suffering and pain. Please fill me with your Spirit so that I may learn from Job's faith—to love you, to praise you, to thank you, and to trust you in every circumstance, knowing that suffering can result in a deeper fellowship with you. I willingly submit to your direction in my life. I pray this in Jesus' name. Amen.

ISAIAH

His Name Means "The Lord Has Saved"

His Work:	An eighth-century B.C. prophet, Isaiah's message was primarily directed toward Judah and Jerusalem, warning God's people of coming judgment on their sins.
His Character:	He was a learned man of principle and integrity and of deep humility.
His Sorrow:	Isaiah was grieved that God's people were unwilling to repent.
His Triumph:	Isaiah had a vision of God that profoundly shaped his long prophetic ministry.
Key Scripture:	Isaiah 6

Monday

HIS STORY

"Thus says the LORD," Isaiah called out to anyone who cared to listen. "Hear, O heavens!" he cried through scarred lips. "Listen, O earth! For the LORD has spoken."

Out of curiosity, people sometimes gathered to watch. They found it fascinating—a man standing in a public place, shouting at the top of his voice. Though their intent was simply to gawk, Isaiah's audience was never passive once they heard his message. How could they be?

"Sinful nation!" Isaiah summoned them. "You are a people loaded with guilt, a brood of evildoers, children given to corruption!"

"Mind your own business, you self-righteous bigot," people shouted back. "Stay out of our lives. What difference does it make to you anyway?"

But Isaiah was undaunted. He delivered his message of condemnation, promising God's judgment on the Jews if they refused to repent. "Zion will be redeemed with justice, her penitent ones with righteousness. But rebels and sinners will both be broken, and those who forsake the LORD will perish."

"Loudmouthed hypocrite!" he heard, day after day. "Judgmental old fool!"

But the prophet continued, seemingly impervious to their mocking. He knew this was his calling, because he had been commissioned in a life-altering way.

As a devout Jew, it was Isaiah's custom to make morning visits to the temple. For sixty years he went there to pray and seek courage and solace from God.

One morning Isaiah arrived at the temple at an hour so early there were no other worshipers. The sound of his sandals slapping against the stone floor echoed from the walls and timbered ceiling of the great structure.

Suddenly he saw something—something so remarkable that it would change him forever. There, in the temple, Isaiah saw the Lord. He froze in his tracks. He could not believe his eyes. The sight of the Lord in his glory was almost beyond his telling.

The position of the Sovereign One was high and exalted. The train of the Lord's robe spread out to fill the sanctuary. It was a magnificent sight.

Isaiah stood motionless, taking it all in. Hovering over God were angel-like creatures, each with six wings, but they used only two of them to fly. The other wings sheltered their faces in wonder and covered their feet in humility. And like children hollering over a hedgerow, they called to each other over the Lord's visible presence: "Holy, holy, holy is the LORD Almighty; the whole earth is full of his glory." The sound was so powerful that the building shook. The doorframes and thresholds trembled at the volume of their voices.

Isaiah was stunned. He had spent his childhood learning of the Holy One, but he had never glimpsed his glory. He was amazed at the splendor of it all. Then the reality of his situation hit him, and his delight turned to terror. "What am I doing here?" he whispered. "What am I doing here?" he said again, crushed by his own shame.

"I have no business standing in the presence of the living God," Isaiah finally said. "I am a sinner . . . a man with a filthy mouth. How dare I use these lips to tell of this Holy One? And now I have seen him," he cried. "I am ruined. I am finished."

At this, one of the angels flew to the altar and, with a pair of tongs, picked up a burning ember. The angel flew toward Isaiah's face with his arm outstretched, the coal glowing and smoking as the air raced past its burning surface.

The sight petrified Isaiah. Although he wanted to turn his face, he could not. The angel laid the fiery coal against Isaiah's mouth. His head snapped back as the cinder hissed when it met his lips. The smell of burning flesh turned his stomach. The pain was excruciating, but he did not cry out.

Then the Lord spoke. "Now that this has touched your lips, your guilt is taken away; your sins have been forgiven."

The pain of the flaming coal was quickly forgotten as Isaiah remembered his own sin—his unworthiness to stand in the presence of this holy God.

As the angel flew back to the altar with the smoldering coal, the Lord spoke. The sound of his voice was a beautiful blend of certainty and gentleness, of authority and kindness.

"Whom can I send to the people?" the Lord asked. "Who will go?"

"I will," Isaiah replied. "I will go," he repeated. "Please send me."

Tuesday

A LOOK AT THE MAN

Eyewitness to the Glory

The people noticed the difference in Isaiah. Rumor had spread that he had seen a vision in the temple that day. No one knew exactly what—or whom—he had seen, but whatever had happened, Isaiah was a changed man.

What Isaiah had experienced in the temple was one of history's most profound commissioning ceremonies, and because of its power, Isaiah's course was changed like a flood tearing down a riverbank.

Isaiah had grown up on the right side of the tracks. His family was from the royal tribe of Judah. His pedigree and command of the language marked his stature and his message. After the vision in the temple, for almost sixty years his assignment included ministry in the courts of the kings Uzziah, Jotham, Ahaz, and Hezekiah. So naturally Isaiah might have been tempted to place himself above the people to whom he preached. But because of the temple visitation, the preacher never forgot that he too was counted among the sinners. Just because he had been gifted and called to deliver God's message didn't excuse him from the need for repentance.

Isaiah had witnessed something very few mortals have seen before his time or since. He was allowed the privilege of seeing a glimpse of God's glory. The experience tore away any shroud of pride that may have covered him, replacing it with a sense of wonder and humility. It was as though the living God was saying to the prophet, "Don't forget who you're talking about, Isaiah. Never forget whom you serve."

And there was the searing heat of the burning ember. *Why couldn't God have just told me of my forgiveness? Why the coal? Why this pain?* Isaiah must have wondered over the succeeding weeks as the scabs on his lips slowly healed. But God had a purpose in this, too. He wanted Isaiah to remember the pain of repentance, the agony of confession. And he touched the part of Isaiah's body that he was using to represent the Holy One of Israel: his mouth. No doubt it was several weeks, perhaps months, before Isaiah could speak without physical pain. God's mission had been perfectly accomplished.

And now Isaiah's message of the people's sinfulness included the promise of redemption in the coming of the Savior: "For to us a child is born, to us a son is given. . . . And he will be called Wonderful Counselor, Mighty God, Everlasting Father, Prince of Peace."

The sparkle in Isaiah's eyes didn't come from a strident preacher who delighted in shouting condemnation, but in the words of deliverance through the Son of God who would come to save the people from their sins—including the sins of the woeful prophet.

Wednesday

HIS LEGACY IN SCRIPTURE

Read Isaiah 11:1–9.

1. "A shoot will come up from the stump of Jesse." To whom was Isaiah referring?
2. As he entered the temple to worship, Isaiah saw God's glory with his own eyes. These verses repeatedly mention the "fear of the LORD." What was the connection between Isaiah's vision and this fear? What does this say about our attitude in worship?
3. This passage forecasts some of the Messiah's public policy positions. What are they?

GOING DEEPER

Read Isaiah 34:1–3 and 40:28–31.

4. Isaiah's message was direct. He minced no words as he told the people that their conduct would result in complete destruction. But he also reminded them of God's grace. Why are both of these ingredients critical in the same sermon?
5. Isaiah was among a privileged few. God was extremely selective in revealing his glory throughout Scripture. Why?

Note: A number of biblical scholars believe that Isaiah 40–55 should be attributed not to Isaiah but to an anonymous prophet. Regardless of questions of authorship, the message of the book of Isaiah is best understood as a whole.

Thursday

HIS LEGACY OF PROMISE

There can be a great deal of danger in truth telling. Lost people prefer entertainment to confrontation. But Isaiah was a truth teller. At the risk of ridicule and scorn, he was fearless in his delivery. Why? Because Isaiah had seen God's glory and heard his voice. This encounter was a complete surprise.

So it was from his own experience, like a child playing hide-and-seek, that Isaiah told the people that God was on his way, "ready or not." The living God would reveal himself to them even if they didn't ask.

And the book of Isaiah told that this visitation would be in flesh and blood. It even predicted that John the Baptist would come right before the Messiah.

Promises in Scripture

The people walking in darkness
have seen a great light;
on those living in the land of the shadow of death
a light has dawned.

—Isaiah 9:2

Surely God is my salvation;
I will trust and not be afraid.
The LORD, the LORD, is my strength and my song;
he has become my salvation.

—Isaiah 12:2

You will keep in perfect peace
him whose mind is steadfast,
because he trusts in you.

—Isaiah 26:3

The Son of Man came to seek and to save what was lost.

—Luke 19:10

Friday

HIS LEGACY OF PRAYER

> "O LORD, you are my God;
>> I will exalt you and praise your name,
> for in perfect faithfulness
>> you have done marvelous things,
>> things planned long ago."

—Isaiah 25:1

Reflect On: Isaiah 25:1–5

Praise God: For his sovereignty and power, for his mercy and his grace.

Offer Thanks: For calling us to repentance and for providing a Savior.

Confess: Our casual attitude about being in his holy presence in worship and our cavalier attitude about our own sin.

Ask God: To give you a glimpse of his glory—an understanding of what Isaiah must have experienced that day in the temple. Tell him that you're willing to be sent, to be his ambassador, his mouthpiece.

Isaiah's encounter with God is one of the great moments in the Bible. It reminds us of our sinfulness, our call to serve, and, most important, of God's awesomeness.

God gave Isaiah something he grants very few people—a glimpse of his glory. We understand how being in the presence of someone famous or powerful affects our conduct. Now imagine the impact of an audience with the living God.

Father, show me your glory. I dare to make this request, knowing that my experience of you will change everything. Forgive me when I forget who you really are. Remind me of your indescribable goodness and your hatred of sin. And fill me with your love, giving me the courage to take the wonder of your grace to a lost world. I pray this in Jesus' name. Amen.

JEREMIAH

His Name May Mean "Yahweh Has Exalted" or
"Yahweh Has Established"

His Work: Though Jeremiah's prophecies were primarily directed toward Judah, the Lord also gave him prophetic messages for other nations of the world. His ministry took place during the last forty years of Judah's existence, from 627–586 B.C.

His Character: Jeremiah has often been called "the weeping prophet." He struggled with feelings of insecurity, doubt, and alienation. Because of the constant opposition he faced, he became so depressed that he cursed the day of his birth. Despite the cost to himself, he spoke the word of the Lord with uncompromising honesty.

His Sorrow: Though the date and place of Jeremiah's death are uncertain, Jewish tradition holds that he was stoned to death by fellow Jews while living in Egypt after the destruction of Jerusalem. Despite their misfortunes, those who had taken refuge in Egypt remained unrepentant, blaming their troubles not on their idolatry, but on their failure to worship Ishtar, the Queen of Heaven.

His Triumph: It is hard to find evidence in the book of Jeremiah that the prophet enjoyed any sense of personal triumph throughout the course of his ministry. Though he may have felt vindicated when his prophecies about Jerusalem came true, such feelings would have been small comfort in light of the suffering that had befallen his people.

Key Scriptures: Jeremiah 1; 20; 36; 37:16–21; 39:1–14

Monday

HIS STORY

"Before I formed you in the womb I knew you, before you were born I set you apart; I appointed you as a prophet to the nations."

Jeremiah lay flat on the ground, his face pressed into the dirt, remembering the words he had heard as a youth, words from heaven that had at first reassured him and then shaken him, unmaking his plans for his life.

"But, LORD, I do not know how to speak; I am only a child," he had objected.

"Do not say, 'I am only a child,'" the Lord replied. "You must go to everyone I send you to and say whatever I command you. Do not be afraid of them, for I am with you and will rescue you. Tell me what you see."

"I see a boiling pot, tilting away from the north."

"From the north disaster will be poured out on all who live in the land," the Lord said. "Today I have made you a fortified city, an iron pillar and a bronze wall to stand against the whole land—against the kings of Judah, its officials, its priests, and the people of the land. They will fight against you but will not overcome you, for I am with you and will rescue you."

In the thirteenth year of Josiah's reign, this word of the Lord came to Jeremiah, a youth who, like the boy king of Judah, had suddenly been called into service. Prophet and king—Jeremiah and Josiah—the two were like brothers sharing the same passion, working for the same cause. But when Josiah died, Jeremiah was suddenly left alone, lamenting the loss of the man who had bolstered his hope that Judah might one day return to the Lord.

Jeremiah rolled over, staring at the darkness of his dungeon prison. He could smell the dank earth, feel its chill clinging to him like ice coating a stick. He had not eaten for some time. Food was scarce in a city under siege. *How long had he been here?* he wondered. *A long time,* was his conclusion. No wonder the Lord had forbidden him to marry. What future was there for children born into a world that was falling apart? What future was there for children of an outcast?

With the exception of Josiah, Judah's kings had hated Jeremiah. They had tried silencing him by the usual methods—bullying him, beating him, placing him in stocks, and shutting him away in prison. But nothing had worked. Jeremiah kept on speaking the word of God, standing in front of them like a bronze wall that could not be breached, just as the Lord had said.

One day a scroll containing the prophecies of Jeremiah was delivered to King Jehoiakim while he was sitting in his winter apartment warming himself in front of a burning firepot. Jehoiakim leaned back lazily in his chair and ordered his official to read it to him. After a few columns were read, the king leaned forward with a scribe's knife in his hand and sliced off a portion of the scroll, throwing it into the firepot. Then his official resumed reading. After each section was read to the king, he cut it off, consigning it to the fire until the entire scroll was burned up. Like a spoiled child covering his ears to the voice of an angry parent, Jehoiakim refused to listen to the chastening words of God. Instead, he ordered Jeremiah's arrest. For his part the prophet simply dictated another scroll while in hiding from the king's men.

At times Jeremiah had grown so weary of the struggle that he had tried to stop prophesying. But each time he kept silent, the words became like a fire shut up in his bones. Exhausted from the struggle of holding them in, he thundered on: "Flee for safety, people of Benjamin! Flee from Jerusalem! Sound the trumpet. I will destroy the Daughter of Zion, so beautiful and delicate. Cut down the trees and build siege ramps against Jerusalem. This city must be punished; it is filled with oppression. As a well pours out its water, so she pours out her wickedness. Take warning, O Jerusalem, or I will turn away from you and make your land desolate so no one can live in it."

After Jehoiakim came Jehoiachin and then Zedekiah, the last king of Judah. This king was no better than the others. When Jeremiah warned him that Babylon would attack Jerusalem and burn it to the ground, Zedekiah had him imprisoned, this time in a dungeon.

Now, lying in the darkness of his cell, Jeremiah heard a lock turning in the door. Shielding his eyes from the sudden onslaught of light, he squinted at the man who stood at the opening. "Come with me," the guard ordered. "Zedekiah wishes to meet with you privately."

Zedekiah greeted Jeremiah as he walked through the door to his private apartment. The king studied his prisoner carefully, noting the tall, narrow build covered by a filthy robe. Straggly gray hair and beard framed a deeply lined face, out of which stared eyes calm and sane as any man's. Holding a handkerchief to his nose to ward off the smell, the king inquired of Jeremiah. *Did he,* Zedekiah wondered, *have a word from the Lord, perhaps a softer word than the ones he had delivered before his long imprisonment?*

The old man stood straight as a rod and then spoke slowly, deliberately, as though addressing someone whose hearing had been permanently damaged: "I do have a word for the king. You will be handed over to the king of Babylon. If you surrender to the officers of the king of Babylon, your life will be spared and this city will not be burned down; you and your family will live. But if you do not surrender, this city will be handed over to the Babylonians, and they will burn it down; you yourself will not escape from their hands."

It wasn't the word Zedekiah had been hoping to hear. Stubborn as many of the kings who preceded him, he ignored the warning, refusing to surrender Jerusalem to its enemies.

When the Babylonians finally broke through the city wall, Zedekiah and his soldiers fled under cover of darkness, but they were soon captured in the plains of Jericho. Then Nebuchadnezzar, the king of Babylon, made him watch as one by one his own sons were slaughtered along with all the nobles of Judah.

Zedekiah closed his eyes, bracing himself for the sword that would end his life. But death was too great a mercy for him. Instead, Nebuchadnezzar had his eyes gouged out and then bound him with bronze shackles to take him captive to Babylon, where he would have ample time to recall the scene he had just witnessed.

After that, Nebuchadnezzar burned Jerusalem to the ground, taking many of its citizens captive. As Jeremiah had foreseen forty years earlier, Babylon had been that boiling pot, tilting away from the north, which had finally boiled over and destroyed the kingdom of Judah.

After the destruction of Jerusalem, Jeremiah too found himself in chains, lined up with the others about to be transported to Babylon. But the commander of the guard spotted him and recognized him as the prophet who had foretold Jerusalem's destruction. Speaking kindly, he reassured him, saying, "Today I am freeing you from the chains on your wrists. Come with me to Babylon, if you like, and I will look after you; but if you do not want to, then don't come. Look, the whole country lies before you; go wherever you please."

Then the commander of the imperial guard gave him provisions and a present and let him go, and Jeremiah chose to remain among his own people.

Tuesday

A LOOK AT THE MAN
Linking Judgment to Hope

Jeremiah is often considered a prophet of doom, a man who warned God's people of the grievous consequences of their sin. Yet it would not have been possible for him to thunder on about impending judgment if he had despaired of the possibility that Judah might actually repent and be saved. Surely it was hope that kept him going.

This hope was made tangible during Babylon's sustained siege of Jerusalem. One day Jeremiah heard the Lord telling him that one of his cousins would soon ask him to buy a field belonging to him. *But why,* he must have wondered, *should he waste precious silver purchasing property that was about to be overrun by a foreign invader?* Before he had time to puzzle out the answer, he saw his cousin approaching. Sure enough, the man was selling his field and wanted Jeremiah to buy it. So Jeremiah did.

As the prophet tried to make sense of this impractical business transaction, God spoke again, telling him, "I will surely gather [my people] from all the lands where I banish them in my furious anger and great wrath; I will bring them back to this place and let them live in safety. They will be my people, and I will be their God. I will give them singleness of heart and action, so that they will always fear me for their own good and the good of their children after them. I will make an everlasting covenant with them: I will never stop doing good to them" (Jeremiah 32:37–40).

Jeremiah's hope was based on the knowledge that nothing is ever too hard for God, not even restoring the fortunes of a people whose future seemed utterly wrecked. So, like a good contrarian investor, he ignored the conventional wisdom and bought the field. His purchase proved valuable, for the Lord eventually brought many of his people back to Jerusalem, a people chastened, purified, and eager to live once again in the land of the promise.

Wednesday

HIS LEGACY IN SCRIPTURE

Read Jeremiah 1.
1. Why do you think God spoke to Jeremiah so clearly about his call and about the divine protection that would follow?
2. Have you ever felt too young, too insecure, or too ill-prepared to do something God called you to do? Describe the situation and your response.

Read Jeremiah 20:7–18.
3. How does Jeremiah's prayer strike you—accusatory, honest, self-pitying? What does it reveal about his experience of serving the Lord? About his relationship with God?
4. How honest are your own prayers?

Read Jeremiah 32:6–15.
5. Why was land such an important feature in Israel's covenant relationship with the Lord?

GOING DEEPER
6. The book of Jeremiah is filled with beautiful poetry, striking phrases, and powerful symbolism. Like the prophet Ezekiel, Jeremiah often used symbolic actions to drive home the seriousness of his prophetic message. For examples, read:

Jeremiah 13:1–11 the ruined belt
Jeremiah 16:1–4 the command not to marry or have children
Jeremiah 19:1–12 the broken potter's jar
Jeremiah 27:1–11 the yoke of straps and crossbars

Thursday

HIS LEGACY OF PROMISE

Jeremiah didn't sit down every week to determine what he would preach about. Neither did he spice up his preaching with humorous stories in hopes of warming up his audience. He simply spoke the word of the Lord as it came to him. Over and over, he kept on speaking it, even though people hated him for it, thinking his words too harsh. Jeremiah's prophetic warnings make no sense outside the larger context of God's love, outside the bigger picture of his overall intentions. As we read the story of Jeremiah, we need to remember that God's judgment is always tempered by his mercy. How merciful would it have been, after all, if God had allowed his people to stray so far from him that they might never find their way back? Through Jeremiah, God called to the people he loved, pleading with them, begging them to repent, revealing his heart through the words of the prophet.

Promises in Scripture

I have loved you with an everlasting love;
I have drawn you with loving-kindness.
I will build you up again
and you will be rebuilt, O Virgin Israel.

—Jeremiah 31:3–4

"The time is coming," declares the LORD,
"when I will make a new covenant
with the house of Israel
and with the house of Judah. . . .
"This is the covenant I will make with the house of Israel
after that time," declares the LORD.
"I will put my law in their minds
and write it on their hearts.
I will be their God,
and they will be my people."

—Jeremiah 31:31, 33

"The days are coming," declares the LORD, "when I will fulfill the gracious promise I made to the house of Israel and to the house of Judah.

> *"In those days and at that time*
> *I will make a righteous Branch sprout from David's line;*
> *he will do what is just and right in the land.*
> *In those days Judah will be saved*
> *and Jerusalem will live in safety.*
> *This is the name by which it will be called:*
> *The LORD Our Righteousness."*

—Jeremiah 33:14–16

Friday

HIS LEGACY OF PRAYER

"Why did I ever come out of the womb
to see trouble and sorrow
and to end my days in shame?"

—Jeremiah 20:18

Reflect On:	Jeremiah 20:7–18
Praise God:	For his relentless love.
Offer Thanks:	That he will never fail or forsake us.
Confess:	Any tendency to try to hide your thoughts or feelings from God.
Ask God:	To help you develop a deep and honest relationship with him.

Jeremiah's prayer is so honest, raw, vulnerable. One moment he is calling God a mighty warrior who's always with him, and the next he's wishing he had never been born. What kind of prophet is this, what kind of man of God? Jeremiah, like anybody else, had feelings, hopes, and needs. He wasn't a cardboard cutout nor a saint on a pedestal; he was a man who exposed his heart in God's presence. Like Jeremiah, we need to be honest with God, to stop hiding from him if that is our habit. Though God can easily penetrate our defenses, he often waits until we're ready to come to him, just as we are, without the fig leaves, without the pretense, without the need to defend ourselves in his presence.

Lord, give me the grace of honest prayer. Help me to present myself not as I think I should be but as I am. Give me the humility to bring you every-thing—the confusion, the doubt, the ugliness, the anger. I don't want to hide anything from you. Help me to trust that you love me, warts and all.

DANIEL

His Name Means "God Is My Judge"

His Work:	He was a Jew who became a governor in Babylon.
His Character:	Daniel was an exile who exhibited great discipline and faithfulness to his God in adverse circumstances.
His Sorrow:	Daniel experienced the tearing of his people from their homeland to be exiled in Babylon. He was never able to return to the land he loved.
His Triumph:	God used his faith and his godly diligence to win the loyalty of kings and kingdoms.
Key Scriptures:	Daniel 1–6

Monday

HIS STORY

"Let us in!" the men shouted, pounding on the door. "Open up," they demanded. "Open this door immediately!"

But no one answered. And the longer they waited, the more frantic the group became. These men were respected leaders, not common street thugs. But like sharks drawn to blood, the closer they got to the home of their victim, the more frenzied they became. Any semblance of peace or logic was lost.

The door slowly opened. An old man stood in the doorway. His hair and beard were immaculate, his robes tidy and clean. He smiled, his eyes filled with a disarming gentleness. He opened his arms wide, as though welcoming dear friends.

For a moment the band of vigilantes stood motionless. Then one of them spoke. His tone was wooden and stilted, as though he had carefully memorized each word but had started offbeat and then couldn't find his rhythm. "Daniel, . . . on the order of King Darius and in accordance with his royal edict that no one shall pray to anyone but the king, you are hereby charged with treason in the first degree. You have been found guilty, the penalty is death, and we have come to arrest you."

"Long live King Darius," one of the men shouted from the back. "Long live King Darius," another returned. Soon the men were chanting and jostling each other, eager to capture the man who had dared to keep praying to his God in defiance of the king's order.

Daniel nodded, calmly stepping across the threshold of his home. He turned and deliberately closed the door behind him. As he moved into the mob, the men grabbed him as though he were trying to escape. They pulled at his beard and robe, and he stumbled forward as someone shoved him from behind.

By the time the group had reached the rock cavern, Daniel's captors were celebrating like a pack of jackals, pushing each other and laughing at their easy success. Two of the men ran ahead to slide back the large rock that covered the mouth of the cave. Daniel knew this place. Everyone knew this place.

The furious roars of lions shattered the air. At the sound, the men stopped. Then Daniel walked to the edge of the hole and, with one last backward look, disappeared into the darkness below. The men quickly slid the stone back into place. After a few halfhearted laughs and furtive glances that displayed their disappointment that Daniel hadn't put up more of a fight—hadn't given them some physical satisfaction—the group disbursed.

Daniel covered his face with his hands as he stumbled and tumbled into the darkness of the den. He could hear lions nearby, pacing, sniffing. The hair on the back of his neck stood on end.

His mind raced with the treachery of the moment—these would be his last conscious seconds. He had to concentrate, think of the things that mattered, nothing else. The lions were so close now, he could hear them padding forward, circling. "The living God be praised!" Daniel prayed. "God be praised!"

He held his breath, listening, his body aching from the tension. Suddenly he felt something warm and moist on the back of his neck. *Was it a lion? Was the beast so close he could feel his breath?*

Daniel rolled over quickly, scooting his body to the side and adjusting his eyes to the darkness. Just inches away he could make out the silhouette of the largest animal he had ever seen. Its nostrils flared with each breath, and its penetrating eyes transfixed the man. But the creature did not roar, did not even bare its teeth.

Slowly . . . ever so slowly . . . Daniel rose to his knees. In the dim light, he could see bones littering the cave floor. Then he caught sight of something even more alarming. Dozens of lions had surrounded him. Some were standing close, as if wondering what had just tumbled into their lair. Others were lazily lying around the perimeter licking their fur like house cats. Each was completely calm.

Daniel sat where he was, leaning backward against a rock, trying to make sense of what was going on. Several lions moved in closer as though vying to be near him. Tentatively, Daniel reached out and stroked the thick mane of one of the huge animals that had lumbered over and then sat down next to him like a friendly old dog. Daniel laughed under his breath. *Could this really be happening?*

Then he laid his head back on the rock and looked up into the darkness. "God be praised," he said aloud. "God be praised," he sighed. Suddenly weary beyond measure, Daniel closed his eyes to sleep.

"Daniel! Daniel!"

The sound of a man's voice eased Daniel from his dream, and he sat up and squinted against the harsh light of morning pouring in from the cave mouth. "Daniel, servant of the living God," the voice sounded again. Then Daniel recognized the voice of his old friend and grinned. "Has your God, whom you serve continually, been able to rescue you from the lions?" his friend called.

"Good morning, King Darius," Daniel returned, finally able to see his friend. "My God sent his angel, and he shut the mouths of the lions. I am unhurt."

The king was overjoyed.

"Lift Daniel from the cave," the king ordered his servants. "Bring him out now!"

Embracing him, the king examined Daniel and found that not even the slightest of wounds had been inflicted by the lions. Darius pulled his head back and laughed, his heart filled with gratitude. But no one was more grateful than Daniel.

Tuesday

A LOOK AT THE MAN

Sleeping with the Enemy

Daniel's life was filled with unpleasant—and sometimes tragic—surprises.

When he was a young man, the Babylonians laid siege to his homeland, tearing down the walls and buildings of Jerusalem. Even the sacred temple was ransacked and destroyed. Along with the other Israelites who had survived the carnage, Daniel was taken as a prisoner of war back to Babylon.

Knowing that the future of his nation rested on the shoulders of the brightest young men in the land—including Hebrew men—Nebuchadnezzar the king called for the finest in the land: "young men without any physical defect, handsome, showing aptitude for every kind of learning, well informed, quick to understand, and qualified to serve in the king's palace." Among these carefully chosen Jews was a young man named Daniel, along with three of his friends.

The young men lived in the palace. It was Daniel's first experience of sleeping with the enemy, but it would not be his last.

To more fully indoctrinate the men, Nebuchadnezzar gave them Babylonian names. Then Daniel and his friends were placed under the instruction of the teachers of Babylon, and the four young men gained "knowledge and understanding of all kinds of literature and learning." So remarkable were these men that when they were presented to King Nebuchadnezzar for his review, he found them "ten times better than all the magicians and enchanters in his whole kingdom."

But it was to Daniel alone that God gave the special gift of interpreting visions and dreams of all kinds. And it was this ability that granted Daniel a place of honor in the kingdom. After a while, Nebuchadnezzar had a dream that haunted him. He sought an interpretation from all the wise men in the land—magicians, enchanters, sorcerers, and astrologers. Infuriated by their inability to help him, Nebuchadnezzar ordered the execution of all the wise men in Babylon.

Upon hearing of this decree, Daniel begged for an audience with the king, pleading for his life and the lives of the wise men. Then

Daniel interpreted Nebuchadnezzar's troubling dream. In thanks the king promoted Daniel as the ruler of an entire Babylonian province and "lavished many gifts on him."

But in spite of the power and wealth bestowed on Daniel, his love and loyalty to the God of Abraham, Isaac, and Jacob were unaltered. His daily regimen included three visits to an upstairs window facing his precious homeland, where he knelt and prayed. Daniel's faithfulness to God—and his divine gift of interpreting dreams—placed him in great prominence in the kingdoms of Nebuchadnezzar, Belshazzar his son, and Darius.

Under Darius, Daniel rose to power over one-third of the kingdom. It was, in fact, in the king's plan to place Daniel over all of Babylon. But the other rulers seethed with envy over the king's favor of this Hebrew. And so they plotted to destroy him under the sanction of the kingdom.

These men went to the king with a flattering plan. "Issue an edict and enforce a decree," they proposed to Darius. "Anyone who prays to any god or man during the next thirty days, except the king, shall be thrown into the lions' den." Seeing an opportunity for glory and believing that there would be no harm in such a plan, the king put the decree in writing and secured it with his seal. Unfortunately for Daniel, the king himself could not reverse his decision.

Without regard to the consequences, Daniel prayed at his window. Facing prosperity or the threat of execution, he would not let his heart be drawn away from the God whom he loved and served. And his reward for this act of obedience was yet another restful night—in a cave of death for anyone but a man of God.

Wednesday

HIS LEGACY IN SCRIPTURE

Read Daniel 1:8–17.

1. Like Joseph in Egypt, Daniel was taken against his will to a foreign land. And like his ancestor, he prospered there. What adjustment was Daniel unwilling to make in his new home? What were his reasons?

2. Not only were Daniel and his three friends vulnerable to the temptations of Babylon, a godless culture, but they may have been surrounded by fellow Jews who failed to take a stand. If so, which group do you think provided the more crushing pressure on these four men? Why?

3. Give examples of these two kinds of pressures from your own experience.

GOING DEEPER

Read Daniel 6:1–5.

4. We live in a culture that often seems conciliatory to our faith, including decrees from statesmen that genuinely honor God. But appearances can be deceiving. From a spiritual viewpoint, how does our society—including Christians surrounded by a pagan culture—parallel Babylon?

5. Daniel's conniving adversaries knew how to corner him. They set a trap because they knew that Daniel would not defy God's laws regardless of the consequences. They chose his prayer life as their target. If your adversaries set a trap for you, what, if any, spiritual disciplines might they choose to attack?

6. What spiritual disciplines have you neglected that you should begin pursuing again?

Thursday

HIS LEGACY OF PROMISE

What more can be said about a man whose unfettered loyalty was to the God of his fathers and whose passion was prayer? Whether it was in the selection of his food or in the interpretation of complex dreams, we know that prayer was included in Daniel's daily routine.

> *Three times a day he got down on his knees and prayed, giving thanks to his God, just as he had done before.* —Daniel 6:10

A man living as an exile—a prisoner of war—Daniel had control over very few things, at least as a young man. But he could maintain a daily diet of worship. Whether with his friends or alone, Daniel prayed. Whether in the safety of his own land or living amid spiritual hostility, Daniel prayed. This habit and the intimacy with the Lord that it provided gave Daniel the wisdom, courage, and faith that sustained him. This faithful man provides a great example for us to follow—praying on his knees three times every day.

Promises in Scripture

> *I sought the LORD, and he answered me;*
> *he delivered me from all my fears.*
> —Psalm 34:4

> *His dominion is an eternal dominion;*
> *his kingdom endures from generation to generation.*
> —Daniel 4:34

> *I tell you, whoever acknowledges me before men, the Son of Man will also acknowledge him before the angels of God. But he who disowns me before men will be disowned before the angels of God.*
> —Luke 12:8–9

> *The prayer of a righteous man is powerful and effective.* —James 5:16

> *If we confess our sins, he is faithful and just and will forgive us our sins and purify us from all unrighteousness.* —1 John 1:9

Friday

HIS LEGACY OF PRAYER

"I issue a decree that in every part of my kingdom people must fear and reverence the God of Daniel.

> *"For he is the living God*
> *and he endures forever;*
> *his kingdom will not be destroyed,*
> *his dominion will never end."*

—Daniel 6:26

Reflect On: Daniel 6:19–28

Praise God: For his power and ability to change hearts.

Offer Thanks: For the faithful prayers of "the great cloud of witnesses" that have gone before us.

Confess: Our lack of spiritual discipline—our pretense of spiritual devotion rather than our daily practice of it.

Ask God: To fill you with a burning desire to know him.

Daniel's example of faith and loyalty to God is one of the most profound examples of courage and discipline in all of Scripture. In the midst of oppression and temptation, he and his three friends refused to succumb to the pressure of a culture hostile to their God.

The Lord gave them wisdom, and they persevered. Their lives provide us with a benchmark of faithfulness and triumph.

Father in heaven, you set up kings and you take them down. Your decrees fill the whole earth. You are faithful. Forgive me for my lack of courage and discipline to stand for what I know is right and true. And please draw me so completely to yourself that I will not wander from your presence no matter what temptations come my way.

HOSEA

His Name Means "Yahweh Has Delivered"

His Work:	Hosea was a prophet in Israel. Like other prophets, his charge was to call the people to repentance. However, he was also called to show them by his own life what it felt like to be a forgotten and yet merciful God.
His Character:	In obedience Hosea was willing to abandon his own dreams and marry a harlot. His love foreshadowed Christ's love for the church.
His Sorrow:	His unrepentant and unfaithful wife left him with their three children and a deep, aching hurt.
His Triumph:	Because of his selflessness and his willingness to forgive, his wife Gomer was restored.
Key Scriptures:	Hosea 1–3

Monday

HIS STORY

"Have you seen my wife?" the man asked the busy people in the Jezreel marketplace. He touched a passerby's arm, desperation creeping into his voice. "Excuse me, have you seen Gomer?"

Ordinarily, men and women milling about in the bustling market had little sympathy for beggars or lonely hearts. For anyone else they'd look the other way. "Get out of my shop!" busy merchants would bark. "You're bothering my customers."

But this man was no stranger. His name was Hosea. He was a local prophet, and nearly everyone knew him—and his pathetic story. When they saw Hosea on the dusty street and heard his plea, some were filled with pity and compassion. Others tried to be direct. "Give up on her," they'd counsel. "She's a waste of your time." Some even tried to help. "We'll ask around about her," they'd encourage. Neither they nor Hosea knew where Gomer was, but they knew she wasn't alone.

Long before Hosea had taken Gomer to be his wife, she had been a harlot, a *zonah*—a prostitute. Some men who had slept with her felt a tinge of shame when they saw her; others wantonly looked her over. Every woman despised the sight of her. The townspeople knew Gomer all too well.

A prostitute hadn't been Hosea's first choice for a wife. When the time had come for him to marry, Hosea, like his friends, had wanted to marry a young Jewish virgin, an inexperienced and mysterious woman whose innocence created wonder with each of her lover's advances—a woman whose husband's ways would have been unfamiliar adventures. This is what Hosea had longed for.

But God had other designs.

"Go, take to yourself an adulterous wife," the Lord commanded his servant.

Hosea's heart sank. *How could God tell me to do such a despicable thing?* he wondered. *Does he know what he's asking?*

But Hosea did not argue. His unquestioning obedience overshadowed his doubts.

"Will you marry me?" Hosea asked Gomer, a woman hardened by her craft but outwardly beautiful. He stood before her outside the tent of prostitutes, his hands holding hers, his eyes, his heart, and his words pleading with the woman, "I will love you, and you will bear our children."

Gomer hesitated, fascinated by the man's earnest proposal. Her immediate reaction was to send him away, have the guard throw him out of the city gates. But to be perfectly honest, home and hearth was what she had longed for. For years she had given in to insecurity and fear. Her occupation gave witness to that. Commitment to one man and having a family to cherish sounded appealing but far-fetched. Unbelievable. She stared back at Hosea. He was serious, intent on having her as his wife. Perhaps with him she could gain some respectability, glimpse normalcy again...

"Yes," she told her suitor, "I will be your wife."

So Hosea and Gomer were married, and soon a son was born. Hosea set aside his disquiet about his wife's past. So thoroughly had he forgiven her that the disgrace of her former life no longer entered his mind.

Then a daughter was born . . . and another son.

Hosea could not have been more pleased. In God's mercy and grace, he had given Hosea a wife and had blessed him with children.

But Gomer was growing restless. The daily demands of motherhood were wearing her thin; the better memories of her former life—of fine, rich robes and prepared food and flattering attention—lured her away. And so late one day, when Hosea returned to his home, he discovered that Gomer was not there. Her abandonment of his family would have been painful enough, but Hosea knew exactly where his wife had gone. She was back on the street soliciting the pleasures of other men. He winced at the thought and then screamed at the sky in hurt and fury.

Night after night Hosea ran his hand over the cold side of their once-shared bed, longing for her to return. But she did not. Soon his loneliness became rife with anger. *She deserves to die for what she has done to me and to our children.*

Still, Hosea's heart was strangely drawn to Gomer, loving his wayward wife far beyond her deserving. After some time had passed, God spoke to Hosea once again. "Go, show your love to your wife again, though she is loved by another and is an adulteress."

"She has become someone's concubine," Hosea moaned. "She has fallen in love with another man." He ached to think of her with one man. It was even more than thinking of her with many. But he had been told, and Hosea was obedient to the Lord's command. He gathered some money and grain as payment for her ransom and set out to find his wife.

When Hosea found Gomer, he pled, "Please come home to me and our children again. You don't need to live like this. I love you; I want to spend the rest of my days with you."

So Hosea paid the ransom for Gomer, and she returned to the family that loved her. There, day by day, she relearned the pleasure of intimacy and fidelity, the joy of being with her husband and the children who needed her. Hosea's persistent love had finally drawn her home.

Tuesday

A LOOK AT THE MAN

A Living Parable

Telling stories is often the most powerful way to communicate truth, and speaking in parables was Jesus' method of choice. But sometimes in the Bible, God asked people not only to tell stories but to *live* them, to *be* the parable. This was the lot of Hosea.

The thought of falling in love with a prostitute is repugnant to any man. The thought of marrying her is even more revolting. But this is precisely what God ordered Hosea to do.

How can I love a woman who has "loved" so many? he must have wondered. *How can I make a covenant with someone whose conduct deserves condemnation, not forgiveness?*

But regardless of his questions, Hosea did exactly as the Lord told him. Hosea married a common harlot, a woman who knew nothing of virtue or faithfulness. As a learned man, Hosea knew that he could not reply to the Almighty's directive, "You don't know what you're asking me to do." He knew full well that God knew exactly what he was doing. As a prophet, Hosea had been called to preach repentance to God's people. He had tried to fill his message with the passion of the sovereign God, whose provision, love, and mercy had been scoffed at or ignored. These Jews were even worshiping other gods. The chosen people were playing the harlot.

Now, with this assignment, Hosea would come to understand what this felt like. His love would be poured out to a woman who by the laws of the time deserved nothing less than a public execution for her blatant transgressions. But God took Hosea and made him the fool—the lover of the undeserving, the keeper of the vows, and the redeemer of the repeat offender. And though the people could not see God, they saw in the life of this man a compelling example of divine love—bold and just, yet relentlessly merciful.

Wednesday

HIS LEGACY IN SCRIPTURE

Read Hosea 1:1–7; 3:1–3.

1. Hosea will forever be known as the man who was given an almost impossible assignment. Why was it so difficult?
2. What was God's reason for telling Hosea to do such a painful thing?
3. To the people who knew him, Hosea was a visible example of God's grace. Think of someone who is this same kind of example. How does this person reflect God's mercy and love?

GOING DEEPER

4. How does Hosea's life experience parallel that of Jesus Christ?
5. How could God use you to be a parable on his behalf? What might that assignment look like?
6. What is keeping you from stepping out in faith and taking on this challenge?

Thursday

HIS LEGACY OF PROMISE

Hosea was told to marry a prostitute so he would know how it felt to be the faithful God of a wayward people. The message of Hosea is twofold: For those who are sinners, the call is for contrition, salvation, and right living. Repent of your unfaithfulness: "Return, O Israel, to the LORD your God." And for those who have received salvation, the directive is to spread the Good News and welcome home those who have fallen. Fill the message of repentance with compassion and grace.

Promises in Scripture

> How great is your goodness,
> > which you have stored up for those who fear you,
> which you bestow in the sight of men
> > on those who take refuge in you.

—Psalm 31:19

> You will receive power when the Holy Spirit comes on you; and you will be my witnesses in Jerusalem, and in all Judea and Samaria, and to the ends of the earth.   —Acts 1:8

> Christ's love compels us.   —2 Corinthians 5:14

> This is how God showed his love among us: He sent his one and only Son into the world that we might live through him. This is love: not that we loved God, but that he loved us and sent his Son as an atoning sacrifice for our sins.   —1 John 4:9–10

Friday

HIS LEGACY OF PRAYER

"Come, let us return to the LORD.
He has torn us to pieces
but he will heal us;
he has injured us
but he will bind up our wounds. . . .
Let us acknowledge the LORD;
let us press on to acknowledge him.
As surely as the sun rises,
he will appear;
he will come to us like the winter rains,
like the spring rains that water the earth."

—Hosea 6:1, 3

Reflect On: Hosea 3:1–3

Praise God: For his love for you.

Offer Thanks: For God's relentless pursuit of his unfaithful and
                 wayward children.

Confess: Your own sinfulness and your spirit of judgment
                 rather than compassion for others.

Ask God: To fill you with Hosea's kind of willingness to serve
                 and his mercy and love.

As though we were sending messages from an ivory tower, sometimes our prayers are filled with requests to God "to empower missionaries and all *those* in ministry." We forget that every believer has been called not just to pray but also to go, and not only to go but to *be.*

God calls his children not just to tell others about him or to preach repentance. He calls us to live in such a way that our witness parallels our walk, that our words match our lives. More important than the message he delivered as God's prophet, Hosea's personal example was his most persuasive ministry.

Father in heaven, I have been unfaithful to you. I have been distracted from following you. I have found and worshiped other gods. Thank you first for loving me in my trespasses and sins. Thank you for your pursuit. Now, because I am surrounded by others who are lost, I pray that you will give me the courage to go and to be. I want my life to reflect your love.

JONAH

His Name Means "A Dove"

His Work:	He was a northern kingdom prophet.
His Character:	Jonah must have been a gifted communicator. Why else would God choose him to preach repentance and grace to the pagan city of Nineveh? But Jonah was a proud man, a rebellious prophet, and a sulker.
His Sorrow:	Jonah was sad that the Ninevites had repented and that God had granted them mercy. Jonah would have preferred seeing these pagans punished for their sinfulness.
His Triumph:	That God had spared his life from the belly of the fish.
Key Scriptures:	The book of Jonah; Matthew 12:38–41

Monday

HIS STORY

The sun was barely cresting the horizon, silently chasing the morning darkness from the seacoast. "Cast off," the captain bellowed, and the massive craft slid silently away from the dock. When the boat had cleared its mooring, he called out again, ordering his men to hoist the sail.

The wind rippled through the folds of the mainsail as it was raised on the mast. Like a soldier snapping to attention, its creases and wrinkles disappeared into seamlessness. The ship lurched forward as the sailors secured the boom. With his hand on the tiller, the captain turned the bow, tacking the ship westward.

"To Spain," he hollered, thrusting his fist into the cool daylight air. "To Spain," the crew shouted back.

As with every launch, there was a sense of festivity among those on board. But as the ship sliced through the warm waters of the Mediterranean, the celebration subsided. A seriousness took hold. The captain knew these waters. He had made this voyage before. Though the skies were clear enough this morning, he knew that storms and treacherous seas lay in wait.

Everyone stood on the deck watching the land disappear as the boat headed out to sea—everyone, that is, but one man who was still fast asleep in the belly of the ship. He was a traveler who had paid his fare and boarded the ship the day before. The crew hadn't paid much attention, except to note that he looked more like a sage than a sailor.

By midday clouds began forming to the north, bringing some welcome shade to passengers but worry to both crew and captain. The winds were worse than the clouds, whipping first in one direction and then another, becoming more frenzied as time went on. Soon huge waves came crashing across the deck.

For several hours the ship fought its way through the angry waters, wave by wave, as the storm grew worse. Before long it didn't matter if the voyage would prove a commercial success. To keep from sinking, the captain ordered all the cargo to be thrown overboard. Terrified sailors called out to their gods for mercy. But the storm shrieked all the louder.

On word that there was a stranger sleeping in the ship's hold, the captain himself paid a visit. "How can you sleep?" he shouted. "Get up and call on your god! Maybe he will take notice of us, and we will not perish."

Wondering if this treacherous storm might be a god's punishment of someone on board, the sailors called to everyone. "Let's cast lots to find out who's responsible for this calamity," they said. The lot fell on the stranger.

"Who are you? What do you do? Where do you come from? From what people are you?" Their panicked questions came pouring out.

"My name is Jonah. I am a Hebrew, and I worship the LORD, the God of heaven, who made the sea and the land. I am a prophet and have disobeyed this God." Jonah winced at what he had just said. "I am running from his presence."

The sailors were horrified. "Then what should we do to you to make the sea calm down for us?"

"Pick me up and throw me into the sea," Jonah replied. "And it will become calm."

Not wanting to murder the man, the sailors grabbed oars, attempting to bring the ship around toward land. But it was no good. No matter how hard they struggled, the winds were a wall they could not scale.

"O LORD, please do not let us die for taking this man's life," they prayed. "Do not hold us accountable for killing an innocent man, for you, O LORD, have done as you pleased." Then, picking up Jonah by his hands and feet, they threw him over the gunwale. Already soaked from the storm, Jonah hardly felt himself strike the water's surface. He held his breath as his body sank through the turgid waters, his mind shouting a desperate prayer. "O merciful LORD," he cried. "Forgive me . . . save me."

Below the surface, something threw itself around him from behind, like a warm, heavy blanket encompassing his body. And then Jonah felt himself being drawn down a fleshy passageway and into a small area. He opened his mouth and gulped in air, glad—and amazed—to be alive. But then it dawned on him. He was entombed in the stomach of a sea creature.

Jonah was inside the fish for three days and three nights, plenty of time to think about the circumstances that had landed him there.

Tuesday

A LOOK AT THE MAN

Getting Ready to Pray

Prophets often scandalized God's people, ill-prepared as they were to hear the unvarnished truth about their spiritual condition. But in Jonah's case it was the prophet who was scandalized, not by another prophet, but by God himself. For one day he heard God issue an incredible command: "Go to the great city of Nineveh and preach against it, because its wickedness has come up before me."

Could God possibly mean it? It was one thing to endure mockery and ridicule from your own people whenever you preached repentance, but going to the capital city of Assyria was dangerous, perhaps deadly. The Ninevites, after all, were a violent and ruthless people who had already brutalized many Israelites. What's more, Jonah despised them. So, like a rebellious teenager, he ran away, except that he wasn't fleeing his parents, he was running from the Creator of the universe.

But, as Jonah soon discovered, you can't outrun God. Instead, he found himself surrounded by the entrails of a great fish. There in the darkness, Jonah was ready to pray.

"In my distress I called to the LORD, and he answered me. From the depths of the grave I called for help and you listened to my cry. . . . You brought my life up from the pit, O LORD my God. . . . Those who cling to worthless idols forfeit the grace that could be theirs. But I, with a song of thanksgiving, will sacrifice to you. What I have vowed I will make good."

From inside the fish, Jonah was calling his fear, his defiance, his pride, and his willful disobedience by a new name: "idols." And he was identifying the ship, the storm, and the fish as something they had never been called before: "grace." And once Jonah acknowledged these truths, God gave him another chance to obey, and the great fish vomited Jonah onto dry land. Even though Nineveh was probably more than five hundred miles away, Jonah headed for the city.

In the same way he had prepared the fish to swallow the prophet, God prepared the people for Jonah's message. "The Ninevites believed

God. They declared a fast, and all of them, from the greatest to the least, put on sackcloth to show their sorrow for their sin."

But now, instead of rejoicing at the way God had used him, Jonah acted like a spoiled child. Although he had taken God's message to the Assyrian capital city, he had no mercy for the people himself. He would have much rather watched Nineveh burn than have seen its people repent and avert God's judgment. He believed God's gift of grace belonged exclusively to his own countrymen.

How little did Jonah perceive the nature and intentions of the living God for whom he spoke. His running and his sulking demonstrate how little he understood about God's great compassion and his desire to forgive anyone who repents of his or her sins.

Wednesday

HIS LEGACY IN SCRIPTURE

Read Jonah 1:8–12.

1. What was the sailors' response to Jonah's confession?
2. Why is this significant?

Read Matthew 12:38–41.

3. A man surviving a three-day stay in the belly of a fish? It's preposterous—except that Jesus Christ himself refers to this story. What equally outrageous future event was the Savior preparing his audience for?
4. What are the parallel truths of the two stories of Jonah and Jesus: their call, their survival, and their mission?

GOING DEEPER

Read Jonah 4:1–11.

5. Because of Jonah's preaching, the entire population of Nineveh was transformed. But Jonah's reaction to Nineveh's repentance is surprising. How does he react?
6. What does this tell us about the prophet's motives? What lessons are to be learned from what Jonah did?

Thursday

HIS LEGACY OF PROMISE

The story of Jonah is the account of the sovereignty and grace of the living God. So powerful are these truths that the accounts of the prophet, the ship, the storm, the fish, and the godless city are almost secondary. And like so many who lived before him and who have followed him, God gave Jonah another chance to obey.

Promises in Scripture

> Great is his love toward us,
>   and the faithfulness of the LORD endures forever.
> Praise the LORD.
>
> —Psalm 117:2

> I am the LORD your God,
>   who churns up the sea so that its waves roar—
>   the LORD Almighty is his name.
>
> —Isaiah 51:15

> Call to me and I will answer you and tell you great and unsearchable things you do not know.
> —Jeremiah 33:3

> I knew that you are a gracious and compassionate God, slow to anger and abounding in love.
> —Jonah 4:2

> As Jonah was three days and three nights in the belly of a huge fish, so the Son of Man will be three days and three nights in the heart of the earth.
> —Matthew 12:40

Friday

HIS LEGACY OF PRAYER

*"When my life was ebbing away,
I remembered you, LORD,
and my prayer rose to you,
to your holy temple."*

—Jonah 2:7

Reflect On: Jonah 2

Praise God: For his grace—in its many forms.

Offer Thanks: For God's call on your life and his willingness to make certain that you hear his voice.

Confess: Your own foolishness and rebellion, remembering that nothing escapes his watchful eye.

Ask God: To fill you with a renewed gratitude for his presence and love for the lost.

No one in recorded history has prayed from a more disgusting sanctuary than Jonah, trapped in the belly of a fish. But it was there that he finally named his idolatry, confessed his sin, and identified God's gracious intervention in the ship, the storm, and the sea creature.

Forced to stop running from God, Jonah reestablished his promise of obedience, and he did not forget to thank God for his mercy.

By way of his Word, his messengers, or the still small voice, God calls his children to obedience. If they disobey, his pursuit is relentless. Nothing will get in his way.

Father in heaven, I have treated your commands casually. Or I have chosen to rebel. Forgive me. Thank you for using me to fulfill your will in the world. Please renew my love for all those whom you love. Thank you for sending life's storms to wake me up and keep me completely dependent on your hand of mercy. I humbly pray this in Jesus' name. Amen.

JOSEPH

His Name Means "May He [God] Add"

His Work:	Joseph was a working man who supported his family through the trade of carpentry.
His Character:	A man who traced his ancestry back to David, Joseph was just, compassionate, and obedient to God. Though poor, he was a good husband and father, providing for and protecting his family.
His Sorrow:	That Herod the Great tried to murder his son, Jesus.
His Triumph:	To be used by God to protect and provide for the world's Savior. Through him, Jesus could trace his ancestry to King David and the tribe of Judah.
Key Scriptures:	Matthew 1–2; Luke 2

Monday

HIS STORY

Joseph had no complaints. Nazareth kept a carpenter of his skill and reputation as busy as he cared to be, making plows, yokes, roofs, doors, and window shutters. He loved the smell and heft of the wood, the unique pattern and possibility of each board hewn from the greenwood. Once dried, the oak planks were sturdy and reliable, like the man himself.

Working alone in his workshop gave Joseph time to think and to remember. He recalled a day more than twelve years earlier that had almost shattered him, the day he discovered that Mary, the woman he had been engaged to, had become pregnant. Strangely, Joseph had felt no rage, only a great disappointment that settled like a permanent knot in his chest, weighing him down and making it hard to breathe.

How could his judgment have been so flawed, so far from the mark? He had looked forward to marrying the young woman whose character and temperament had made her seem all the more likable.

Rather than dragging her before the elders, Joseph had decided to divorce Mary quietly. Her life would be hard enough without a husband, and he had no need to watch her suffer publicly for what she had done. But before he had the chance to carry out his plan, Joseph had a dream, and in it he saw an angel who told him, "Joseph son of David, do not be afraid to take Mary home as your wife, because what is conceived in her is from the Holy Spirit. She will give birth to a son, and you are to give him the name Jesus, because he will save his people from their sin." Rather than brushing off the dream as a product of the previous night's meal, Joseph took it to heart, bringing Mary home as his wife.

But before they could settle in, Caesar Augustus ordered every man in his vast empire to register in a census. For Joseph, that meant traveling south to Bethlehem, the city of David, his ancestral home. *But would Mary, now several months pregnant, be strong enough for the trip,* he wondered. Perhaps he should leave her in Nazareth in the care of her family. But that would expose her to all the mean-spirited gossip already circulating about her pregnancy. No, he could not bear to part with his wife.

So the couple set out for Bethlehem, finding the roads jammed with people hurrying to comply with the census. The closer they came to the town, the more worried Joseph became. With so little money and so many people on the move, how would he find a place for them to stay? Once in the city, his fears seemed justified as house after house refused them. "Sorry, we're full." "Try the inn down the street, why don't you?" "I feel bad about your wife, buddy, but we're already packed so tight we can hardly breathe."

In the small town of Bethlehem, the city of David, there was no room for Joseph, no room for his wife, and no room for the child who was to be born—the one the angel had said would save the people from their sins.

Finally, someone told Joseph about a cave full of animals. At least it was dry, it would keep the wind off for a while, and it would cost little. Sweeping out a corner of the cave, the couple lined the ground with blankets and hay and then unpacked their few provisions. Exhausted from the journey, they at last had a place to lay their heads, a place where Mary could give birth. When her labor was finally over, she wrapped the baby in long strips of cloth to keep him warm and then handed him to Joseph. Awkwardly at first, he took the boy, brushing a large fingertip across the small lips, the perfect nose, the wrinkled brow. Then he hugged the baby to his chest, feeling a strange sense of pride, a fierce love rising up in him. What a thing of wonder this child was—his son to cherish and protect.

The next night, Joseph was surprised to see strangers approaching the cave. He could tell by the look and smell of the ragtag bunch that they must be shepherds. One of the men stepped forward eagerly, deferentially. "We want to see the baby, sir." Craning his neck as if to see through the shadows, the man pointed. "Is that him there?"

Joseph invited the men inside. But how had they heard about the child, and why were they so agitated? He didn't have long to wait for an explanation, because each man was eager to share his version of what had taken place the previous night.

"We were minding our sheep out in the field," one man piped up.

"Suddenly the whole sky lit up," said another.

"I fell on my face because I thought it was the end of the world," said the roughest of the bunch.

"Even the sheep fell over." They all laughed as they recalled the scene, though no one had laughed at the time.

Joseph and Mary listened carefully as the shepherds told them about the glorious angel who had tried to calm them by saying, "Do not be afraid. I bring you good news of great joy that will be for all the people. Today in the town of David a Savior has been born to you; he is Christ the Lord. This will be a sign to you: You will find a baby wrapped in cloths and lying in a manger." Then more angels had come, praising God and saying: "Glory to God in the highest, and on earth peace to men on whom his favor rests."

In the time that followed, Joseph had more strange encounters—an old man and an old woman in the temple in Jerusalem; Magi following a star from the east; an angel warning him in a dream to take the boy and his mother and flee to Egypt; another angel telling him when it was safe to return home. What it all meant, Joseph did not know for certain. He only knew how glad he felt to be the father of this boy and the husband of this woman. Surely the holy God who had cared for them so well would continue to watch over his son, the one who was to inherit the throne of David and save the people from their sins.

Tuesday

A LOOK AT THE MAN

Everything a Father Should Be

Three times Joseph saw angels in his dreams. In the first appearance, the angel announced something impossible: Mary had become pregnant, though she had not been unfaithful to him. In the second, the angel warned him to flee to Egypt to escape Herod's plan to murder the boy Jesus. Later, an angel sounded the all clear, informing Joseph of Herod's death so that he could return to Israel with Mary and Jesus.

Though we know little of Joseph from the Scriptures, we know at least of his remarkable faith and obedience. Each time the angels appeared to him, they revealed something he could not have known without divine revelation. But each new revelation presented him with a choice. Would he do as the angel instructed, or would he rely on his own understanding and do as he thought best? It would have been so easy to brush off the first dream. When in the history of the world had a woman ever become pregnant without sleeping with a man? Common sense would have told him to proceed with his plan to set Mary aside and marry someone else. Instead, he heeded the angel and, by doing so, said yes to God's surprising plan for his life.

Did Joseph comprehend the enormity of the decisions he was making? Possibly. But certainly he could not foresee the strange mixture of blessing and suffering that lay in store for him and his family. His yes would cost him many sleepless nights, but it would also involve him in the greatest miracle ever.

Centuries later we celebrate Joseph's life, knowing that he was everything a father should be—spiritually perceptive, compassionate, humble, faithful, loving and protective toward the family the Lord had given him.

Wednesday

HIS LEGACY IN SCRIPTURE

Read Matthew 1:18–21.

1. As a carpenter, Joseph was a man with physical strength. But what do these verses tell us about the strength of Joseph's character?

2. Even more painful than the news that Mary was pregnant by someone other than himself was the knowledge that he had been betrayed. How would you feel if you were in Joseph's situation?

3. What did Joseph have the right to do? What did he decide to do? What were his motives?

GOING DEEPER

Read Ephesians 6:1–4.

Joseph was the earthly father of Jesus, the Messiah. God had chosen Mary to be the mother of the Savior, and God had chosen Joseph to take this very important role in the life of the growing boy.

4. Fathers are told not to exasperate or provoke their children to anger. How do they frustrate their children?

5. Fathers are to bring their children up in the training and instruction of the Lord. What specific things should you do to obey this admonition?

Thursday

HIS LEGACY OF PROMISE

In some circles, Joseph is one of the great unsung heroes of the Bible. During the formative years of the Messiah's childhood, Joseph lived a consistent and exemplary life of faithfulness and obedience to God. Imagine how important it was that Jesus grew up with a father whose character was worthy of emulating. Years before he was recognized as—or confessed to being—the Son of God, Jesus was known as the son of Joseph.

Promises in Scripture

If . . . you seek the LORD your God, you will find him if you look for him with all your heart and with all your soul. —Deuteronomy 4:29

Be strong and very courageous. Be careful to obey all the law my servant Moses gave you; do not turn from it to the right or to the left, that you may be successful wherever you go. —Joshua 1:7

*Humility and the fear of the LORD
bring wealth and honor and life.*
—Proverbs 22:4

You did not choose me, but I chose you and appointed you to go and bear fruit—fruit that will last. Then the Father will give you whatever you ask in my name. —John 15:16

Friday

HIS LEGACY OF PRAYER

An angel of the Lord appeared to Joseph in a dream. . . .

So he got up, took the child and his mother during the night and left for Egypt.   —Matthew 2:13–14

An angel of the Lord appeared in a dream to Joseph in Egypt. . . . So he got up, took the child and his mother and went to the land of Israel.
                                                —Matthew 2:19, 21

Reflect On:	Genesis 39:1–5 (This is an account of another Joseph, but the similarities between these two obedient men and God's gracious blessing is striking.)
Praise God:	For offering a love that constrains us to obedience.
Offer Thanks:	For blessing you with the responsibility of leading and directing the lives of young people—children, nieces, nephews, grandchildren, neighbors.
Confess:	Your sin and willful disobedience.
Ask God:	To give you a heart that is drawn to him in love and compliance to his perfect will and to empower you in the task of leading these young ones in his ways.

In the Gospels, Jesus challenges his disciples with the words, "From everyone who has been given much, much will be demanded; and from the one who has been entrusted with much, much more will be asked" (Luke 12:48). Joseph was entrusted with the responsibility of raising the eternal Son of God. What an incredible charge! But never forget, *every* child is a miraculous gift and every parent's responsibility is a sobering one.

Father, thank you for calling great men like Joseph to be your servants. Thank you for entrusting him with your blessed Son as you have entrusted me with those under my care. Lord, please grant me wisdom and understanding. I confess my sins and ask that you draw me to yourself by your mercy. Make me a worthy ambassador of your love. In Jesus' name I humbly pray. Amen.

JOHN THE BAPTIST

His Name May Mean "Yahweh Has Been Gracious"

His Work:	He was the forerunner of Jesus, called to live in the spirit and power of Elijah. John prepared the way by preaching the need for repentance.
His Character:	John was completely focused on his assignment, unaffected by anything other than his message. And he wasn't willing to take on this duty without plenty of preparation.
His Sorrow:	A prophet's greatest joy is in preaching. But John spent the final days of his life in prison, unable to do what God had called and gifted him to do.
His Triumph:	God chose John to baptize his Son. No greater honor has ever been given a man.
Key Scriptures:	Luke 1:5–25; 3:1–20

Monday

HIS STORY

Standing waist deep in the Jordan River, John looked at the crowds gathered on the banks and lifted his voice: "Repent and be baptized, for the kingdom of heaven is near." The words echoed across the Judean landscape. It had been a long time—ages—since anyone had spoken like this prophet, and many were fascinated by what they heard and saw.

His name was a common one, but his appearance was strange. Even wild. Although John was barely thirty, his rough-hewn face revealed years of exposure to the desert sun from living in the wilderness. His hair was coarse and long, his beard unkempt. He wore animal skins, the pelts held together with a strip of leather tied at his waist.

To many of the people, John must have looked like a new Elijah. And like that most fearless of prophets, John himself was unafraid, boldly confronting the people with their need for salvation and slamming the religious establishment for its hypocrisy.

"You bunch of snakes!" John shouted at the crowd. "An ax is already at the root of the trees, and every tree that doesn't produce good fruit will be cut down and thrown into the fire."

From the time he was a small boy, John had known the story of his birth, how his father Zechariah had been performing the daily sacrifice of incense when the angel Gabriel suddenly appeared, scaring him half to death.

"Who are you? What do you want?" Zechariah inquired.

The angel comforted the old priest. "Don't be afraid," he said. "I have good news for you."

Gabriel told Zechariah that his prayers had been answered. A son was going to be born to Zechariah and Elizabeth. "He will be a joy and a delight to you, and many will rejoice because of his birth," the angel announced. "For he will be great in the sight of the Lord; and he will be filled with the Holy Spirit even from birth."

"He will go on before the Lord," Gabriel continued. "In the spirit and power of Elijah, your son John will turn the hearts of the fathers to their children and the disobedient to the wisdom of the righteous—to make ready a people prepared for the Lord."

Zechariah was stunned. He wanted to believe. "How can I be sure of this?" he asked. "I am an old man, and my wife is old, too."

"Do you know who I am?" the angel replied. "I am Gabriel. I regularly stand in the presence of Almighty God, who sent me to give you this good news. Because you don't believe me," the angel said, "your voice will be silent until the day this happens."

Zechariah tried to argue, but the words stayed frozen inside his mouth. Unable to speak, the old man knew that the angel really had come from God and had spoken the truth. A son *was* to be born who was to have a sacred assignment.

John never grew tired of hearing the story. He loved hearing his mother Elizabeth's version as well, her telling of her special kinship and friendship with Mary, the mother of the Messiah. She told him that before he was born, he had kicked for joy inside her when Mary had come to visit, pregnant with his cousin Jesus.

These accounts gave John a sense of purpose, of calling and destiny, a sense that compelled him to seclude himself for many years in the desert. He could not call the people to repentance until his own heart was ready.

But John's time had finally come. Today, as he looked at the riverbank, he saw Jesus standing there. He watched as his cousin stepped into the Jordan River and then waded out toward him. Though the water was warm, John felt a chill pass through him. "Baptize me," Jesus said to him.

"How can *I* baptize *you?*" John asked, having inherited some of his father's skepticism. "*You* should baptize *me.*"

But Jesus insisted.

So John wrapped his arm around Jesus, around the very one who had created the universe, slowly lowering him into the water. And then, as John lifted him from the water, the sky opened, and everyone heard a voice saying, "This is my Son, whom I love; with him I am well pleased."

John watched as Jesus made his way back into the crowd, a smile spreading across his face as he saw every head turning in the Messiah's direction.

Tuesday

A LOOK AT THE MAN

Preparing the Way

People in Israel were expecting the Messiah. The prophet Malachi had spoken of a redeemer, saying, "See, I will send you the prophet Elijah before that great and dreadful day of the LORD comes"; this long-awaited day of the Lord had melted into years, decades, centuries. Generations had come and gone, and still there was silence. God's voice was not heard.

But then came John with the clear-cut assignment pronounced centuries earlier by the prophet Isaiah: "A voice of one calling in the desert, 'Prepare the way for the Lord; make straight paths for him.'" John's voice was so strong and so persistent that it was heard even in the king's palace. When Herod learned that John had pronounced judgment on his illegal and immoral marriage to his brother's wife, he threw the prophet in prison.

While imprisoned, John felt the need of reassurance about the one whose way he was preparing. Had he, like so many others, secretly hoped the Messiah would be like other great kings, using military force to overthrow his adversaries? But Jesus had assembled no armies. *Perhaps,* he may have thought, *Jesus would use political force.* But civil reform would never prove to be part of Jesus' agenda.

When John's emissaries questioned Jesus, they found him at work, curing diseases, giving sight to the blind, delivering those who were possessed by evil spirits. Jesus merely replied to their questions with the command: "Go back and report to John what you have seen and heard."

Imagine how John must have been pleased with this message. *This is not what I expected in the Messiah,* he may have thought. *But Jesus must be from God. No one could do these things unless he was the one we have waited for.*

A short time later, John was beheaded by Herod. By his life and by his death he prepared the way of the Lord, whose kingdom was not of this earth. Jesus said of John: "I tell you the truth. Among those born of a woman there has not risen anyone greater than John."

John said of Jesus, "One more powerful than I will come, the thongs of whose sandals I am not worthy to untie. . . . He must become greater; I must become less." A perfect summary of what it means to prepare the way of the Lord.

Wednesday

HIS LEGACY IN SCRIPTURE

Read Luke 3:1–19.

1. Why do you think the Bible almost always includes historic information about rulers and kings?
2. Given John's message, oratorical style, and personal appearance—coupled with four centuries of silence since the last prophet had spoken—what kind of responses would he have received from commoners? From religious leaders?
3. John's call was simple: prepare the way, declare the way, get out of the way. What could have been John's personal challenges at being the best man instead of the groom? What things tucked away in his memory bank would have kept him on course?

GOING DEEPER

4. John was a truth teller. His evangelism style was attention-grabbing, fascinating, and interesting, but it certainly wasn't loving, winsome, or kind. Or was it? Explain your answer.
5. What did John tell the people to do once he had their attention? What does this suggest true repentance and conversion should look like for you and me? (Reread Luke 3:10–14.)

Thursday

HIS LEGACY OF PROMISE

John the Baptist's life is a study in good news—and bad news.

The good news was that prophets had foretold his coming and an angel had announced his birth. How's that for building self-esteem? But the bad news was that John would spend his life in a wilderness, at first physically and then relationally. Who wants to be friends with someone like that? In fact, his final wilderness was prison and then execution at the hand of a spineless king.

But John was born to fulfill a mission. He was focused and he was faithful. For him nothing else mattered.

Promises in Scripture

> Blessed is the man
>> who does not walk in the counsel of the wicked
> or stand in the way of sinners
>> or sit in the seat of mockers.
> But his delight is in the law of the LORD,
>> and on his law he meditates day and night.
>
> —Psalm 1:1–2

> Commit to the LORD whatever you do,
>> and your plans will succeed.
>
> The LORD works out everything for his own ends.
>
> —Proverbs 16:3–4

> He must become greater; I must become less. —John 3:30

> We have the word of the prophets made more certain, and you will do well to pay attention to it, as to a light shining in a dark place, until the day dawns and the morning star rises in your hearts. —2 Peter 1:19

Friday

HIS LEGACY OF PRAYER

"A voice of one calling in the desert,
'Prepare the way for the Lord,
make straight paths for him.'"

—Luke 3:4

Reflect On: Luke 3:7–14

Praise God: For his faithfulness.

Offer Thanks: For God's plan of salvation, for the obedience of John the Baptist, and for sending his Son.

Confess: Your fear of boldness in speaking the truth and in telling of your love for God and your faith in him.

Ask God: For opportunities to tell others of his mercy and for courage to speak.

Although we do not have the text of any of John's prayers recorded in the Bible, it's clear that his life was a prayer. It was a prayer of humility for being chosen and called to a world-changing task. It was a prayer for courage to speak the truth and face the predictable consequences. And it was a prayer of thanksgiving for the privilege of being God's mouthpiece to a lost world.

John's mission and ours are alike. We are called to remind people of their lostness and tell them of God's provision and mercy. Then as we "get out of the way," God's Holy Spirit does the work and changes people.

Father in heaven, you have called me to tell of your coming. But too often I have hidden from this responsibility. Please give me the boldness of John and the words from your Spirit to tell others of your saving grace. And please help me to renew my own heart in solitude, alone with you. I humbly pray this in Jesus' name. Amen.

JESUS

His Name Means "Yahweh Is Salvation"

His Work:	Although a member of the Holy Trinity who participated in the creation of the universe, his assignment was to come humbly to earth as a man to serve as Redeemer and Lord.
His Character:	Fully God, fully man; sinless perfection.
His Sorrow:	Taking upon himself the sins of every human being to satisfy the wrath of a holy God—the sins of those who lived before his birth, those who lived during his lifetime, and those who were to follow.
His Triumph:	The completion of his mission as the Savior of the world.
Key Scriptures:	The Gospel of John

Monday

HIS STORY

The house was overflowing with people. The bride and groom had exchanged their vows, and were now "husband and wife." Amid shouts of congratulations, the guests noisily greeted the newlyweds and each other. Chatter and revelry spilled into the streets of Cana as old friends and family members embraced, laughing, drinking, and dancing. This was the third day of a weeklong wedding celebration.

The Roman occupation of Palestine may have put a damper on ordinary life. But not even Rome dared interrupt a wedding feast, everyone's favorite party. Men and women moved about the crowd with trays of food and pitchers full of wine. Mary was there along with her son, Jesus, and his disciples. After a while she overheard the servants whispering among themselves. Distressed by what she heard, she went straight to Jesus. "They have no more wine," she said to him, keeping her voice low so the news wouldn't spread to the other guests.

"Dear woman, why do you involve me?" Jesus replied. "My time has not yet come."

And then, as though Jesus had promised to resolve the bride and groom's embarrassing problem, Mary presumptuously spoke to the servants. "Do whatever he tells you to do."

Like soldiers awaiting orders, the servants stood before Jesus. With a resigned smile, he told them to fill six stone jars with water. *But what good would that do*, they may have wondered; *the party needed wine, not water*. Still they did as he said. Then Jesus instructed them to draw some water out and take it to the master of the banquet.

With a puzzled look, the man dipped a ladle deep into the container and lifted it to his lips. His eyes widened. He drew the ladle close to his face, savoring the aroma. Then, closing his eyes, he drank again. This was no ordinary wine; it was the best he had ever tasted. "What a wonderful surprise!" he said to himself.

The master of the banquet went straight to the groom. "Usually at parties like this, the choice wine is served first. Then, when the guests have had too much to drink, the host serves the cheaper wine and the guests don't know the difference," he said as he filled the groom's goblet. "But you have saved the best till now."

The groom lifted his goblet and drank deeply. He had no idea what the master was talking about, but it didn't matter. "This *is* excellent wine," he replied, a quizzical smile crossing his face. "I hope we have enough."

The disciples were exhausted. They had eaten the Passover meal with Jesus but not before he had washed their feet. There was an air of suspicion and uneasiness about the whole evening. Jesus had announced that one of them would betray him. "Surely not I, Lord?" each man had responded. Their questioned response let Jesus know that they were weary of the journey and eager for him to publicly declare his messiahship.

But Jesus had identified Judas as the one, and he had slipped away into the night.

Then the disciples followed Jesus into Gethsemane. Three times he left them to pray by himself, and all three times they had fallen asleep. "Stay here and keep watch with me," he had asked Peter, James, and John. But they were overcome with fatigue and had fallen asleep.

After the third time, Jesus woke the disciples. "Are you still sleeping and resting?" His voice was filled with strength and resolve. "Enough! The hour has come. Look, the Son of Man is betrayed into the hands of sinners. Rise! Let's go! Here comes my betrayer!"

Three years had passed since the wedding at Cana where Jesus had told his mother, "My time has not yet come." But now he was ready to fulfill his appointed mission—to be delivered into the hands of sinners and to die for their sins.

Now he was ready to finish the work he had begun. God's grace was abundant and lavish. And like the wine at the wedding, there would be more than enough to go around.

Tuesday

A LOOK AT THE MAN
It Started with a Party

The *first* day of school, the *first* day on a new job—these are land-mark moments, times to celebrate, to give your best, to set a pattern for the days to follow.

Jesus could have begun his public ministry with a healing service or a deliverance session. He could have gathered twice as many people as John the Baptist had and begun by excoriating the religious leaders for their sins. Instead, he performed a miracle, turning water into wine so that a bride and groom could avoid embarrassment, so that a party could continue.

Didn't Jesus have more important things to attend to? What was he thinking? What about all the hungry people who needed feeding, the blind who needed to see? What about restoring worship in the temple, freeing the demon-possessed, silencing gale-force winds, and walking on water?

Jesus knew the time would come for him to confront the ugliness in people's hearts. He knew about the suffering that lay ahead and the resistance he would face. But right now it was time for a party. True, the bridegroom hadn't been quite ready for the wedding, running out of wine before the celebration was half finished. Jesus wasn't quite ready either.

But three years later, as he hung on a Roman cross dying for our sins, it was a completely different story, because now the Bridegroom was ready. That day Jesus declared his work "finished," for the purpose of his life and ministry was to prepare his people to become his spotless bride.

At Cana he had changed water to expensive wine. On the night before he died, he lifted a cup of wine, saying to his friends: "This is my blood, shed for you." On the cross he turned the costly wine into his own precious blood.

After Jesus' resurrection, the Spirit of God moved on the disciples so powerfully that three thousand people became believers in one day. Jesus, through the power of the Holy Spirit at work in his followers, was drawing people to himself, changing the course of history, giving us the best news we could ever hear, throwing the greatest party anyone had ever attended.

Wednesday

HIS LEGACY IN SCRIPTURE

Read Luke 2:21–35.

1. To every parent the birth of a child is a wonderful event. But Mary and Joseph knew that the circumstances surrounding their son's birth were extraordinary. Both of them had had a personal encounter with an angel before his birth, but, being devout Jews, how do you think they felt when they heard Simeon's words? What was good and what would have been frightening to Mary and Joseph about what Simeon said?

2. There are only two short passages that tell us about Jesus' early years: Luke 2:40–51 and Luke 2:52. What qualities characterized this young man?

GOING DEEPER

Read Colossians 1:15–24.

3. In these verses the apostle Paul presents one of the most succinct overviews of Jesus' life and purpose found in Scripture. Summarize this text in your own words.

4. What does verse 16 mean?

5. Every bride is beautiful on her wedding day. Verse 22 is a portrait of the bride of Christ. Who is she and what does she look like? What can you do to help her get ready?

Thursday

HIS LEGACY OF PROMISE

Jesus came to earth as a man. He also came to speak and to embody a special message: God's grace is sufficient. And it's not just adequate. Like the wine at the wedding reception, the quality of God's grace is abundant and the quantity is excessive—more than we can imagine.

Promises in Scripture

Jesus said, "Let the little children come to me, and do not hinder them, for the kingdom of heaven belongs to such as these."
—Matthew 19:14

Jesus answered, "I am the way and the truth and the life. No one comes to the Father except through me."
—John 14:6

My grace is sufficient for you, for my power is made perfect in weakness.
—2 Corinthians 12:9

I turned around to see the voice that was speaking to me. . . . When I saw [Jesus], I fell at his feet as though dead. Then he placed his right hand on me and said: "Do not be afraid. I am the First and the Last."
—Revelation 1:12, 17

Friday

HIS LEGACY OF PRAYER

Going a little farther, he fell with his face to the ground and prayed, "My Father, if it is possible, may this cup be taken from me. Yet not as I will, but as you will."   —Matthew 26:39

Reflect On: Matthew 26:36–46

Praise God: For his love.

Offer Thanks: For his Son—the child born of a virgin, the boy who grew in character, the one who lived a sinless life and died to redeem us—the groom who not only loved his bride but gave his life for her.

Confess: The temptation to forget who Jesus really is and to treat his life as only an example of right living rather than to fully embrace his purpose for coming to earth.

Ask God: To fill you with his Spirit, to live as a person who has been redeemed by the blood of Jesus, to teach you to pray and to celebrate.

Many of Jesus' prayers are recorded in the Gospels. The prayer most often repeated is the one he taught his disciples to pray. It must have been that Jesus' prayer life was so compelling to his close friends that they didn't have the patience to wait for him to tell them about prayer. They asked him to teach them. Our request ought to be the same— that he would teach us to be people whose lives are filled with prayer.

Jesus lived in perfect communion with his Father. As we pray we are joining him in this sacred fellowship.

Father in heaven, I praise you and thank you for sending Jesus, a gift too wonderful for words. Thank you for loving me like a smitten groom who loves his beautiful bride. Please give me a heart that longs to hear your voice, a heart that willingly obeys your commands, and a heart that loves others the way you loved them. I want to celebrate your lavish and abundant grace. I pray this in Jesus' name. Amen.

MATTHEW

His Name Means "Gift of Yahweh"

His Work:	Matthew was a tax collector who was awarded by Herod Antipas a contract to extract tariffs from his own people.
His Character:	A successful businessman whose encounter with Jesus profoundly changed his life and vocation forever.
His Sorrow:	Alienation, first from his own people because of his profession and then from religious leaders because of his vocation.
His Triumph:	A carefully organized, accurate, and convincing apologetic for the veracity of Jesus Christ as the Messiah.
Key Scripture:	Matthew 9

Monday

HIS STORY

Matthew was delighted. His carefully crafted proposal had persuaded the local authorities that he could successfully collect the commercial taxes they depended on to help fund the empire. To make a decent living, he had only to extract more money from the people than the authorities required, pocketing the difference. The more money he squeezed from every commercial transaction, the better he would live. That's how the game was played, and it was all perfectly legal.

One day as Matthew was collecting taxes at his stand, a crowd passed by. Matthew loved large gatherings because they afforded more opportunities for goods to be exchanged, and that meant more duty to collect. Like any tax collector worth his salt, Matthew was on the alert.

The crowd parted, and a man walked toward his booth. Matthew had heard about this one whom many were calling the Messiah. The crowd grew silent as Jesus addressed Matthew. Some poked each other in anticipation hoping for a confrontation. Perhaps the Teacher would rebuke this crook, administering the public tongue-lashing he deserved.

"Greetings, Matthew," the rabbi said.

Matthew did not speak.

Jesus eyes were fixed. "Follow me," he said.

The people were shocked. What was Jesus thinking? A man like Matthew cared nothing for spiritual things. He would never follow the rabbi, not at the cost of leaving his business behind.

But Matthew smiled and nodded as though he had been waiting for just this invitation. He began to collect his papers and stuff them into a sack. Lowering the awning that protected him from the hot sun, he slung the bag over his shoulder and hustled to catch up. No one could believe it.

Hurrying after Jesus, Matthew said, "Come to my house tonight. I'll invite my friends. We'll have a great feast. Please come," he pleaded. The look on his face let Jesus know that Matthew would hardly take no for an answer.

But those standing close by knew what Jesus would say. No self-respecting rabbi would ever lower himself to eat with a "lowlife" like Matthew—much less eat with the man's friends.

"I would love to come to your house," Jesus said without hesitation. "And I look forward to meeting your friends."

That night—invited or not—the Pharisees and teachers of the law showed up and surrounded the perimeter of Matthew's home, waiting to see what would happen. They were dismayed to realize that Jesus really was eating with Matthew and his friends. Not only that, but he was enjoying himself, laughing and talking with sinners. Scandalized, they pulled his disciples aside. "Why do you eat with tax collectors and 'sinners'?" they griped.

Hearing what they had said, Jesus replied, "It's not the healthy who need a doctor, but the sick." Matthew was impressed. *Jesus has just called these arrogant leaders "healthy." How could they argue with that?*

"I have not come to call the righteous, but sinners to repentance," Jesus added.

Oddly, neither Matthew nor his friends felt insulted by Jesus' words. They hadn't spent their lives posturing to make themselves acceptable to the religious elite. They knew who they were. But here was a man who was treating them with kindness, enjoying their company, teaching them, challenging them, and loving them—someone who wanted to heal them, not condemn them.

Matthew had never considered himself a religious man, yet he had yearnings and aspirations that no amount of money would ever satisfy. When Jesus called him that day, he was ready to leave his well-laid plans behind—ready to employ his talents for a greater purpose, for a remarkable enterprise, for the work of spreading the gospel to all who would listen. Matthew had convinced Herod that he should be the one to collect taxes, and he knew he could convince his own people that Jesus was the Messiah. He could think of no more profitable task in all the world.

Tuesday

A LOOK AT THE MAN

Building a Convincing Case

Matthew was good at making money. But there was a downside to getting rich as a tax collector in Palestine: People hated you for it. It made it hard to have any friends besides tax collectors or other ne'er-do-wells. He had learned to ignore the looks, to pretend he didn't hear the epithets—to conclude that these were the necessary costs of doing business.

Tax collectors were answerable to no one. There were no regulations to guide their procedures. Whatever they could extract from the people—over and above what the authorities required—was theirs to keep. It wasn't that Matthew didn't care about people, it was just that he cared *more* about his own prosperity. No wonder he was hated.

Matthew knew this when he chose his profession. In fact, in his writing, Matthew grouped tax collectors with prostitutes in social rank. But he was willing to pay this price for financial success.

But in spite of his choice of occupation and his pleasure with its material benefits, everything changed the day Jesus invited Matthew to be one of his disciples. And the wisdom of following the Master was confirmed in Matthew's heart the night Jesus won the affection of his friends.

Matthew knew that his decision was one he could never withdraw. He had set his life on a new course that could not be changed. Unlike the other disciples who had temporarily left their fishing nets—and could return to them at a later time—he knew it would be difficult for him to go back to his tax collecting. But Matthew was not halfhearted about his decisions. He had paid a heavy price among his countrymen when he chose tax collecting; now he would be asked to do the same in following Jesus.

Imagine how Matthew's transformation became a confirmation of the power and the authenticity of the Messiah's message. "Have you seen Matthew recently?" Jews would say to each other in the marketplace. "Something has happened to him."

Matthew was swept away with Jesus the man, the messenger, the Messiah. His gospel includes more references to Old Testament prophecy than any other. *This* truly was the one the prophets had foretold. And his thorough coverage of Jesus' most important sermon reminds us that Matthew was awed by the power of the Savior's words.

Very little is recorded in the Gospels as to Matthew's specific activities. Except for his invitation for Jesus to join him and his friends for dinner, we read of no conversation or dialogue. But this does not diminish Matthew's prominence during the days of Jesus' ministry on earth. For nothing speaks more profoundly than the testimony of a changed life—especially one that makes waves in the marketplace.

Wednesday

HIS LEGACY IN SCRIPTURE

Read Matthew 9:1–17.

1. Jesus had just returned to Capernaum when some men approached him carrying their paralyzed friend. At first Jesus did not heal him. What did he do instead? Why was this so threatening to the "teachers of the law"? What did Jesus do to prove his point?

2. According to Matthew's chronology, the healing of the paralytic happened just before Jesus called Matthew to be his disciple. Assuming that news of this event had reached Matthew, how might it have influenced his decision to leave his tax collecting to follow Jesus?

3. Matthew follows the story of the party at his home with a question to Jesus about the discipline of fasting. In answer to John's disciples' inquiry, Jesus refers to himself as the "bridegroom." What does he mean?

GOING DEEPER

Read Matthew 10:37–39 and 19:28–30.

4. These are challenging and sobering words. From personal experience, Matthew knew all about this. What are some of the implications of this for you?

5. How did Matthew take his skills and experience and invest them wisely?

Thursday

HIS LEGACY OF PROMISE

The story of Matthew is a story of self-denial and sacrifice. Before his encounter with Jesus, he must have had money to burn. But suddenly money was no longer important. Something else was. He left all of this to follow Jesus, but he did not abandon his talents in obeying the Savior; instead, he offered them, and God put them to good use.

Promises in Scripture

> Listen, my son, accept what I say,
>> and the years of your life will be many.
>
> I guide you in the way of wisdom
>> and lead you along straight paths.
>
> When you walk, your steps will not be hampered;
>> when you run, you will not stumble.
>
> —Proverbs 4:10–12

Do not store up for yourselves treasures on earth, where moth and rust destroy, and where thieves break in and steal. But store up for yourselves treasures in heaven, where moth and rust do not destroy, and where thieves do not break in and steal. For where your treasure is, there your heart will be also. —Matthew 6:19–21

If you want to be perfect, go, sell your possessions and give to the poor, and you will have treasure in heaven. Then come, follow me. —Matthew 19:21

Who is going to harm you if you are eager to do good? But even if you should suffer for what is right, you are blessed. "Do not fear what they fear; do not be frightened." But in your hearts set apart Christ as Lord. Always be prepared to give an answer to everyone who asks you to give the reason for the hope that you have. But do this with gentleness and respect. —1 Peter 3:13–15

Friday

HIS LEGACY OF PRAYER

As Jesus went on from there, he saw a man named Matthew sitting at the tax collector's booth. "Follow me," he told him, and Matthew got up and followed him.
—Matthew 9:9

Reflect On: Matthew 9:9–13

Praise God: For his transforming power.

Offer Thanks: For the impact that the message of Jesus Christ has on those who are willing to believe and follow the Messiah.

Confess: An unwillingness to turn from our drive for economic success and to submit to the Spirit's direction—to resist being inconvenienced by the call of the Savior.

Ask God: To come to your workplace—your tax-collector's booth. Ask him to repeat the same words he spoke to Matthew, and ask him to give you the courage to respond as Matthew did.

There must always be a connection between belief and behavior—a bridge from what we say to how we live. Everything changed when Matthew met Jesus. He quickly realized that his occupation was not consistent with the message he was hearing and believing. So he walked away from it all. As a tax collector, Matthew would have been a visible character in his community. But in his role as a follower of Jesus, Matthew was willing to quietly serve.

May the Savior have the same impact on us for his glory.

Father in heaven, thank you for calling ordinary people to be your disciples. Thank you for those who have set an example of total commitment to following you. Please give me the courage to be faithful to you first. I want my life to count for eternity, not just for material gain. I submit to your will and want to follow you. I pray this in Jesus' name. Amen.

JAMES AND JOHN

John's Name Means "Yahweh Has Been Gracious"

*James's Name, a Form of Jacob, Means
"He Grasps the Heel" (Figuratively, "He Deceives")*

Their Work:	James and his younger brother John were career fishermen working in their father's business on the Sea of Galilee.
Their Character:	James was quiet and analytical; John was verbal and open. Both of these hardworking men were profoundly changed when they met Jesus. Not only did they follow him, but they were brought into his inner circle along with Peter, their friend and business associate.
Their Sorrow:	Following Jesus cost them everything. They left their family business, their familiar surroundings, their friends, and even their families to walk with the Savior.
Their Triumph:	What may have started as pure adventure—following the Teacher—ended in a revolution that changed the world.
Key Scriptures:	Matthew 4:18–22; 16:13–17:9

Monday

THEIR STORY

"Good morning."

James and John looked up from mending their fishing nets to see who had spoken.

"Good morning to you," John said with a friendly smile, while his older, more analytical brother slowly looked the stranger over.

They talked for a while—of the weather, of fishing, of the communities nearby—then Jesus calmly said, "Leave your nets and come, follow me."

James and John stared at the man's back as he walked slowly away, then at each other in bewilderment. The suggestion could not have been more outrageous. *Leave our nets? Why? And for how long? What will we do for work? Our families depend on us; what will they do if we go?*

But as Jesus took each step away from them, their hearts beat faster. Who was he? And why were they so drawn to him?

With a hurried good-bye to a sputtering, flabbergasted father, and with nothing but the clothing on their backs, they left the shores they had known all their days. They could do nothing less than what Jesus asked of them.

The next few years were filled with remarkable experiences. They watched Jesus heal people of life-threatening diseases. Blind people regained their sight, lame people walked again. When Lazarus, four days dead, came out of his tomb, James and John clung to each other and then hooted and hollered in amazement and joy. Jesus was the most remarkable man they had ever met; they considered it a privilege to be counted among his closest friends.

But something troubled them. Jesus kept sidestepping questions about who he was and how he could perform such miracles. Obviously, he was favored by the God of Abraham, and he could do little other than talk of his "Father," teaching them, always teaching. Late at night the disciples often whispered about it. Was Jesus a reincarnation of one of the prophets? Or was he the Messiah sent from God to redeem Israel?

Then Jesus asked them outright, "What are people saying about me? Who do they think I am?"

The disciples had been waiting for a long time to have this conversation, but openly discussing it with Jesus made them feel uneasy. As James and John stared into Jesus' eyes, they sensed a shift, as though the earth was about to move beneath their feet. From the time they were little boys, they had been taught by their parents and by the priests in the temple about the Messiah. But was Jesus the one?

And now, in this place called Caesarea Philippi, more than ten miles from their home in Capernaum, near the foot of Mount Hermon, Jesus was finally getting to the reason he was with them, the reason why he was on earth at all. They were filled with anticipation.

"Some people are saying that you're John the Baptist come back to life," a disciple said from the back of the group. "Some people say that you're a great prophet, like Elijah or Jeremiah," another right beside James bravely said.

Then Jesus asked the question they hoped he wouldn't ask. "But what about you? Who do *you* say that I am?" All twelve men froze in silence.

James and John caught each other's eye, then looked around at their friends, then back at Jesus, into eyes that seemed to speak of ancient knowledge and of peace. To a man, the disciples had *hoped* that Jesus was the Messiah. They *wanted* him to be the Messiah. But why was he asking *them?* If he really was the Messiah, why wouldn't he just come right out and say it?

Jesus gazed back at them as though he knew exactly what was in their hearts.

Peter broke the silence. "You are the Christ, the Son of the living God," he said. He spoke with forcefulness, a confident resolve in his tone.

The disciples held their breath.

"Congratulations, Peter," Jesus said. "You're right, but you didn't come up with this yourself. The living God has revealed it to you." The disciples were stunned. This was the first time that Jesus had actually laid claim to being the Son of Man—the Messiah.

At the end of the week in Caesarea Philippi, Jesus gestured toward James, John, and Peter. "Come with me," he said to the three men. So together the four men walked to the base of Mount Hermon and began to climb. They were largely silent as they ascended, apprehensive, perhaps, at what might lay ahead.

When the foursome reached the pinnacle of the mountain and paused, something happened to Jesus. Suddenly his face and clothing began to glow. The men shaded their eyes from the intensity of the light, their hearts pounding with excitement. Then two men suddenly appeared out of nowhere—on either side of Jesus—and began chatting with him as though they were old friends.

Although they had never seen these men before, somehow James, John, and Peter knew exactly who these two were—Moses and Elijah! All at once the six men were enveloped in a white fog so dense they could hardly see one another. And then they heard a voice. It was clear and strong—the most powerful sound any of them had ever heard—so loud that the ground shook but so mysterious that they found themselves straining to make out every word.

"This is my Son, whom I love; I am completely satisfied with him." There was a pause. "Listen to Jesus."

The next thing James, John, and Peter knew, they were facedown, crying like little boys, terrified by an experience they did not understand. Then someone touched them, and they lifted their heads, looking into Jesus' face. They were alone with him again. The fog had lifted; the blinding light was gone. "Get up, my friends," Jesus said with a smile. "Don't be afraid."

Tuesday

A LOOK AT THE MEN

Brothers in Arms

Life was good for Zebedee. He owned a prosperous fishing enterprise, and he and his wife, Salome, had two sons who were partners with him in the business.

Although it must have been a blow to their fishing company when James and John left their nets to follow Jesus, there is no evidence that Zebedee and Salome resisted their sons' decision. "After all," they may have said to each other, "think how good this will be for the boys to be seen with the Teacher. Maybe it will even be good for business."

For their part, James and John would never look back. They lived with the Savior. They walked hundreds of miles with him and saw him perform awesome miracles, all the while wondering who he was. Whenever he was asked by commoners and Pharisees, he sidestepped their questions. *Why doesn't he just go ahead and declare his messiahship?* the disciples wondered.

And then, after two years of being with Jesus, Zebedee and Salome's sons went to the mountain with their friend Peter and saw the light. These men caught a glimpse of the glory of God. And like Moses and Isaiah before them, they were completely dumbfounded. This was the Messiah. They no longer doubted.

From that moment forward, Jesus had a special relationship with James, John, and Peter. He put them in his inner circle as his closest associates. When James and John reported this to Zebedee and Salome, they must have been proud. But Salome took a step beyond good sense when she went to Jesus with an ill-advised request. "One day, when you come into power," she said to the Savior, thinking he would one day be an earthly king, "could you give my sons the highest rank in the land? So lofty would be their positions that one would sit to the right of your throne and one would sit to the left."

This request wasn't just coming from a doting mother. She and her sons had discussed it, for when Jesus said, "You don't have any idea what you're asking," the answer was in the plural. "Yes, *we* do!" they answered.

When the other disciples heard about James's and John's request, they were outraged—probably because they had wanted these positions of prominence for themselves!

And then, in one short moment, history's most profound lesson in leadership was delivered. Jesus' words must have seared the disciples' hearts. "Heathen leaders take their power and cram it down the throats of their subjects," he told them. "But you're not to do this."

James's and John's faces must have flushed. Jesus was talking to all twelve of the disciples, but it was these two brothers who really felt the sting of his words. Sideward glances from the others made it worse.

"Whoever wants to be great among you must be your servant, and whoever wants to be first must be your slave." James and John were transfixed by Jesus' words, but he wasn't quite finished. "I, the Messiah, did *not* come to be served, but to serve," Jesus said. Then he added, "And to give my life as a ransom for many."

Following Jesus' resurrection, James, John, and five other disciples were back on the sea late at night. They fished all night but caught nothing. As the morning sun peeked over the horizon, they saw a man standing on the shore. "Throw your net on the right side of the boat," he hollered to them. When they did, they couldn't pull the net in because it was so full of fish. "It's Jesus," John said, recognizing the cadence of his voice and the power of his words. "It's Jesus!"

Once on shore, the disciples and Jesus had breakfast together. His final words after the meal, although directed at Peter, were surely for each of the seven disciples who were there. They are words for us as well. "You want to lead?" Jesus asked. "Then feed my sheep."

Wednesday

THEIR LEGACY IN SCRIPTURE

Read Matthew 4:18–22; 17:1–8.

1. Though James and John were hardworking businessmen, they left everything behind to follow Jesus. Why? What happened when they saw Jesus and heard his voice?

2. What were the risks involved in following Jesus? What were the risks in *not* following him?

3. There may have been days when James and John doubted their decision to follow Jesus. How do you think they felt about their choice after they had seen the incredible spectacle on the mountain?

4. Why was God so careful about revealing his glory to people?

GOING DEEPER

Read Matthew 20:20–28; John 13:1–8.

5. In the cold light of day, Salome's request is understandable. She only wanted the best for her sons. Of course, James and John were in on this, too. What are the inherent dangers of fame and fortune?

6. Jesus' life and words are filled with countless lessons. The one he taught about leadership and serving is one of the most profound. If Jesus were to ask you to "follow him" in this area, where would be the first place he would tell you to go?

Thursday

THEIR LEGACY OF PROMISE

James and John left their nets—and everything familiar and comfortable—and followed Jesus. This was not a halfhearted decision. They were fully committed. These men had the privilege of seeing, hearing, and touching the Messiah. This was no intellectual exercise, but something completely visible and tactile.

As credible eyewitnesses to the life of the Savior, theirs can be an authentic witness for us.

Promises in Scripture

Once, having been asked by the Pharisees when the kingdom of God would come, Jesus replied, "The kingdom of God does not come with your careful observation, nor will people say, 'Here it is,' or 'There it is,' because the kingdom of God is within you."   —Luke 17:20–21

The Word became flesh and made his dwelling among us. We have seen his glory, the glory of the One and Only, who came from the Father, full of grace and truth.   —John 1:14

When the time had fully come, God sent his Son, born of a woman, born under law, to redeem those under law, that we might receive the full rights of sons.   —Galatians 4:4–5

There is no Greek or Jew, circumcised or uncircumcised, barbarian, Scythian, slave or free, but Christ is all, and is in all.
                                        —Colossians 3:11

Friday

THEIR LEGACY OF PRAYER

"Do not love the world or anything in the world. If anyone loves the world, the love of the Father is not in him." —1 John 2:15

Reflect On: Matthew 4:18–20

Praise God: For God's glory.

Offer Thanks: For the life-changing power of God's presence and holiness.

Confess: Any unwillingness to risk it all to be Jesus' disciple— any temptation to treat Jesus like your buddy or your example rather than the glorified and perfect Son of the living God.

Ask God: To challenge you to acknowledge his presence more frequently. Wherever you are, whatever you're doing, listen to his voice saying to you, "Follow me."

James and John looked up from their busyness and said to Jesus, "Yes, we will follow you." The tug of the Savior was stronger than the draw of their careers. Wherever he calls you and whatever he calls you to, be willing to follow.

Father in heaven, thank you for the example of those who completely realigned their priorities to follow you. And thank you for reminding me of your holiness and your glory. Please draw me into your presence and give me a glimpse of yourself. Help me to feel the wonder and to hear your voice saying, "Don't be afraid." I humbly pray this in Jesus' name. Amen.

MARK

His Name Means "A Large Hammer"

His Work:	An eager journalist whose specialties were serving, following up on details, and making travel arrangements.
His Character:	A man who was willing to serve behind the scenes for others who were in ministry.
His Sorrow:	On his first major assignment as Paul and Barnabas's traveling secretary, Mark returned home, unable to finish the journey. This created a rift between Mark and Paul, as well as between Barnabas and Paul.
His Triumph:	Not only was the relationship breach healed, but Mark had the privilege of penning the first gospel— the good news of Jesus.
Key Scripture:	Mark 14:32–72

Monday

HIS STORY

"Who goes there?"

With a bit of feigned bravado, one of the disciples shouted toward the approaching men who were brandishing swords and lighted torches. The shadows from the flames cast a sinister appearance on the men's faces. And rightly so.

The group entered the clearing in the olive grove where Jesus and his disciples were gathered. These were no commonplace thugs looking for a fight. This eclectic group included several officials of the highest religious order and a few professional soldiers. And to the disciples' horror, their friend Judas was leading the vigilantes right up to Jesus.

When Jesus' friends saw what was happening, they ran for their lives, but Jesus stood his ground. "Who are you looking for?" he said.

"Jesus of Nazareth," they replied.

And although it was Jesus who was about to be arrested, they looked more nervous than he.

Judas stepped forward and kissed Jesus on the cheek.

"Hello Judas," Jesus said with a smile. "What are you doing here?"

"Master," Judas said ruefully.

At that moment, just off to the side, a couple of the soldiers scuffled with a man too young to be a disciple. He had been watching from close range, and some of them recognized him as a sympathizer. They grabbed his cloak, but he escaped into the darkness, leaving his robe in their hands. The young man's name was Mark.

It was the middle of the night—Thursday night of the Passover. As they had done countless times before, Jesus and his closest friends had spent the entire evening together. But this time Jesus had acted curiously. He seemed restless, preoccupied, as though his mind was elsewhere.

In fact, he had surprised his friends when they gathered for dinner by taking a towel and basin and washing the road dirt from their feet. This was something that had been done before, but on this night, Jesus had surprised them all. He ceremoniously poured fresh water into a bowl and went from person to person, gently washing their feet.

Jesus' actions had embarrassed Simon Peter. "You're not going to wash my feet, Jesus," Peter had protested. "I will wash *yours!*"

But Jesus scolded his friend. "If you don't let me do this, then you can't be my friend." Peter's face flushed. Then Jesus added, his voice full of compassion, "You don't understand what I'm doing here, Peter. But someday you will."

During the meal, Jesus and Judas had exchanged a few words, and Judas had slipped out into the night. The disruption put everyone on edge.

While they ate, Jesus had taken some bread in his hands, lifted it heavenward, prayed a short prayer, and broke it into pieces. He had given the pieces to his disciples, saying to them, "This is my body." Then Jesus had poured some wine into his cup. Again he had lifted it, given thanks, and then passed it around the room. "This is my blood of the covenant, which is poured out for many." Jesus had seemed preoccupied—focused somewhere else. The disciples were quiet. They had never seen him quite like this.

After dinner Jesus and his disciples sang a few psalms and headed into the darkness. No one knew where Jesus was going, but trailing him into the night was all they wanted to do. Mark followed from a safe distance.

The son of a prominent and wealthy woman in Jerusalem, Mark had met several of Jesus' disciples during one of their visits to the city. Simon Peter singled out the young man and befriended him. It was this special camaraderie that gave Mark access to Jesus' comings and goings. So he followed the disciples from their dinner toward a place called Gethsemane.

Pulling his robe around him to guard against the evening chill, Mark hunkered down a safe distance from Jesus and his disciples. Somehow he knew this would be a night he would remember in great detail.

Several years later Mark was leading a small group of discouraged believers in prayer. The meeting was in his mother's home in Jerusalem. Herod Agrippa had just murdered John's older brother, James. He had also thrown Mark's friend, Simon Peter, in prison. Peter's bold preaching ignited the fury of many Jewish leaders, and they urged Herod to do whatever he could to crush Peter's influence.

Herod's plan was to try Peter in public, but because it was the time of the Passover, he delayed the hearing. In the meantime, Herod ordered sixteen soldiers to guard him day and night. Letting Peter escape from prison was not something he cared to face.

The people gathered in Mark's home pleaded with God to spare Peter's life. Although their prayers were filled with pious words, their hearts held out no hope at all.

Suddenly there was a knock at the door. Perturbed by the interruption, Mary sent a girl named Rhoda to see who was there.

"Is anyone home?" the man said on the other side of the closed door. "Can I come in?"

Rhoda was overjoyed. Recognizing the voice but forgetting to unlock the door, she turned and ran back to the group, interrupting their prayers once again. "It's Peter!" she exclaimed. "I heard his voice myself."

"That's impossible," they chided. "You're out of your mind."

But Rhoda insisted—as did Peter standing outside the locked door. His incessant knocking brought a handful of people. When they opened the door, they couldn't believe their eyes. "It's Peter! It's Peter!" they shouted.

"Shhhh," Peter said, lifting his finger to his lips as he stepped into the house and closed the door behind him. "Bring him something to eat," Mary said to the servants as Peter sat down, his friend Mark by his side. "What a night," Peter said as he explained his escape from prison. "It was incredible."

Mark sat quietly, drinking it all in. Somehow he knew that this, too, would be a night he would remember in great detail.

Tuesday

A LOOK AT THE MAN

An Eyewitness Account

Just as soon as he had gathered all the information, Mark sat down and began to write. He was the first of the gospel writers★—Matthew, Mark, Luke, and John—to do so. As a young spectator, Mark was awestruck by Jesus. And because of his mother's influence, he was able to meet the disciples during the time of the Savior's ministry. This gave him special behind-the-scenes access, and he kept a record of what he saw.

Mark served quietly and unobtrusively. When Paul and Barnabas, Mark's cousin, traveled from Jerusalem to Antioch, they took Mark along as their assistant. When they set out for their first extensive missionary journey, again they asked him to come along. In this role, Mark advanced their trip by arranging for travel, food, and lodging. But when they got to Perga, Mark left the troupe and returned to Jerusalem, although the exact reason he left isn't known.

When Paul and Barnabas decided to revisit the cities they had traveled to on their first missionary journey, Barnabas wanted to take Mark along again. But Paul wasn't interested, so he chose Silas as his traveling companion. Barnabas asked Mark to join him on his trip to Cyprus, where he was given the chance to serve again.

The conflict between Paul and Mark was eventually healed. Ten years later Paul asked the people in Colosse to receive Mark with a welcome. In his letter from prison to Philemon, he called Mark "my fellow worker." And in Paul's final letter to his protégé, Timothy, he asked him to "bring Mark with you; he is helpful to me in my ministry."

Mark's special relationship with Simon Peter is mentioned in Peter's first letter to the new Christians scattered throughout Asia Minor. Mark must have been on the road with Peter in Rome, because Peter sent greetings to the believers from Mark and called him "my son." It was most likely during this time that Mark penned the gospel.

★Although some scholars question the authorship of Mark's gospel, the early church unanimously attributed it to John Mark.

Traveling with Simon Peter, certainly the most zealous and emotive of the disciples, Mark reviewed his notes about Jesus' life. This, combined with his own firsthand experiences as a young man, gave him a special passion as he recalled the life of this Nazarene.

Mark's mission was to be sure that anyone reading his account would know that Jesus was the incarnate Son of God—the Messiah. The activities and miracles of Jesus were just as important to Mark as his words. The proof of his deity was in his person.

Mark followed Jesus as an observer. His perspective was real. He saw Jesus' humanity with his own eyes—exhausted (4:38), amazed (6:6), disappointed (8:12), displeased (10:14), angry (11:15–17), and sorrowful (14:34).

Moving quickly from scene to scene, Mark's account is filled with youthful impatience and urgency—"And straightway coming up out of the water" (1:10 KJV); and "At once the Spirit sent him out into the desert" (1:12).

In spite of what he saw at Gethsemane, Mark didn't give up on the possibility of the resurrection. If Jesus would *really* do what he implied during his ministry—conquer death—imagine what would happen!

Wednesday

HIS LEGACY IN SCRIPTURE

Read Mark 14:43–52.

1. The scene of Jesus' arrest is filled with great drama. How do you think the disciples felt as they ran from the garden of Gethsemane? As a young man and as an eyewitness to many of the events recorded in the Gospels, what unique perspective would Mark have had on Jesus' life?

2. In his gospel, Mark never refers to himself in the first person. What might this tell us about the man? How does this approach stand in contrast to much of what seems to motivate Christian leaders in our day?

GOING DEEPER

Read Romans 12:1–8.

3. In this passage Paul the apostle reminds us of the variety of gifts that God bestows on his followers. How would Paul have described Mark's gifts? What have others told you about your gifts?

4. Paul makes it clear (v. 3) what our attitude about our gifts ought to be. What is this attitude?

5. Some gifts are more publicly visible, like Paul's and Peter's. Others find their expression without fanfare or notice. What should be our attitude toward others' gifts?

Extra: Nothing is said about Mark's father. It's possible that Mark was raised by a single mother who, because of her faith, encouraged her son to be a follower of Jesus. The spiritual influence a mother has on her children cannot be overestimated.

Thursday

HIS LEGACY OF PROMISE

It's easy to become complacent about our faith. We often treat God's presence in our lives with the same enthusiasm as we do hot running water or light fixtures that produce all the illumination we need.

And then we run into someone like Mark. Reading his gospel is like listening to a wide-eyed youngster describe his first ride on a roller coaster or a new father recalling the birth of his child. For Mark, this was what it was like to follow the Savior.

So the young believer took what he had seen and committed his life to ministry—serving, helping, and documenting his experience with Jesus for the edification of believers for generations to follow.

Promises in Scripture

> The LORD bless you
>   and keep you;
> the LORD make his face shine upon you
>   and be gracious to you;
> the LORD turn his face toward you
>   and give you peace.

—Numbers 6:24–26

Everything is possible for him who believes.   —Mark 9:23

Blessed are those who have not seen [Jesus] and yet have believed.
—John 20:29

Who shall separate us from the love of Christ? Shall trouble or hardship or persecution or famine or nakedness or danger or sword? As it is written:

> *"For your sake we face death all day long;*
>   *we are considered as sheep to be slaughtered."*

No, in all these things we are more than conquerors through him who loved us.   —Romans 8:35–37

Friday

HIS LEGACY OF PRAYER

"O LORD, our Lord,
how majestic is your name in all the earth!"

—Psalm 8:1

Reflect On: Psalm 8:1–9

Praise God: For his holiness.

Offer Thanks: For his presence that fills you and his love that con-
strains you to follow him.

Confess: Your indifference to his power, your willingness to
reduce your relationship to him to the ordinary and
the mundane rather than delighting in the thrill and
wonder of it all.

Ask God: To fill you with his empowering Spirit so that the
gifts he has given you will be fully used for his glory.

From all appearances, Mark was an ordinary young man. But once
he had seen the Savior, everything changed. He resolved to follow
him whatever the cost. Mark's life is an example of faithfulness, sacrifice, and service in ministry.

———————————

Father in heaven, thank you for your power to change lives. Thank you for
the witness of people who were willing to set aside their own plans and dreams
to follow you. Please forgive me for becoming complacent about my love for
you. Inspire me through your Holy Spirit to a new zeal to be your faithful
disciple. I humbly pray this in Jesus' name. Amen.

PETER

His Name Means "Rock"

His Work:	A career fisherman on the Sea of Galilee.
His Character:	Peter was a determined and impetuous man who became bold in his witness to the resurrection of Jesus Christ.
His Sorrow:	Like many impulsive people, Peter's greatest enemy was his mouth—speaking without thinking. This landed him in all kinds of trouble.
His Triumph:	The leadership of the disciples, the spread of the gospel to the Gentiles, and his martyrdom for the Savior he loved.
Key Scripture:	Luke 9

Monday

HIS STORY

For Simon Peter it was just another miraculous day with the Master.

Jesus and his disciples had crossed the Sea of Galilee together. Being followed by hundreds of people was not unusual, but when they reached the shore, they were astonished to find a literal multitude—more than ten thousand—waiting to see Jesus. Finding a remote place to dock well beyond the city of Capernaum wasn't enough to keep the crowd away. Even though Jesus was physically and emotionally spent (having just received the news that John the Baptist had been executed), he was filled with compassion for these people.

Over the next few hours he moved through the crowd, listening to the tales of the dispirited and touching the broken bodies of the lame, the deaf, and the blind. Then the disciples took Jesus aside. "Master," they quietly advised, keeping their voices among themselves, "it's late in the day, and we're too far from civilization to find enough food to feed these people. Why don't you send them away so they can get something to eat?"

"They don't need to go away," Jesus replied. "You can feed them."

The disciples looked at each other and shook their heads. "It would take eight months' worth of work to pay for food for this many people," Philip said, underscoring their frustration.

"Here, I have five barley loaves and two small fish," Andrew said, extending a small basket toward his big brother, Simon Peter. Peter looked down at the meager rations and smiled cynically. A few of the disciples snickered at Andrew's naïveté.

"Bring them over here," Jesus said to Andrew, having overheard the conversation among the brothers.

Jesus spread the word for the crowd to be seated. After a few minutes, each person was sitting on the plain next to the sea. Except for festivals in Jerusalem, this was more people than any of the disciples had ever seen at once.

Jesus raised his hands toward heaven and prayed, "Blessed are you, O Lord our God, who brings forth bread from the earth. Amen."

"Amen," the crowd echoed, the word reverberating through the glen and glancing off the faces of the surrounding cliffs: "Amen. Amen. Amen."

Jesus picked up one of the loaves and broke it in half, handing half to Peter. Then Jesus tore another half from the piece left in his hand. Peter blinked as Jesus handed him another piece of bread the same size as the preceding one. Looking into Jesus' hand, Peter saw that he still held half of the first loaf. Before Peter could say anything, Jesus twisted off another half and handed that to him. Peter lifted his robe, creating a makeshift basket large enough to hold all the bread.

Jesus continued to do this with the same first loaf until Peter's "basket" was completely full. Peter's arms and legs tingled with the wonder of what he was seeing. Jesus directed him to step back, and another disciple moved forward. Again Jesus tore halves of loaves from the same half and filled the disciple's robe with pieces.

He took the fish and did the same, filling a few of the disciples' outstretched garments with seafood instead of bread. When all the disciples had their robes filled, they began walking among the people, who reached in and helped themselves. As their "baskets" emptied, the disciples returned to Jesus, who filled them again.

This they did until the people—all ten thousand—were filled.

When they were finished, the disciples scattered to claim any food that had not been eaten.

In a few minutes, they were standing in the presence of the Lord, all twelve of them with their robes overflowing with food. They sat down and enjoyed as much as they could eat. Very little conversation came from these men. Even Peter was quiet. What they had just seen was too fantastic to put into words.

The crowd began to disperse. "Go, get in your boat and row to the other side of the sea," Jesus told the disciples. They didn't understand why he didn't want to come along with them, but they were too wonder-struck to speak. Together the disciples walked to the shore, boarded their boat, and cast off into the sea.

At about three o'clock the following morning, the wind picked up and the boat began to pitch and yaw. The disciples looked out over the water. "What's that," one of them hollered, his voice barely audible above the sound of the wind. "It's a ghost," another shouted, seeing what looked like a form of a man standing on the water.

"Take courage! It is I," Jesus called. "Don't be afraid."

Peter stood up. "Lord, if it's *really* you," he shouted, "tell me to step out of the boat and walk to you."

"Come on, Peter," Jesus replied.

Lifting one leg and then the other over the side of the boat, Peter stood on the surface of the water. The other disciples were stunned.

Gingerly, Peter began to walk toward Jesus, his mind reeling. *I can't believe it. Jesus has given me the power to actually walk on the water.* Looking up, Peter saw the intimidating waves in front of him, their white-caps glistening in the moonlight. The sheer heft of the swells made his legs weak. He became increasingly afraid and slowly began to sink.

"Please, Lord, save me," Peter screamed. "Save me."

Jesus reached out and took Peter's hand, and together they stepped into the boat. The instant their feet hit the deck, the winds became completely still.

On this single day Peter had seen Jesus feed ten thousand people from a handful of food, walk on the water and give him the power to do the same, still the storm, and calm his soul. This was more than Peter could take. He fell on his face at Jesus' feet and worshiped him. Each of the others did the same.

It was just another miraculous day with the Master.

Tuesday

A LOOK AT THE MAN

The Rock

Simon Peter had heard about Jesus. Living close to the Sea of Galilee, as Peter did, it would have been hard to miss him. But Peter's career kept him busy. Being distracted by the Teacher wouldn't be good for business.

Then one morning, as Jesus walked along the shore with the usual crowd of people surrounding him, he stopped and, without warning or permission, stepped into Peter's boat. Imagine the fisherman's shock when Jesus said to him, "Push out into the deep and drop your nets."

"But, Master," Peter protested, surprised that Jesus knew his name. "We've been up all night fishing and haven't caught anything."

Jesus turned to look at Peter with a glance that for the next three years would become familiar.

"Okay," Peter sighed. "Because it's you, I'll do it."

The moment the nets drifted below the water's surface, they filled with fish. Peter called for a second boat. But the nets were so full of fish that both boats nearly sank. Suddenly Peter made the connection between the miracle and his own wickedness. "Go away, Lord," he pleaded as he fell to his knees. "I'm a sinful man."

The Master must have instantly bonded to this rough but tender-hearted fisherman. "Don't be afraid, my friend," Jesus said to him. This may have been the first time anyone had ever said these words to this brave man. Then Jesus added, "Follow me."

The most outspoken and visible of Jesus' disciples, Simon Peter was a remarkably complex man. He was impulsive, brash, thickheaded, courageous, tough—and fearful. But there was a special place among Jesus' closest followers for this man. We have no record of there being an election of officers, but the gospel writers put Peter's name first when they list the disciples. He was their designated leader.

And there was a special place in Jesus' heart for Peter as well. He was the only disciple who received a new name—a nickname. "Blessed are you, Simon son of John," Jesus announced to him one day. "Now you are Peter, and on this rock I will build my church. And against my church, the gates of hell don't have a chance."

But like the man who carried the name, the word *rock* had many faces. Certainly there was the kind of rock that provided stability— bedrock on which the church was to be built. But there was the *rock* that represented shallowness—an impediment for the seed to grow. There was the *rock* that got in the way of progress—the stumbling stone of offense. And there was the *rock* that was many Jews' weapon of choice. And in a contemporary setting, *rock* sometimes refers to a precious gem. Jesus couldn't have given Simon a more appropriate moniker.

But any instability that marked the man prior to Jesus' resurrection was permanently erased once he touched the risen Savior and heard his call once more: "Follow me!" It was Peter who stood at Pentecost and preached a radical conversion message. It was Peter who, like his Lord, healed the sick—even his shadow had healing power! It was Peter who confidently stood before the antagonists in the Sanhedrin, the same men who later murdered Stephen. "Salvation is found in no one else but Jesus," he declared. "There's no other name under heaven by which we must be saved!"

It was Peter who was singled out for an extremely unpopular assignment—to take the message of salvation to non-jews. Peter, whom King Herod imprisoned for his refusal to stop preaching the Good News, was miraculously set free by an angel. And it was Peter whose death, Jesus said, would "glorify God."

While ministering in Rome, Peter was arrested by Nero and was later tried and crucified. However, unwilling to be killed in the same sacred way his Master had died, Peter requested that he be crucified upside down. His wish was granted, and God was glorified.

Wednesday

HIS LEGACY IN SCRIPTURE

Read Luke 5:1–11.

1. Simon Peter was minding his own business—until Jesus came by. He went fishing again despite his better judgment. Why did he go ahead?
2. What happened when Peter dropped his nets into the sea? Why did he connect two boatloads of fresh fish with his own sinfulness?
3. Why is our awareness of our sin intensified when we're in God's presence? What does this tell us about our walk with him?

GOING DEEPER

Read Matthew 16:13–37.

4. Jesus was secretive about his deity. Why?
5. In this passage Jesus explains to his disciples that he will suffer and die at the hands of the chief priests and the teachers of the law. Peter scolds him for predicting this, and Jesus calls Peter "Satan." Why is Jesus so pointed in his rebuke?
6. "Whoever wants to save his life will lose it," Jesus said. "But whoever loses his life for me and the gospel will save it." What do these words mean to you?

Thursday

HIS LEGACY OF PROMISE

There was no disciple more fascinating than Simon Peter. An uneducated fisherman—we smile at his childlike questions. An impetuous man—we understand his outspokenness. A devout man—we admire his courage. A sinful man—we identify with the battle between what he believes and how he acts. And in spite of his physically demanding occupation, we see Peter as a tender man who truly loves the Savior.

There is no disciple more widely recognized, no follower of Jesus more revered.

Promises in Scripture

I love you, O LORD, my strength.

The LORD is my rock, my fortress and my deliverer;
my God is my rock, in whom I take refuge.
He is my shield and the horn of my salvation, my stronghold.
I call to the LORD, who is worthy of praise,
and I am saved from my enemies.

—Psalm 18:1–3

The LORD is good to those whose hope is in him,
to the one who seeks him.

—Lamentations 3:25

Whoever acknowledges me before men, the Son of Man will also acknowledge him before the angels of God.   —Luke 12:8

No one has ever seen God; but if we love one another, God lives in us and his love is made complete in us.   —1 John 4:12

Friday

HIS LEGACY OF PRAYER

"Like newborn babies, crave pure spiritual milk, so that by it you may grow up in your salvation, now that you have tasted that the Lord is good."

—1 Peter 2:2–3

Reflect On: 2 Peter 4:12–13

Praise God: For his love.

Offer Thanks: For the wonder of a Savior who meets us where we are and transforms us by his Spirit.

Confess: Your inconsistency in wanting to follow him but so often neglecting to be his unfailing and faithful ambassador.

Ask God: For the will to be in his presence daily and to find in that encounter his redeeming power.

Simon Peter lived without inhibitions. His words came freely and unguarded. His zeal was impassioned. Even his confessions were bold. And Peter's life and message became a beacon of hope for the lost. Would that our lives may be filled with the same passion for Jesus Christ and our activities so significantly count for eternity.

God in heaven, thank you for your loving-kindness. Please draw me into your holy presence. Call me and change me. Let me see my sinfulness in the light of your love and grace. And pull me away from whatever I'm doing that keeps me from knowing the wonder of who you are. I pray this in Jesus' name. Amen.

LUKE

His Name Means "Light-Giving"

His Work: He was a Gentile by birth, a physician by trade, and a journalist by calling.

His Character: A humble man willing to be used rather than lauded.

His Sorrow: An eyewitness to the sinfulness and jealousy of the religious elite in their support of the torture and execution of many faithful believers.

His Triumph: The opportunity to chronicle the story of Jesus and the account of the founding of the church.

Key Scriptures: Luke 1–2; Acts 27

Monday

HIS STORY

Luke pored over his notes. Bits of parchment and papyrus were stacked in neat piles. Journals from various trips—and notes from conversations with eyewitnesses—covered the floor of his temporary Roman dwelling, a gift from Theophilus, a wealthy Gentile and the patron of this publishing venture. To a casual visitor, it appeared to be controlled chaos, but for Luke it was all artfully organized.

In the same way, Luke was meticulous about his writing, enjoying the scheduled, sedate pace. The rigors, dangers, and spontaneity of travel were not Luke's forte. *This is the work I love,* he mused.

As the apostle Paul's traveling companion and beloved friend, Luke ventured for years throughout Asia Minor and the countries of the western Mediterranean Sea. Now, because of Paul's arrest in Jerusalem and his request—as a Roman citizen—to have his venue changed to Rome, the pair had made the voyage together to Italy.

A Gentile, Luke understood why he hadn't been included in their inner circle. But he eventually proved himself by being a consistent, loyal friend. The ability to administer medical treatment to the disciples was also a welcome boon.

Luke knew he wasn't the only one to assume the daunting task of putting Jesus' story in writing. There were hundreds, thousands, who needed to hear the Good News!

Inspiration from God flooded Luke's heart. *And there were shepherds living out in the fields nearby, keeping watch over their flocks at night.* Luke's quill moved swiftly across the papyrus in front of him. *An angel of the Lord appeared to them, and the glory of the Lord shone around them, and they were terrified.* He sat back in his chair and smiled, letting out a long, noisy sigh. The flame of his lamp danced with the sudden burst of air. He looked up at the low ceiling in gratitude, knowing that other writers had decided not to detail the miraculous birth of the Savior. This was going to be wonderful!

"What did you see?" he queried the air, envisioning the shepherds years before, the very ones who tended their sheep on the Judean hillside that holy night. "What did you do when you heard the angel's voice? What was it like when you saw the Christ child?"

As a physician, Luke was familiar with the enchantment, the mystery, and the anxiety of a women's pregnancy. He may have spoken at great length with Mary, the mother of Jesus, collecting the details of her story. Luke would have remembered her telling him of the Messiah's birth.

Luke may also have spent time with Elizabeth, Mary's cousin and the mother of John the Baptist. "What did you think when Mary announced to you that she was pregnant by the Holy Spirit? What did you do? What did your preborn son do?" On and on he had gently questioned the elderly woman. Suspecting that the other writers would overlook many of these details, especially those close to a woman's heart, Luke resolved to tell the tender side of the story.

As Luke penned the gospel, he included many of the accounts his counterparts had written. But like his singular telling of the Savior's birth, Luke looked for moments in the life of Jesus that the others might overlook—like the account of the Good Samaritan. To Luke, this parable was one of the cornerstones of Jesus' ministry. As a Gentile, he knew the pain of prejudice, and as a physician, he knew the Samaritan's gentle healing touch. Luke knew that Jesus' words meant that his followers' beliefs and creeds must be demonstrated in good deeds.

A special audience with Mary and Martha in Bethany may have given the physician deep insight into the hearts of these two women whom Jesus loved. The account of the Master's challenging words to the busy Martha and tender words to the worshipful Mary were entrusted only to Luke.

One Sabbath day Jesus encountered a woman outside the synagogue, crippled and bent from a debilitating disease. He had compassion on the woman and healed her on that holy day, much to the outrage of the devout people standing by. Only Luke filed this account.

When Paul prepared for his second missionary journey, he sent word to Luke. "Please join me in Troas," he wrote. Luke, a good man and fellow laborer, was the perfect traveling companion. "Only my faithful friend Luke is with me," Paul wrote from the Roman prison to his young protégé Timothy. "And that is enough," he could have added. Luke found the man's devotion to Jesus contagious and invigorating and his invitations impossible to ignore. Traveling with Paul must have brought Luke renewed insight and the determination to record the most miraculous life ever lived. For years he had kept copious notes, perhaps knowing that one day he would craft them into prose.

Picking up a page, Luke leaned back as he read from his notes. "Nain: Jesus encounters a funeral procession. Woman who has already buried her husband has lost her son. 'Don't cry,' Jesus said. Raises boy from the dead. People filled with awe. 'God has come to help his people.'"

Luke had himself experienced the wonder of the story he told. He knew that in Jesus, God *had* come. All alone, he prayed earnestly for the Holy Spirit to empower him to tell the story of God's incredible love for his people, made manifest through the life, death, and resurrection of his Son, Jesus Christ. Then, picking up his quill, Luke dipped it into the stone inkwell and continued to write.

Tuesday

A LOOK AT THE MAN

Putting It in Writing

Luke may have been born in Antioch, just across the northeast corner of the Mediterranean from Paul's birthplace in Tarsus. There is no record of how Luke was converted to Christianity, but it may have been through the witness of Nicolas, who, along with Stephen, was one of the seven deacons selected by the apostles to care for the Greek-speaking believers.

Luke accompanied Paul to the city of Troas during Paul's second missionary journey. They were compatible traveling companions, so Luke joined Paul as often as he could, eventually becoming his full-time associate.

As a professional accustomed to disciplined study, Luke decided to undertake a massive assignment—writing an account of Jesus' life and chronicling the founding and early development of the church. Two years of waiting for Paul's trial in Rome gave him ample solitude to organize the documents and memories from his experiences and travels—then to document them in writing.

Before their voyage to Rome, Luke had also accompanied Paul during his two-year imprisonment under the custody of the Roman governor in Caesarea. During that time he had begun to organize his notes for his gospel and the Acts of the Apostles. He probably traveled throughout the region during those years to collect the material he would need to pen the gospel account. An accomplished historian, Luke knew the value of personally interviewing eyewitnesses. He carefully organized his work to insure accuracy.

Once Paul had been ordered to travel to Rome, Luke joined him on the harrowing voyage across the Great Sea. On their way, their ship was destroyed near the island of Malta. Everyone aboard narrowly escaped with their lives. So it was with a great deal of emotion, once they arrived in Rome, that Luke began writing.

Because Luke had personally visited many of the cities Paul had visited, he could collect detailed accounts of what happened as the Holy Spirit descended at Pentecost and the message of Jesus spread throughout the known world. Visits with apostles and witnesses along the way gave Luke not only the information but also the inspiration to finish his task.

Luke soberly accepted his God-given assignment. He was fully aware that his account would be the only one penned by a non-Jew. Luke's greatest desire was that the truth of the message would go beyond its provincial beginnings to touch the souls of those who had never seen or heard for themselves. He probably hoped to reach hundreds, maybe thousands. What he couldn't have known was that these two documents—the Gospel of Luke and the Acts of the Apostles—would be read and studied by millions for generations to come.

Wednesday

HIS LEGACY IN SCRIPTURE

Read Matthew 23:12.

1. In this verse, Jesus is admonishing people who are "great" to become servants. As a physician, Luke probably would have held a prominent place in his culture, but his life is marked with humility. How does this run counter to our culture? What are the dangers of self-exaltation?

Read Luke 10:25–37.

2. Like grace, "inheritance" is not earned. It's a gift from our Father. It's our reward for being born again. Why is this truth so difficult for many people to accept?

3. As a Gentile surrounded by Jews, why was Luke interested in making certain that this story was included in his gospel?

4. Is there a conflict between the gift of inheritance and the Samaritan's good deeds? Why or why not?

GOING DEEPER

Read Luke 10:38–42.

5. Just in case someone missed the power of the truth that inheritance is a gift and cannot be earned, Luke follows the story of the Good Samaritan with the account of Mary and Martha. What truth of the previous story does this account underscore?

6. How do "Marys" view "Marthas"? How do "Marthas" view "Marys"? Do you tend to be a "Mary" or a "Martha"?

Read 1 Corinthians 13:1–3.

7. Luke's good friend Paul penned these words. He could have written, "If I'm a priest and not a Good Samaritan, I gain nothing." Or he could have said, "If I'm a Martha and have no Mary, I'm wasting my time." How could you apply this truth to your own life?

Thursday

HIS LEGACY OF PROMISE

As a Gentile, Luke saw Jesus from a different perspective. As an educated man, he saw the value of constructing Jesus' life story in such an organized way. (He also wanted these things to be elegantly documented.)

As a tender and humble man, Luke was eager that his authorship would not draw attention to himself. So, although he is credited with writing a significant portion of the New Testament, Luke did not write his own name or make any references to himself at all. Not one single time.

Promises in Scripture

> Many, O LORD my God,
>> are the wonders you have done.
> The things you planned for us
>> no one can recount to you;
> were I to speak and tell of them,
>> they would be too many to declare.
>
> —Psalm 40:5

> His mercy extends to those who fear him,
>> from generation to generation.
> He has performed mighty deeds with his arm;
>> he has scattered those who are proud in their inmost thoughts.
> He has brought down rulers from their thrones
>> but has lifted up the humble.
>
> —Luke 1:50–52

> If you then, though you are evil, know how to give good gifts to your children, how much more will your Father in heaven give the Holy Spirit to those who ask him! —Luke 11:13

> For the Son of Man came to seek and to save what was lost.
>
> —Luke 19:10

Friday

HIS LEGACY OF PRAYER

"Love the Lord your God with all your heart and with all your soul and with all your strength and with all your mind"; and, "Love your neighbor as yourself."
—Luke 10:27

Reflect On: Psalm 95:1–7

Praise God: For his majesty.

Offer Thanks: For calling you to obedience and service.

Confess: Your eagerness for significance rather than your passion for submission.

Ask God: To give you a servant's heart, to serve him with gratitude.

Luke's legacy was not to be significant, but useful. He preferred obedience to acclaim, service over commendation. So God selected Luke to be the only non-Jew—an outsider—to write his Son's biography. God took Luke's skills and willingness to be used and brought glory to himself. If our hearts and our motives were this pure, our work might be this noteworthy.

God in heaven, thank you for using unlikely messengers to tell your story. Please forgive me for choosing human applause rather than your blessing. I want to use my talents and gifts to tell your story to those around me. Please use me to bring honor to your name. I pray this in Jesus' name. Amen.

THE MAN BY THE POOL

His Work:	Since the man by the pool was an invalid, he may have made his living by begging.
His Character:	His role in the story seems almost entirely passive, perhaps in keeping with his character. He showed evidence neither of faith nor gratitude after the miracle of his healing and even went so far as to give evidence against Jesus to men who were hostile toward Jesus. Sin appears to have played a role in his condition.
His Sorrow:	To have been paralyzed for nearly forty years.
His Triumph:	To have been instantly healed.
Key Scripture:	John 5

Monday

HIS STORY

The man lay on a mat near the pool of Bethesda. Though *Bethesda* meant "house of mercy," he had, for the last thirty-eight years, felt himself beyond the reach of mercy. Only his arms were good for anything, not powerful but adequate for dragging his body from place to place and for stretching out a beggar's cup to anyone who passed by. On good days, his friends would carry him to the pool, where he waited along with other poor souls for its healing waters to be stirred.

It was said that the first to reach the pool after the water began moving would be healed. Today a large crowd of those who were blind, lame, and paralyzed had packed together at its edge, their numbers increased by men and women who had come to Jerusalem to celebrate the feast.

Suddenly the lame man heard a stranger addressing him. "How long have you been an invalid?" the man asked.

He was tempted to tell him to mind his own business, but then beggars had no business offending able-bodied men since they made their living on the pity of others. So he merely looked up at the man and replied, "I've been like this for the last thirty-eight years."

"Do you want to get well?" the stranger asked.

How could the man ask such a question? Did he have any idea what it was like to live in his skin, a beggar whose steady diet consisted of nothing but rude stares and condescending remarks? How could he not want to get well?

But for a reason the lame man did not fully understand, he felt paralyzed to say so, unable to assure the man that his one desire was to be well again. Instead, he replied, "Sir, I have no one to help me into the pool when the water is stirred. While I am trying to get in, someone else goes down ahead of me."

Expecting pity, he got none, only a command: "Get up! Pick up your mat and walk."

As suddenly as he heard the words, the man experienced a jolt of such tremendous power that it seemed as though someone had kicked him. To the amazement of the watching crowd, he crawled to his knees and then stood up. The man who had been unable to walk for nearly four decades now bent over, picked up his mat, and walked away as nimbly as any other man.

Oddly, no one slapped him on the back to congratulate him for his good fortune. No one threw arms in the air to praise God for the miracle just witnessed. Instead, a few men stopped him. Crowding around, they began to accuse him: "Why are you carrying that mat? Don't you know it's the Sabbath? It's forbidden!"

As though to deflect their criticism, he replied, "The man who made me well said to me, 'Pick up your mat and walk.'"

When they asked him who had dared to do such a thing on the Sabbath, the man told them he had no idea. He had never seen the stranger before. Turning to point him out, he found that his healer had already slipped away into the busy crowd.

After that, the man made his way to the temple, surprised to meet the stranger once more. "Now that you are well again," Jesus told him, "stop sinning or something worse may happen to you."

The man went away and told the Jews that it was Jesus who had made him well.

Tuesday

A LOOK AT THE MAN

Rejecting Mercy

"Do you want to be healed?"

It was an outrageous question to ask a man who had been paralyzed for thirty-eight years, a man forced to beg for a living.

But there was a reason for the question. Perhaps, in fact, the paralyzed man wasn't happy about the prospect of being healed. Maybe his disability offered a certain kind of security, enabling him at least to make a living as a beggar. His sudden cure would have undermined his many dependencies, his familiar routine, his ingrained view of himself. He would have had to start life all over again.

Or maybe he was offended by Jesus' warning against sin. Perhaps he thought it would do Jesus good to receive his comeuppance at the hands of the religious leaders.

The story of the man by the pool reminds us that displays of God's power are not enough to create faith in a person's heart. Though the man had suffered for many years, he showed no evidence of gratitude and no evidence of belief. We expect him to fall on his knees when he is miraculously healed. But he doesn't. We expect him to show some kind of curiosity about the person who healed him. But he doesn't even ask Jesus his name until their second encounter. We expect him to protect Jesus against his detractors, to be scandalized by their blindness and self-righteousness. Instead, he reports Jesus to men he knew to be hostile toward Jesus.

In Matthew's gospel, Jesus denounces the cities that had witnessed most of his miracles, because the vast majority of people there had failed to repent (Matthew 11:20). His words remind us that, even though miracles are evidence of God's power and compassion, without faith we are still free to reject them, still free to conclude that his offer of mercy is irrelevant or unnecessary.

Though none of us know what went on in the heart of the man who was healed, we are troubled by the way he responded and the way he failed to respond to the miracle he experienced. We may even wonder if by his own choice he finally succeeded in placing himself beyond the reach of God's mercy. Only God knows.

Wednesday

HIS LEGACY IN SCRIPTURE

Read John 5:1–15.
 1. The question Jesus posed to a man who had dragged his pathetic frame along the ground for almost forty years seemed scandalous. But *was* it? What did this newly able-bodied man have to do now?
 2. It's fashionable to accuse others for our own condition. "My father mistreated me." "My schoolmates mocked me." "My spouse doesn't understand me." These excuses both cripple us and give us a logical explanation for our conduct. Then Jesus shocks us with his words. "Do you want to be healed?" "Do you want to stand on your own two legs and live without the luxury of blaming others?" What might it mean if Jesus spoke these words to you?
 3. "Stop sinning or something worse may happen to you." Jesus added insult to injury. Or did he? Explain your answer.

GOING DEEPER

Read Ephesians 2:1–10.
 4. God's grace—Jesus' blood shed for us and his atonement for our sins—is truly amazing. It's a gift. But these verses (especially 8 and 9) tell us that something else is a gift. What is this gift?
 5. The man by the pool experienced the gift of healing, but even this astonishing miracle wasn't enough to force him into believing in Jesus. What was he missing?

Thursday

HIS LEGACY OF PROMISE

Scripture makes it abundantly clear. Like the man by the pool, we are crippled by our sin, unable to stand in God's presence. Fortunately, Jesus' death and resurrection reverses our condition. He not only grants us the ability to get up from our mats of self-pity and shame but gives us access to God's presence as well. Because of his great love, we can stand before him spotless, receiving his gifts of faith and healing.

Promises in Scripture

[Jesus said,] "Everything is possible for him who believes."

Immediately the boy's father exclaimed, "I do believe; help me overcome my unbelief!" —Mark 9:23–24

This righteousness from God comes through faith in Jesus Christ to all who believe. There is no difference, for all have sinned and fall short of the glory of God, and are justified freely by his grace through the redemption that came by Christ Jesus. —Romans 3:22–24

If you confess with your mouth, "Jesus is Lord," and believe in your heart that God raised him from the dead, you will be saved. For it is with your heart that you believe and are justified, and it is with your mouth that you confess and are saved. —Romans 10:9–10

Friday

HIS LEGACY OF PRAYER

"Now that you have been set free from sin and have become slaves to God, the benefit you reap leads to holiness, and the result is eternal life. For the wages of sin is death, but the gift of God is eternal life in Christ Jesus our Lord." —Romans 6:22–23

Reflect On: Psalm 86:1–8

Praise God: For his grace, mercy, and the faith to believe.

Offer Thanks: For the blessings of healing and wholeness.

Confess: Any tendency you may have to blame others rather than to admit your own sinfulness and receive Christ's pardon.

Ask God: To give you courage to stand, face those crippling hurts, and live with freedom and hope.

The scene along the edge of the pool called Bethesda is stunning. The figure of a faithless man standing after thirty-eight years of paralysis is just as pathetic as his broken body lying on his mat. His gnarled legs were now straight and strong, but his soul was hopelessly weak. When we pray, our request to the Father must be not only to receive his gift of forgiveness but also the gift of healing faith—the ability to understand and believe.

Lord God, thank you for loving me. Thank you for offering to me your generous gifts of grace and faith. Please forgive me for hiding from the accountability of my own sin. Purify my body and my soul. I confess my sins and my inability to believe. Fill me with faith to believe. Thank you for hearing my prayer. In Jesus' name, I pray. Amen.

LAZARUS

His Name Means "God Helps"

His Work:	Lazarus was the brother of Martha and Mary, the family who hosted Jesus in their home when he traveled through Bethany.
His Character:	Little is known about Lazarus other than that he was one of Jesus' close friends.
His Sorrow:	Lazarus had a terminal illness and eventually succumbed to it.
His Triumph:	Very few have had the experience of hearing Jesus' voice from the tomb. Lazarus was such a person.
Key Scripture:	John 11

Monday

HIS STORY

"Mary ... Martha." The words that squeezed through Lazarus's parched lips were barely audible. "Bring me some water."

The voice was quiet, but Mary and Martha, the sisters of the sick man, were on the alert. Hearing his request, they rushed to Lazarus's bedside. Carefully lifting his head, they gently poured cool water into his mouth.

Lazarus swallowed hard, laid his head back, and looked at them. It was a look of gratitude for their kindnesses, but it was also filled with resignation. Lazarus was about to die, and he knew it. Although he had bravely challenged death, the ravages of his illness had prevailed.

Once more he gathered enough strength to speak. "Go ... bring Jesus," he whispered.

Martha jumped to her feet and ran from the room. But Mary did not move, staying on her knees beside the bed and tenderly holding her brother's hand.

Over the next few hours, Lazarus could hear people coming and going from his room, but he could not open his eyes or speak to them. He simply didn't have the strength. As he lay there, the intensity of his pain quietly subsided. He felt completely calm. Lazarus slowly paged through his memory bank and saw the faces of his lifelong friends. He reminisced about the good things, and his heart was filled with a deep sense of joy and gratitude.

And then everything became unfocused. Murky. Like a book slowly closing, the memories ended. The noises of the busy people around him faded into silence. Lazarus drifted off.

"Your friend Lazarus is very sick, my Lord," the messenger gasped. He had hurried from Bethany to Perea, on the other side of the Jordan River, where Jesus was teaching. "He may die very soon."

The disciples gathered around Jesus to comfort him. They knew of the Master's intimate friendship with Lazarus and his two sisters, Mary and Martha. Staying in their home was customary when Jesus was in Bethany. Certainly he would be crushed by the news of his friend's impending death.

"He's not *that* sick," Jesus responded. His words weren't rude, but his frankness shocked everyone. The disciples' faces flushed with embarrassment. The messenger stood aghast. *How could he say that?* they all wondered. *He's not been to Bethany for weeks.*

Jesus thanked the messenger for the information and sent him on his way. "We'll travel to Bethany the day after tomorrow," he said to the disciples. They couldn't believe that Jesus wouldn't drop everything to hurry to his ailing friend. But after almost three years of being with Jesus, they had learned not to question his judgment.

"Our friend Lazarus has fallen asleep, and I'm going to wake him up," Jesus announced to his disciples as they prepared for the trip to Judea two days later.

"But Master, if he's only sleeping, then he'll get better," they answered.

"No," Jesus said. "That was just a figure of speech. What I mean is that Lazarus is dead." And then he added, "And for your sakes, I'm glad that I didn't go earlier. This is going to be a big faith experience for you."

The disciples scratched their heads in wonder. Just when they thought they had Jesus figured out, he surprised them again.

Many hours later as they walked along the Jericho road, the disciples could see the village of Bethany in the distance, tucked up against the foot of the Mount of Olives. When they reached the outskirts, they stopped for a drink. Someone recognized Jesus and ran into town with the news that the Master had arrived.

Martha was the first to hear the report. She rushed to see Jesus. "Lord, if you had been here a few days ago, Lazarus would not have died." Then she said, "But I know that it's not too late for you to ask God to bring him back."

"Lazarus will rise again," Jesus said with a smile.

"That's not what I mean," Martha replied, a hint of frustration in her voice. "I *know* he'll rise again in the last day. I'm talking about *now.*"

"*I'm* the resurrection and the life," Jesus said evenly. "He who believes in me will live, even though he dies; and whoever lives and believes in me will never die." Jesus looked directly into the woman's eyes. "Do you believe this, Martha?"

"Yes, Lord," she said, an unfamiliar twinge of emotion touching her voice as she spoke.

Martha turned and hurried back to her house. She wanted to tell her sister that the Master had come. When Mary heard the news, she ran with all her might and fell at Jesus' feet. "O Lord," Mary sobbed, "if you had been here, my brother wouldn't be dead."

Jesus tenderly reached down and put his hand on Mary's head. Then scanning the grieving crowd, Jesus asked, "Where's his body?"

"Come this way," someone volunteered, leading Jesus and his disciples to the burial site.

As Jesus walked toward the tomb, he was filled with overwhelming emotion, a strange mixture of pain over the loss of his friend and the depth of bereavement these people had over Lazarus's untimely death. Jesus also felt sorry for these people who were without any hope.

In a few minutes, Jesus was standing in front of the tomb. He asked for the stone that sealed the crypt to be rolled away.

Out of nowhere, semiconscious thoughts went racing across Lazarus's mind. *Was that a voice? Is someone calling me? I must get up to see who needs me.*

Slowly he opened his eyes. Lazarus had never experienced such blackness in his life. The pungent smell of perfume flooded his senses. *Something is over my face,* he thought. He tried to remove it, but he could not move his hands. His body was wrapped tightly from head to foot.

Lazarus took a deep breath, sat up, and struggled to his feet. The dank floor sent a shiver through his bare feet and up his spine. He shuffled in the direction of the voice he had heard. A balmy glow surrounded his cold body—he could see light through the cloth over his face. Lazarus was standing in the afternoon sunlight. He had never felt such warmth.

The sounds of people speaking to each other could be heard all around. Some were whispering, some were gasping, and others were shrieking with delight. "Unbind him," a familiar voice said. "Take off the grave clothes and let him go."

Lazarus's heart raced with anticipation.

Tuesday

A LOOK AT THE MAN
Memoirs of a Dead Man

The story of Lazarus's resurrection is filled with ironies.

We know where Lazarus lived—Bethany—and the names of his two sisters—Mary and Martha—but we have no record of a single word he spoke or even a mention of what he was like. We don't know his occupation, who his parents were, or, if he was married, the names of his wife and children.

If it hadn't been for his special friendship with the Savior, Lazarus's death wouldn't even have merited a footnote in the gospel account. Yet his story is one of the most well-known in all of Scripture.

When word reached Jesus that Lazarus was deathly ill, Jesus seemed unaffected—almost cavalier—about it. Of course, people bringing bad news to Jesus would have been a nonstop event during his waking hours, but Lazarus was his friend—his good friend. Jesus suggested that he and his disciples *should* visit Bethany—in two days!

Like a wife kindly taking her husband aside to challenge his bad manners, we can imagine the disciples suggesting that Jesus might want to reconsider his decision. "How will this look to the family?" they may have counseled.

"I'm doing this for you," was Jesus' perplexing response.

At the same time, the disciples were not eager to travel west to Bethany. No doubt, they would have to go through Jerusalem where, just a few days before, a handful of Jewish leaders had threatened to stone Jesus. He had said, "My Father and I are one," and these people weren't willing to accommodate a man who claimed to be equal with God.

Two days later the disciples were willing to take their chances. Helping a desperate friend like Lazarus was more urgent than any danger they may have encountered. As they reached the outskirts of Bethany, first Martha and then Mary ran to meet Jesus, reporting the news he already knew. Once again Jesus did not seem eager to help—at least not within Martha and Mary's time frame.

Jesus asked where Lazarus's body was entombed and made his way to the site along with a cadre of curious—and a few cynical—

onlookers. At no point in this story, however, did he seem to be in a hurry.

Soon he arrived at the cemetery. Can you envision Jesus standing in front of his friend's burial cave? It had been four days since Lazarus had died. His two sisters, now standing at Jesus' side, were in a quandary. They were hoping for a miracle, but they were just as concerned about how much their decaying brother's body would smell. The people who had come, standing behind Jesus and Lazarus's sisters, completed the picture.

Everyone stopped talking as Jesus lifted his head to the heavens to pray. "Father," he began, "I thank you that you have heard me. I knew that you would. But for the benefit of these people standing here, I especially thank you for listening this time."

People shifted nervously in their places, but no one spoke. Those in the back of the crowd craned their necks to see what might happen next.

"Lazarus, come out!" Jesus said in a voice much louder than anyone had ever heard him use. The living God had just spoken. If he hadn't identified his friend by name, every crypt in the entire cemetery would have emptied.

And then Lazarus appeared. In his own time and with only the sound of his voice, the Messiah had brought a corpse to its feet.

The final irony was that the Savior raised Lazarus from the dead with his voice but didn't speak the removal of Lazarus's grave clothes. He certainly could have finished the job, but he didn't. Instead, a man wrapped tightly from head to foot stood there in front of his own burial cave—and in front of everyone. "Take off the grave clothes and let him go," Jesus ordered the gawking crowd.

The last act of this incredible miracle—the unbinding and releasing of the man—was left to his family and friends.

Wednesday

HIS LEGACY IN SCRIPTURE

Read John 11:1–6.

1. There is no scriptural record of Martha and Mary attempting to contact Jesus until their brother was almost dead. Why do you think they waited so long to contact the Savior? When have you been guilty of waiting too long to invite the Lord into your situation? Describe what happened.

2. When the messenger returned to Bethany after delivering the news to Jesus that Lazarus was dying, he certainly went to Martha and Mary with the report, "Jesus isn't coming right away." How do you think Martha and Mary felt about this? Have you ever been impatient while waiting for God to send you an answer? Describe your feelings.

3. Scripture gives us some clues as to why Jesus didn't come right away. Why do you think he waited for two days before coming to Bethany?

GOING DEEPER

Read John 11:38–44.

4. Is it possible that Lazarus wasn't happy about being resurrected? Why or why not?

5. What do you think Jesus had in mind by bringing Lazarus forth with the grave clothes still in place, then asking others to loose him and let him go?

6. Do you know someone who has been "healed" but is still bound up? What could you do to loose that person?

Thursday

HIS LEGACY OF PROMISE

Resurrection is certainly among the most astounding of all Bible miracles, perhaps eclipsed only in wonder by Creation itself. Although many accounts of supernatural events are recorded in the Bible, only eight resurrection stories are recorded. In each of these miracles—including Lazarus's account—God's timing was flawless.

The hope of every believer is founded in the resurrection of Jesus Christ. And this hope promises that all who come to the Savior in simple faith, confess their sins, and ask God's Holy Spirit to fill them with his presence will be added to this number of souls that have been brought back from death to life. You and I do not know when this will happen for us or for our loved ones, but we have every assurance that God's timing will, once again, be perfect.

Promises in Scripture

I will lie down and sleep in peace,
for you alone, O LORD,
make me dwell in safety.

—Psalm 4:8

Whoever lives by the truth comes into the light, so that it may be seen plainly that what he has done has been done through God.

—John 3:21

Jesus said to her, "I am the resurrection and the life. He who believes in me will live, even though he dies; and whoever lives and believes in me will never die."

—John 11:25–26

If only for this life we have hope in Christ, we are to be pitied more than all men.

—1 Corinthians 15:19

Friday

HIS LEGACY OF PRAYER

Jesus called in a loud voice, "Lazarus, come out!" The dead man came out, his hands and feet wrapped with strips of linen, and a cloth around his face.

Jesus said to them, "Take off the grave clothes and let him go."

—John 11:43–44

Reflect On: John 11:38–42

Praise God: For his resurrection power.

Offer Thanks: For God's love for you, for calling you by name and redeeming you from darkness into the light of his glory.

Confess: Your complacency, your willingness to make the best of your "tombs" rather than daily abandoning them and walking into the light.

Ask God: To fill you with the same sense of wonder and gratitude that Lazarus felt as he stood in the mouth of his burial crypt. And ask him to show you others who need your hands to unwrap their "grave clothes."

Not many people are allowed the opportunity of living twice. Lazarus was one of those. His life was dramatically separated into two parts: preresurrection and postresurrection.

Spiritually, all are given the opportunity of living twice. Our experience can be divided into two parts: preconversion and postconversion. This was exactly what Jesus explained to Nicodemus one night. He called it being born again—a second birth. When we receive Christ, like Lazarus, we go from death to life, darkness to light, lost to found.

Prayer literally moves us from one sphere into the next. We leave the temporal and are transported into the spiritual. We get up from our places in the tomb and walk into the light.

So many of those who were with Jesus—disciples, friends—were profoundly impatient. They wanted Jesus to act on their timetable. Once we have confessed our sin and invited him into our circumstances, our greatest desire should be for his will to be done—in his time.

———————————

Father in heaven, thank you for your resurrection power. I want to rest in your sovereign hand. I want to be satisfied with your will on your perfect schedule. Please forgive me for my impatience, anxiety, and lack of faith in you and your plan for me. And I ask that you fill me with your Spirit and give me new life each day. I pray this in Jesus' name. Amen.

PRODIGAL SON AND ELDER BROTHER

Their Work:	These men worked for their father, a wealthy landowner.
Their Character:	Both of the brothers were sinners. One committed the sin of unrighteous living and the other the sin of self-righteousness.
Their Sorrow:	Both men were alienated from their father. Geography separated the prodigal from his father, while pride separated the elder brother.
Their Triumph:	The father's open arms and homecoming feast welcomed the prodigal. There was no happiness for the elder brother except the misplaced belief that he was better than his wayward sibling.
Key Scripture:	Luke 15

Monday

THEIR STORY

"Father," the young man called.

"Yes, my son," the old man eagerly replied. Conversations between the two were infrequent and strained these days. But any hopes for a meaningful talk were dashed by his son's next words.

"I don't want to wait for you to die in order to receive my inheritance," the boy said with his defiant chin upraised. "I want you to give it to me now."

Inwardly, his son's words staggered the father. *Insolent child! How could he say such a thing?* Hurt but unwilling to challenge the incorrigible boy, he numbly retrieved the money and handed it to his son. He wanted to warn him not to squander his inheritance. *I don't want to see him throw away his future,* he thought. There was so much that could destroy the young man. But knowing his son would merely ignore his warnings, the father said nothing.

The father watched him—a child he had held within minutes of his birth, a child he had cherished from that day forward—disappear without a backward glance down the road that led from the family home.

When the boy's older brother heard what he had done, he was furious. "How could you do such a thing?" he said, scolding his father. "You *know* what he will do with the money. And you *also* know," the brother added, "that soon he'll come back to you for more."

The father was silent, hoping that the older brother was right. He longed to see his son again, whatever the conditions. Before long, word of the young man's exploits—and his apparent pleasure— reached home, grieving the father all the more.

Meanwhile the boy was having the time of his life. Not only did a pocketful of money buy him all the pleasure and happiness he could want, but he found himself surrounded with the kind of fast-moving friends he had always wished for. No more sleepy farmers. No more dull herdsmen. No more plain and simple female neighbors. This was better than he had imagined.

But soon the young man's fingers touched the bottom of his money pouch. He couldn't believe how quickly the money had vanished. *Now what will I do?* he wondered. *I have no skills for a worthwhile trade.* With mute shock he watched his newfound friends disappear.

Responding to news that a local pig farmer had an opening for a hired hand, the lonely, desperate boy landed a job slopping hogs. Day after day the young man cared for the pigs. And day after day his spirits sank. Then one morning he came to his senses. "What am I doing here?" he asked the swine, as though he expected them to answer. "At least I would be able to eat better than this if I were working for my father." The pigs did not look up from their breakfast. "I will go home and offer to be one of my father's servants."

But would his father have him? How horribly the boy had treated him! He had not honored his father or loved him. Instead, he had lived in a way that denied everything his father had taught him. Would his father ever forgive him? The thought of being turned away set the son's hands to trembling.

What kind of future would he have without a father? Without a home? "What have I done?" he cried.

Late one afternoon, while absently staring out a window, the boy's father saw something in the distance that surprised him—a tiny figure advancing against the horizon in the exact place he had last seen his son. As the figure grew closer, the father wondered, *Could it be? No! Certainly not! But it looks like . . .* The young man's gait was noticeably slower, his shoulders stooped. . . . But make no mistake about it, it was his boy. He was home!

Without hesitation the father ran down the road toward his son, his arms outstretched and his robes flagging in his wake.

When the young man looked up and saw the man running toward him, his knees buckled. He knew who this was. What punishment would his father exact? Whipping? Exile? Pure contrition was his only chance for survival.

"O Father," the boy wept as his father reached him, "I have sinned against God and against you. I do not deserve to be your . . ."

But the man was not listening. "Good news! Good news!" He shouted so loudly that the neighbors could hear. He lifted his shocked son from his knees, pulling him into his arms, laughing and shouting. Servants in the field gawked at them, but his father paid them no heed. "Kill the fatted calf! Break out the wine. We're going to have a homecoming feast tonight." The father took his son's face between his hands and grinned until his son grinned back at him. "My son who was lost has been found." And then he embraced him again.

This time the son clung to his father as eagerly as the father did to his son.

"What's the commotion?" the elder brother asked his servants when he returned from a long day of toiling in the fields. "What's all the noise—the music and the laughter?"

"It's your younger brother, my lord," they answered. "He is home, and your father is throwing a party in his honor."

Shaking his head in disbelief, his body trembling with fury, the man stormed to the receiving room of his father. "What are you doing?" he shouted. "Who is this scoundrel that he deserves your forgiveness, much less a celebration? Haven't you done *enough* for that rascal?"

And then, as though it was an afterthought, he added, "After all I have done for you—and you treat me like this?"

But the father ignored the elder brother's churlishness. His heart had never been this full of gratitude and love . . . for *both* of his sons.

"My dear son," the father said to his eldest child, "you have been with me always, and I thank you for that. But don't keep me from celebrating your brother's return. Come to the party," he pleaded. "Please come and celebrate."

But the elder brother turned and walked away. The injustice! How could this be fair? How could his father be so blind? He would not join in such revelry over someone who deserved so little. Not even at the request of his father.

Tuesday

A LOOK AT THE MEN

The Unrighteous and the Self-Righteous

This biblical account is one of Jesus' parables, often called "The Story of the Prodigal Son." But it's really the story of not one but three men: the prodigal son, the elder brother, and the waiting father. Each plays a critical role in the narrative.

What the younger son asked of his father was unthinkable. Inheritance was paid to a man's sons upon his death, so in prematurely requesting the birthright from his father, the boy was saying that he wouldn't care if his father were dead. His rebellion was open and shameless, a public embarrassment for the entire family. And what he did broke his father's heart.

The older boy was every father's dream. As an employee, his efforts were productive, his work ethic was flawless. Even his conduct was exemplary—and he did not hesitate to review all of these qualities in his father's hearing. He had every confidence that his virtuous behavior earned not only his father's respect and riches but his love as well.

But the elder brother carried a deep grudge. The insolence of his younger brother's words and the slack in his life ground away at the elder brother's soul like a millstone. And the special attention the young son drew from the father turned the older son's grudge into hatred.

As far as the elder brother was concerned, the moment the inheritance payment was made to his sibling, the boy's days as a member of the family were finished. Now the older son was his father's *only* son, and the benefits of his father's wealth would be exclusively his.

Unfortunately for the elder brother, this was not his father's disposition. The younger son, even with his inheritance paid in full, was still a member of the family. Neither open defiance nor running away would have any effect on his father's love for him. This infuriated the elder brother, but his simmering anger was about to be turned into a bubbling cauldron.

The father threw a party. It was bad enough for his absent little brother to keep their father in distress while he was in a faraway land, but to have his father throw a celebration when he returned home was more than the elder brother could bear. In his attempt to punish the father for his grace, he refused to attend the merrymaking, preferring to sulk instead.

In this parable Jesus was declaring all of humankind "sinners," and he divided them into two groups: prodigals and elder brothers—the unrighteous and the self-righteous. And he underscored the fact that the heavenly Father—the living God—loved both and was willing to forgive both.

Contrition for his blatant sinfulness earned the younger brother full forgiveness and a party in his honor. But the older son's inability to see his self-righteousness as sin kept him from receiving the forgiveness his father would have freely extended. So he spent the night alone, overhearing the joyous celebration but experiencing none of it himself.

Wednesday

THEIR LEGACY IN SCRIPTURE

Read Luke 15:11–32.

1. If you had been the father, which of the sons would you have been tempted to love more? Why?
2. Which son did it seem the father in the story loved more? Why?
3. The story of the three men is recorded in twenty-one verses (11–32). Almost half of these verses (25–32) tell us about the elder brother. Why do you think Jesus spent this much time talking about him?

Read Luke 15:1–3.

4. To whom did Jesus tell the three stories found in Luke 15?

GOING DEEPER

Read Luke 15:4–10.

5. The first of these stories is about a lost sheep. How did the sheep get lost? What did the shepherd do when he realized the sheep was lost?
6. The second story is about a lost coin. How did the coin get lost? What did the woman do when she realized the coin was lost?
7. The third story is about a lost son. How did the son get lost? What did the father do when he realized his son was lost?

Thought: There is a sidelight to this story that may be helpful in understanding and healing relationships. When someone wanders off (the lost sheep) or when someone is misplaced—or damaged—by another person's carelessness (the lost coin), aggressive pursuit is advisable. But when a person defiantly rebels and gets lost by his own hand (the lost boy), the appropriate response is to love and wait. Intentional pursuit carries with it the liability that this lost person will be driven further away.

Thursday

THEIR LEGACY OF PROMISE

Although Jesus' account may have been based on a true story, these were nameless and purely fictional characters. But it doesn't matter that these were not actual men, because what Jesus did in telling this parable was to attach one of two names to every one of us: prodigal son or elder brother.

He cleverly reminds us and those who were listening to him that day, "God is your loving father, and every one of you can be divided into two categories—the unrighteous and the self-righteous." The "tax collectors and 'sinners'" knew that they were the prodigal. Their sin had been deliberate and visible. But the "Pharisees and teachers of the law" were the elder brother—and proud of it. They weren't interested in confessing anything, and so, according to the Teacher, they weren't eligible to come to the party.

Promises in Scripture

Do not worry, saying, "What shall we eat?" or "What shall we drink?" or "What shall we wear?" For the pagans run after all these things, and your heavenly Father knows that you need them. But seek first his kingdom and his righteousness, and all these things will be given to you as well.
—Matthew 6:31–33

This righteousness from God comes through faith in Jesus Christ to all who believe. There is no difference, for all have sinned and fall short of the glory of God, and are justified freely by his grace through the redemption that came by Christ Jesus.   —Romans 3:22–24

[Christ] had to be made like his brothers in every way, in order that he might become a merciful and faithful high priest in service to God, and that he might make atonement for the sins of the people. Because he himself suffered when he was tempted, he is able to help those who are being tempted.   —Hebrews 2:17–18

Friday

THEIR LEGACY OF PRAYER

"'This son of mine was dead and is alive again; he was lost and is found.'
So they began to celebrate."   —Luke 15:24

Reflect On: Luke 15:20–31

Praise God: For his mercy.

Offer Thanks: For the picture of the waiting father and how it
                 tells us of the loving heavenly Father who is eager
                 to forgive our sins of unrighteousness and self-
                 righteousness.

Confess: Any tendency to believe that good deeds earn us a
                 place in the kingdom.

Ask God: To change your attitude, to give you a compassion
                 for the lost and to make your obedience to him a
                 response to his love rather than treating it as a way to
                 earn his love.

The story of the prodigal and the elder brother is the story of sin,
repentance, and the loving Father. Although the prodigal's sin of
unrighteousness is far more visible than the elder brother's sin of self-
righteousness, they are equally wicked in the Father's eyes. And they
keep us from the celebration that comes from having a clean heart.

Scripture makes it clear that it is not by our works but by Jesus'
blood and righteousness that we are made right before a holy God.
Our attempts at righteousness will fail. Our holiness can only be a gift
we receive from God.

Father in heaven, I confess my sinfulness. Thank you for the gift of forgive-
ness. Thank you that you place no higher value on self-righteousness than
unrighteousness. Forgive me for believing that my good deeds make me bet-
ter than my lost brother. Please give me a repentant heart so that I may expe-
rience the joy of my salvation. I pray this in Jesus' name. Amen.

His Work: As one of the twelve disciples, Judas's responsibility was to act as the group's treasurer.

His Character: John's gospel indicates that Judas, though chosen by Jesus, was a thief, a man who regularly helped himself to the community purse. Though he would have been on intimate terms with the Lord, he betrayed Jesus by handing him over to the religious authorities, who then had him condemned to death. The motives for his act of treachery have never been clear. His name always appears last in the list of Jesus' disciples.

His Sorrow: Regretting his decision to hand Jesus over to the religious authorities, Judas hanged himself.

His Triumph: He was a member of Jesus' inner circle.

Key Scriptures: Matthew 26:6–16; John 12:1–8; 13:1–30; 18:1–11

Monday

HIS STORY

Judas ascended the stairs to the upper room, the sound of his steps muffled by a flurry of men's voices. The disciples were already engaged in their favorite argument. Like children vying for sweets on a plate, each man argued that he would one day be the greatest in the kingdom of heaven. *What fools,* he thought. The future belonged not to dreamers but to men like himself, men cunning and bold enough to act when the opportunity arose.

Like many in Israel, Judas had fed himself with dreams of a Messiah, a new David who would one day liberate his people and establish his own kingdom. He had waited and watched, impatient for the man to reveal himself. Carefully he had sifted through the impostors, wanting to believe their impossible claims but too shrewd to do so. Then, before cynicism had a chance to displace his hope, he found the man he was looking for.

Jesus was a different kind of rabbi, speaking words that soothed and inflamed Judas, surprising words that constantly threw him off his guard. Judas loved the way he stood up to the religious elite, likening the Pharisees to whitened tombs full of dead men's bones. But it wasn't only the words that impressed him. It was the power. Here was a man who healed the lame and made the blind see, and even raised the dead to life. Judas had seen such things with his own eyes. To serve such a man, he thought, would be to insure one's own place in the coming kingdom. So Judas had become the group's treasurer, entrusted to administer the money that supported Jesus and his twelve disciples.

Judas's hunger for action grew stronger as large crowds began following Jesus—men and women from Galilee, the Decapolis, Jerusalem, Judea, and the region across the Jordan. But instead of using his popularity to build a political movement strong enough to unseat the Romans, Jesus spoke to the crowds in ways incomprehensible to Judas:

"Blessed are the poor in spirit, for theirs is the kingdom of heaven."

"Blessed are the meek, for they will inherit the earth."

"Blessed are the peacemakers, for they will be called sons of God."

Judas tried to take it all in, but he couldn't stop wondering what kind of king would speak such words to his followers. How could a great man's throne ever be established through talk of meekness and peacemaking?

Besides power, Judas had a fondness for money, as much money as he could get his hands on without drawing attention. One day he became indignant watching a woman pour perfume over Jesus' head. Thinking only of what he could do with the money the perfume would have brought, he scolded her: "Why this waste? This perfume could have been sold at a high price and given to the poor."

But Jesus chided him, saying, "Why are you bothering this woman? She has done a beautiful thing to me. The poor you will always have with you, but you will not always have me. When she poured this perfume on my body, she did it to prepare me for burial. I tell you the truth, wherever this gospel is preached throughout the world, what she has done will also be told in memory of her."

Judas felt betrayed. It wasn't only the public rebuke, it was all this talk of death. Had Judas misjudged Jesus, thinking him a king when he was merely a religious dreamer? What good was popularity if the man knew nothing about leveraging it to achieve political ends? Judas was tired of waiting, tired of hearing sermons at odds with his own view of how the world should change. Words were useless. Action was needed to provoke an uprising that would put an end to the Roman occupation of Judea.

So Judas concocted a scheme whereby he would betray Jesus to the high priests, who promised him thirty pieces of silver as a reward for his treachery. Judas watched for an opportunity to hand Jesus over. If Jesus and his followers failed to act, if they failed to seize their moment of destiny, so be it. It was a risk Judas was willing to take. If he succeeded, a kingdom would be won. If not, he would at least be a little bit richer.

That day in the upper room, as the rest of the Twelve argued about who was greatest, Judas held his tongue. He was through playing such games.

During the Passover meal, Jesus said something that astonished his disciples and sent a chill through the man who was scheming against him: "I tell you the truth, one of you is going to betray me." Shortly after that Jesus dipped a piece of bread into a dish and offered it to Judas. Ignoring the plea in Jesus' eyes, Judas stretched out his hand. At that moment the last of his doubts about the plans he had made vanished. He felt darkness wash over him like an incoming tide, fueling his resolve to do what needed to be done.

"What you are about to do, do quickly," Jesus told him.

As soon as Judas had taken the bread, he went out. And it was night.

Tuesday

A LOOK AT THE MAN

Betrayal

Under cover of darkness, Judas led a detachment of soldiers and Jewish officials to an olive grove on the other side of the Kidron Valley, the place where Jesus and his disciples had retired after the Passover meal. There he betrayed the Lord with a kiss, saying, "Greetings, Rabbi!" Then he watched as the soldiers bound Jesus and led him away.

If Judas intended his act of betrayal to be the spark that ignited the revolution, he must have been disappointed. There was no great uprising, no crowds clamoring for Jesus' release, no miracles from heaven to establish the Messiah on his throne. The next morning brought with it only the grim news that Jesus had been beaten, handed over to Pontius Pilate, and condemned to death. Suddenly Judas felt overwhelmed by a tide of grief so great it swept away his previous certainty. Flinging the thirty pieces of silver—blood money now—into the temple, he went out and hanged himself.

The story of Judas is one of the saddest and best known in Scripture. A man chosen by Jesus to become part of his inner circle, he was privy to God's wisdom, power, and love to an unprecedented degree. But Judas valued the privilege so little that he handed Jesus over to his enemies for the paltry sum of thirty pieces of silver, the price of a slave. Jesus himself commented on Judas's situation with a warning Judas failed to heed: "The Son of Man will go just as it is written about him. But woe to that man who betrays the Son of Man! It would be better for him if he had not been born."

Two thousand years later, Judas's name is still a synonym for betrayal. As one of the Twelve, Judas had been offered a place of honor in the kingdom Jesus promised to establish. But by serving his own vision rather than the Lord's vision, he became not an instrument of good but an instrument of evil in the story of salvation.

Wednesday

HIS LEGACY IN SCRIPTURE

Read Matthew 26:6–16.

1. After several years of following Jesus and seeing many miracles with his own eyes, Judas did an unthinkable thing: He betrayed his friend, turning Jesus over to his archenemies. Do you think Judas did this because he no longer believed in Jesus' authenticity, or was he trying to force Jesus to declare his messiahship and get on with the establishment of his earthly kingdom?

2. In either case, it's clear that Judas was primarily concerned with himself—if Jesus was a fraud, at least Judas had scored a small bounty of thirty silver coins. And if Jesus was the Messiah, then Judas knew that he'd have a prominent place in the new kingdom. In what ways do you follow Jesus out of selfish intentions?

Read John 21:15–17.

3. In a conversation with Simon Peter after the resurrection, Jesus summarized what our motives should be in loving and following him—something that Judas missed. What does Jesus tell Peter? How could this command be followed in your own Christian life?

GOING DEEPER

Read 1 Timothy 6:6–10.

4. Judas was the treasurer for the disciples. How might this responsibility have clouded his thinking?

5. Having an income is essential to your survival. But what can you do to avoid "the love of money"?

Thursday

HIS LEGACY OF PROMISE

Judas Iscariot had a case of spiritual coronary disease—that is, his heart loved money and the power it wielded. And there must have been enough early symptoms of this to warn his friends. During a conversation between Jesus and his disciples in Capernaum, Jesus mentioned that one of the twelve he had chosen was "a devil" (John 6:70). But there is no record that the disciples probed further to see who Jesus was referring to. Perhaps they were afraid to ask, thinking that Jesus may have been speaking of them. Or maybe simple complacency kept them from asking more questions. In either case, the story of Judas's failure is also the story of a group of believers who neglected their responsibility of loving one another and holding one another accountable. Your decision to follow Jesus is a personal one. But your growth as a believer must be within a community.

Promises in Scripture

A generous man will prosper;
he who refreshes others will himself be refreshed.
—Proverbs 11:25

As iron sharpens iron,
so one man sharpens another.
—Proverbs 27:17

If one part suffers, every part suffers with it; if one part is honored, every part rejoices with it.
Now you are the body of Christ, and each one of you is a part of it.
—1 Corinthians 12:26–27

Therefore confess your sins to each other and pray for each other so that you may be healed. The prayer of a righteous man is powerful and effective.
—James 5:16

Friday

HIS LEGACY OF PRAYER

When Judas, who had betrayed him, saw that Jesus was condemned, he was seized with remorse and returned the thirty silver coins to the chief priests and the elders. "I have sinned," he said, "for I have betrayed innocent blood."
— Matthew 27:3–4

Godly sorrow brings repentance that leads to salvation and leaves no regret, but worldly sorrow brings death.
— 2 Corinthians 7:10

Reflect On: Romans 5:6–11
Praise God: For redemption and forgiveness through Jesus Christ.
Offer Thanks: For personal salvation and a community of believers to love and from whom to receive love.
Confess: Any tendency toward self-pity rather than true repentance.
Ask God: For a renewed love for his people and commitment to fellowship, transparency, and accountability. Ask him for the courage to speak the truth in love and the grace to receive the same.

The story of Judas is one of the most sobering in the Bible. It is the account of a good man gone sour, an honorable man becoming corrupt and selfish. In his life we see the perils of living in isolation rather than in community. And we are witnesses to the treachery of remorse rather then the cleansing power of humble repentance. These are powerful lessons to be learned.

Father, thank you for your Word and the unforgettable truth it contains. Forgive me for living in isolation instead of in fellowship with others. Give me the courage to lovingly confront others, and grant me the patience to listen when others confront me. I pray for a spirit of humility and repentance so that my life may be a true reflection of your love. Thank you for choosing me to be your disciple and to join you as you build your kingdom on earth as it is in heaven. I pray these things in Jesus' name. Amen.

PONTIUS PILATE

His Name Means "One Armed with a Javelin"

His Work:	He was the Roman governor over the region of Judea.
His Character:	Pilate had all the trappings of power and leadership but was unwilling to exercise that influence for good.
His Sorrow:	He failed to stand for what was right and allowed an innocent man to go to his death.
His Triumph:	When Tiberius Caesar appointed Pilate governor of Judea, Pilate must have been delighted. Perhaps he thought that this was a step toward even greater authority. But his inability to lead denied him that future.
Key Scripture:	John 18

Monday

HIS STORY

It was a morning he would never forget.

Pontius Pilate, the governor Rome had assigned to manage the region of Judea, was interrupted by a mob of religious leaders. He was no great admirer of these men. They had been up all night and reeked of sweat as they crowded into an area outside his private chambers. He had never seen them like this.

These outwardly virtuous men had completely broken character and were acting like a band of stray dogs. They had captured Jesus and were bringing him to Pilate for him to sanction their request for his

execution. Bound at the wrists and having endured a night of emotional brutality, Jesus stood calmly before the governor.

Sitting in an elevated chair that gave him an air of power and
authority, Pilate sat back, thoughtfully stroking his chin and listening.
Deep creases formed across his leathery brow.

"This impostor is guilty of blasphemy," one of the priests began.
"He claims to be the Son of God, and we have no king but Caesar." The priest's own face flushed with the blasphemy he had just
spoken.

"He's a madman," another interrupted. "He's going to destroy the
temple."

"Not only that, Your Excellency," one of the men patronized, "he
opposes paying taxes to Rome. He's subverting our nation." The others murmured their delight at this charge, knowing that the governor
would pay attention to an allegation of treason.

Pilate turned and looked directly into Jesus' face. A hush swept over
the room as everyone waited for Pilate to speak.

"These are serious charges," he said. "What do you say to them?"

Their eyes were fixed on one another, but Jesus did not speak.

"Are you the Christ, the king of the Jews?" he asked, his eyes
pleading with Jesus for an answer.

"Yes, I am," Jesus said quietly through his swollen lips. He showed
no emotion at all.

Just then one of Pilate's personal servants hurried into the room
and approached his throne. "A word with you, my lord," he said. Pilate
extended his hand, and the servant stepped up to the platform where
he was seated. "Your wife, Claudia, has sent word," he whispered. "She
says, 'Do not condemn this innocent man. I have had a tormenting
dream about him.'"

Pilate nodded as the servant stepped down and disappeared
through a large doorway.

The governor paused until the sound of his servant's footsteps
could no longer be heard. "I cannot go along with your plan," he pronounced, considering his wife's warning and knowing that jealousy
was the only reason Jesus had been arrested. "I find nothing here to
support your charges."

The priests and religious leaders were furious. They began shouting and a scuffle broke out among them.

Pilate's head was spinning. *Do I execute this blameless man and keep my authority intact?* he wondered to himself. *Or do I release him and incite a riot among the people?*

"Take him yourselves," Pilate finally said to the men. "Judge him by your own law."

"But we cannot issue a death penalty," they whined. "And this man's crimes are worthy of execution."

Thinking that something less severe might placate their fury, Pilate ordered Jesus to be flogged. Several soldiers led him into the palace, where he was stripped and beaten until his undergarments were soaked with blood. Then someone rushed into the room with several thorny branches from a scraggly shrub. "Look," he shouted, as he bent the branches into a small wreath. Walking over to Jesus, he put the thorns on his head and twisted them into his flesh. Jesus winced from the pain as blood ran down his face. A soldier found an old purple cloth and placed it over his shoulders. "Hail, King of the Jews," one of the soldiers said, bowing in mocked reverence. The other soldiers elbowed each other and laughed. One soldier even walked up to Jesus and slapped his face with an open hand.

Pilate stood back and took it all in. He felt hopelessly trapped. Walking over to Jesus, Pilate asked, "Are you the king of the Jews?"

"My kingdom is not of this world," Jesus calmly replied. "You're right in saying that I'm a king. This is the reason I was born." And then, almost as an afterthought, he said, "Everyone on the side of truth listens to me."

"What's truth?" Pilate sneered.

By this time a crowd had formed outside the palace. Some of the religious leaders had spread the word that an execution was about to take place, and the courtyard was soon filled with hooligans. Pilate called for Jesus to be brought out before the people, hoping that his ghastly appearance would appease them. "I find no basis for a charge against this man," he announced to the crowd.

"Crucify him! Crucify him!" a handful of loudmouths started to shout from the corner of the courtyard. Soon others picked up the chant as it spread across the crowd.

Pilate walked to the center of the balcony overlooking the people. He called for water and a small basin and ceremoniously washed his hands. "I'm innocent of this man's blood," he said. "He's your responsibility."

"That's fine with us," the people shouted back. "We don't care if his blood is on us and our children."

Pilate nodded to his soldiers, and they led Jesus away to be crucified. Pilate stood in his place until the last person had left the courtyard. Then he turned and quietly walked into the palace. Finding a comfortable chair, he sat down and poured himself a drink.

Tuesday

A LOOK AT THE MAN

The Man Who Acquiesced

It was the ultimate paradox. Pilate was faced with two sobering options—neither would lead to a happy ending.

If he would listen to his conscience—and his wife's warning—and free Jesus, he would lose support among the religious elite. And releasing Jesus could have changed these men's verbal outcries into a physical revolt. Such an uprising would reflect poorly on his leadership. Tiberius Caesar might replace him because of such insurrection among his subjects.

But giving in to the people's demands meant that Pilate would be forced to deny his own heart. He knew Jesus was innocent. He knew that these men had arrested Jesus because of their seething jealousy over his popularity among the people. And he didn't need his wife to have a bad dream to confirm his apprehensions, but it *did* make things worse; now he would have to contend with her. This was Pilate's plight, but these are the predicaments of every leader—popularity or integrity, compromise or character.

As the governor of the land, Pilate certainly knew about Jesus' ministry. He may have received warnings from his own associates that Jesus was extremely popular among the people. He suspected that Jesus' message could be threatening to his regime, but he *knew* that Jesus' words and work were foreboding to the religious establishment. The priests and Pharisees were just jealous. They hated Jesus. But was he dangerous—worthy of capital punishment? Should Pilate sanction his execution just to appease these proud men?

Pilate's approach to this terrible dilemma was something we can understand. Once he had listened to the facts, his response was direct: "Jesus is innocent." Oh, how he hoped that approach would work and the religious leaders would shuffle out of his chambers in resignation.

When that didn't work, Pilate got philosophical. "What is truth?" he pondered aloud. *Doesn't truth depend on the situation? Isn't truth sometimes true and sometimes not? Shouldn't group pressure or expediency or convenience have an effect on truth?*

When Pilate saw that plain speaking and philosophy were not going to satisfy the people, he tried to dismiss himself from the responsibility of his decision by washing his hands. Then, in his final feeble attempt to assuage his guilt, he placed the blame on others. "This is *your* fault," he told the priests and Pharisees.

Pontius Pilate had a historic opportunity to do the right thing, but he buckled under the pressure. The heaviness of the situation forced him to acquiesce. As a result, he will forever be remembered as a defective leader, a man with no courage.

Someday Pilate would be replaced as the Roman governor of Judea. No longer would he have to deal with these tricky situations. No longer would he have to make the difficult decisions. And Pilate could continue to ignore his wife. He could even leave her and no longer deal with her opinions. But Pilate would never be able to quiet his conscience. He would never be able to escape the blood of an innocent man and the power of his own conflicted soul. A troubled heart and sleepless nights would be his lifelong companions.

Wednesday

HIS LEGACY IN SCRIPTURE

Read John 18:28–38.

1. How would you describe Pontius Pilate? What kind of a man do you think he was?
2. Everyone who has been in a position of leadership understands this: Whichever decision I make will be unpopular with someone. What do you think Pilate really wanted to do with Jesus? Why didn't he do the right thing?
3. Why is it easier to deny your own conscience than to go against the pressure of the crowd?
4. What if Jesus had answered Pilate's question, "What is truth?" What would he have said to Pilate?

GOING DEEPER

Read Mark 14:60–65.

5. Someone has said, "There's nothing quite as powerful as *unused* power." How did Jesus' restraint make his accusers appear? How did it make him appear?
6. How might this principle work itself out in your life? When have you lashed out and regretted it? When have you held back and been thankful that you did?
7. Leadership is nonnegotiable. You *are* a leader in someone's life—or perhaps in many people's lives. What can you learn from this story about your important role?

Thursday

HIS LEGACY OF PROMISE

Pilate may have wanted to be the governor of Judea. He may even have petitioned Tiberius Caesar for the job. But he didn't ask to be put in the precarious predicament of judging the life and death of the Savior. Nonetheless, he was placed in a position of authority and was given the chance to do the right thing. But he didn't.

This is not a unique story in Scripture. Many kings neglected to rule responsibly. Many leaders did not lead. Many others disobeyed their call and aborted their missions.

Pilate's life will always symbolize great power and great failure.

Promises in Scripture

> Who, then, is the man that fears the LORD?
> He will instruct him in the way chosen for him.
>
> —Psalm 25:12

> Blessed are the merciful,
> for they will be shown mercy.
>
> —Matthew 5:7

> Everyone who hears these words of mine and puts them into practice is like a wise man who built his house on the rock.   —Matthew 7:24

> Judge nothing before the appointed time; wait till the Lord comes. He will bring to light what is hidden in darkness and will expose the motives of men's hearts. At that time each will receive his praise from God.
>
> —1 Corinthians 4:5

Friday

HIS LEGACY OF PRAYER

Guard my life and rescue me;
let me not be put to shame,
for I take refuge in you.
May integrity and uprightness protect me,
because my hope is in you.

—Psalm 25:20–21

Reflect On: Psalm 25
Praise God: For his mercy.
Offer Thanks: For the blood of Jesus Christ and his offer of pardon in spite of our sin and willful disobedience.
Confess: Any willingness to be swayed by the crowd to do— or think—the wrong thing, instead of doing what is right.
Ask God: To give you the courage to be faithful, to fill you with integrity and character that would be pleasing to him. Ask him to make you a worthy ambassador of his truth and his grace.

The story of Pontius Pilate is a tragic one. A man with all the power he needed buckled under the pressure and did the wrong thing. Following Jesus' crucifixion, there is no account of what happened to Pilate. One uncorroborated account tells us that in his later life he was exiled to Gaul and died by his own hand. But if Pilate had seen the error of his ways and had confessed his sin, he would have been forgiven. God's grace expressed in the cross that Pilate inflicted on Jesus would have fully covered his own sin. Pilate's confession would have removed Jesus' blood from his hands and given him a clean heart. The same is true for us.

Father in heaven, thank you for your grace. Thank you for the sobering account of this man who failed to do the right thing. Please forgive me for the times when I have been unwilling to stand against the tide and have sinned against you. Teach me to know the truth, to speak the truth, and to be set free by it. I pray this in Jesus' name. Amen.

STEPHEN

His Name Means "Crown"

His Work:	After Pentecost, Stephen was one of seven leaders chosen to be the first "deacons" to serve the needy.
His Character:	He is a model of readiness and untold courage in the face of his adversaries.
His Sorrow:	In addition to the rocks that came hurling down on him, Stephen must have been struck by the utter lostness of those who should have known better— the religious leaders of his day.
His Triumph:	The privilege of representing, serving, and dying for his Master.
Key Scriptures:	Acts 6–7

Monday

HIS STORY

"Heretic!" the priest shouted as he lifted a boulder above his head and hurled the rock at the man kneeling on the ground.

As the stone struck Stephen on his forearm, everyone standing nearby heard bones snap like dry tinder. Stephen's hand went numb.

Stephen looked up, calling out to the God he loved. As he did, the events from years past roared through his mind like a cascading river.

As was the custom during the Feast of Harvest—Pentecost— thousands of Jews from every nation had come to Jerusalem. When they gathered one day, thunder rumbled across the sky. The people were filled with wonder. Fire came gently lapping down from above them. Immediately the men from Galilee began to speak in languages they had never studied. The Jews in the room from other regions were astonished. "Aren't these just plain-speaking Galileans?" they asked one another. "Then who taught them our native tongues?"

Peter jumped to his feet. Several days before, Jesus had physically ascended into the heavens, but before he did, he had looked into the faces of the eleven disciples. "Don't worry," Jesus had said to them. "I am going to my Father, but my Holy Spirit is going to descend on you, and the power you receive will be unlike anything you've ever known. Not only will you preach to your country and neighboring lands, but your witness will spread throughout the world."

"This is it!" Peter shouted. "This is the gift the Master promised to send." He caught the eye of several others who had been there, and they nodded with knowing smiles.

"Listen carefully to what I have to say," Peter admonished. "Jesus of Nazareth was a man accredited by God to you by miracles, wonders and signs, which God did among you through him, as you yourselves know. . . . God has raised Jesus to life, and we are all witnesses of that fact. . . . Repent and be baptized, every one of you."

Three thousand people responded to the message and were converted. Among them were many Greek-speaking Jews (Hellenists). They had never heard anything like this, and their hearts were immediately drawn to Peter's message.

Over the next several months, all the believers celebrated their faith by sharing food and possessions with one another. However, the Hellenists noticed that many of their clan were overlooked because they didn't speak the local tongue. The disciples met to discuss the problem. They decided to appoint seven men—all believers who spoke Greek—to care for these people. Stephen was their first choice.

He was an unusually capable man, full of God's grace and power. The disciples knew that Stephen was not only a gifted preacher but also a miracle worker in Jesus' name. Highly educated men from all over the region publicly challenged Stephen but were unable to stand up to his wisdom or the Spirit by which he spoke. Such contests won him few friends among the Jewish hierarchy, but then, Stephen wasn't interested in earthly power.

While he was serving the needy one day, a handful of temple thugs attacked Stephen and dragged him before the Sanhedrin, seventy-one of the most powerful Jews in the region. As had happened when Jesus appeared before the high priest, several liars stepped forward to tell stories about what Stephen was supposedly preaching. On and on they went, accusing him of blasphemy. "We have heard him say that this Jesus of Nazareth will destroy this temple and change our customs."

Instead of defending himself, Stephen looked around the chamber and smiled with compassion. As his accusers looked into Stephen's face, they were taken aback. His skin was clear, luminescent, like the face of an angel. It irritated them; he was going down! This was the end of him. How could the man stand there, looking for all the world as though he wasn't *of* the world? As though he had somehow beaten *them?*

The high priest looked at Stephen. "Well," he began, leaning forward and lifting an eyebrow as if to challenge the behavior of a naughty child, "is this true?"

Stephen stood to his feet and looked around the room. "Brothers and fathers, listen to me!" His boldness was breathtaking. No one stirred or interrupted him.

Over the next several minutes, beginning with Abraham, Stephen summarized the story of God's dealings with his people throughout Jewish history. "Time and time again, patriarchs and prophets were rejected and persecuted." The priests were well versed in the familiar stories of many of their heroes. And they were impressed, in spite of themselves, with Stephen's grasp of Hebrew heritage. They listened, enraptured. But the whole presentation, a brilliantly conceived treatise on the authenticity of Jesus the Messiah, was a dazzling setup.

"You're just like them," Stephen boomed, "you bullheaded bigots, deliberately rejecting the Holy Spirit. You're just like your forefathers who killed every man who prophesied the coming of the very one you've been waiting for. You've done it again to Jesus of Nazareth, and you have no excuse!"

In an instant, the Sanhedrin was in an uproar. Like children on a playground, the religious leaders covered their ears and screamed to drown out the sound of Stephen's voice.

Then Stephen exclaimed, "Look, I see heaven open and the Son of Man standing at the right hand of God." A few of them rushed toward Stephen and grabbed his arms, dragging him out.

Once outside the city gates, they lifted huge stones in the air, intent on killing him. By contrast, Stephen knelt quietly. While they were stoning him, he prayed, "Lord Jesus, receive my spirit." Then he cried out, "Lord, do not hold this sin against them." After that, he fell to the ground.

A young man named Saul had been standing nearby, a quiet observer who approved of the death he had just witnessed.

Tuesday

A LOOK AT THE MAN

Famous Last Words

There are only a few men in Scripture of whom you might say to your son, "When you grow up, be exactly like him." Stephen is such a man, a tender and gracious leader with a brilliant mind, a crisp tongue, and a humble yet disarmingly confident air about him.

For the Jewish leaders of his day, Stephen was not a good man to have on the other side.

Because of Peter's triumphant Pentecost sermon and the spread of the gospel throughout the region, people were converted from many different cultures. Many converts in need came to other believers for food and daily provisions. Generosity prevailed. Primarily accustomed to native Israelites coming to Jesus, the disciples were challenged with the right way to handle Jews from other nations who embraced the faith. Some of the Greek-speaking believers were overlooked.

"What we need are committed men who can help these people," a group of believers said to one another one evening. "Is there anyone here who speaks Greek?"

Seven men stepped forward—Stephen and six others. The leaders were familiar with Stephen. A man known for his faith, his oratory skills, and his Spirit-filled power, Stephen's ministry was widespread. He had even performed miracles in Jesus' name. This was one very gifted man.

But there was no glamour in the assignment for which Stephen was volunteering. He would be responsible for distributing food and supplies to Greek-speaking widows and caring for the disabled. Here was a man who was well versed in history and the law and could command audiences with his words. Now he would quietly be taking care of the needs of people who were incapable of taking care of themselves.

To the Pharisees and Jewish leaders, Stephen was a monumental threat. He was winning the minds *and* hearts of the people, and many were being converted. So they collared a few men who were willing to take oaths and lie about Stephen.

"What do you have to say for yourself?" they demanded of him after the false charges had been presented before the Sanhedrin.

It would have been completely understandable if Stephen had taken the opportunity to defend himself. Point by point he could have summarily disassembled the charges against him and the reprobates who had perjured themselves. But he didn't.

Instead, Stephen took the whole council on a walk through history. He identified *their* heroes—Abraham, Isaac, Jacob, Joseph, Moses, David, and Solomon. Stephen acknowledged how God's faithfulness had sustained and prospered these patriarchs. He reminded them of how each of these men had been obedient in spite of terrible odds. This was not the speech they expected, and they were drawn to Stephen's message.

The Sanhedrin leaned forward in their seats, waiting for Stephen to identify *them* as members of the grand sequence of great Jewish leaders. But it wasn't to be. Imagine their horror when Stephen announced that they, like others of God's adversaries, had deliberately tried to thwart his providence—that *they* were the enemy.

Stephen must have known that he had pronounced his own death sentence—that the cost of his courage, of telling the truth before this powerful assembly, would be the loss of his life. Still, Stephen willingly paid the price. He didn't know that his sacrifice would plant a seed in the heart of a man who heard his stirring address and stood there, watching and approving of his brutal assassination—Saul of Tarsus— who later became the transformed Paul, the apostle to the Gentiles.

As selflessly as he waited on the needy, Stephen gave everything he had in service to the risen Lord. As a result, God took his obedience, multiplied it, and eventually the church of all nations was born.

Wednesday

HIS LEGACY IN SCRIPTURE

Read Acts 6:8–15.

1. Prisons around the world are filled with bitter men who blame their parents or their unfortunate circumstances or someone else. In their minds they're "innocent of the charges brought against them." But Stephen *was* innocent. He *was* arrested on a false charge. How did he respond?

2. What do you think "the face of an angel" looked like to his accusers? How do you think this countenance made them feel?

3. How might we resemble "an angel" when we're faced with stress, temptation, or persecution? What can we learn from Stephen's reaction?

GOING DEEPER

Read Acts 7:1–3.

4. The high priest leaned in on Stephen and asked him a question: "Are these charges true?" Did Stephen answer this question? Why do you think he responded as he did?

5. Even though Stephen never directly answered his question, the high priest did not blindside him. Stephen was ready. What did Stephen do to prepare for this question?

6. What are you doing to prepare for the unpredictable "questions" you will be asked about your life, your conduct, or your belief system?

Thursday

HIS LEGACY OF PROMISE

Sometimes the word *hero* is laid at the feet of unworthy people. Not so with Stephen. His giftedness, his selfless service, his courage, and his sacrifice qualify him as a hero. A saint. The writer to the Hebrews would rightly put Stephen in the exclusive category of "the world was not worthy of them."

We have the luxury of looking back on the life of Stephen. We are able to see how God used him to change history. But Stephen saw none of this. His call was to be obedient, one day—one moment—at a time. Stephen never saw the consequences of his faithfulness, but that didn't matter to him. He trusted God for the results.

Promises in Scripture

His master replied, "Well done, good and faithful servant! You have been faithful with a few things; I will put you in charge of many things. Come and share your master's happiness!"   —Matthew 25:21

Just as the Father raises the dead and gives them life, even so the Son gives life to whom he is pleased to give it.   —John 5:21

I tell you the truth, unless a kernel of wheat falls into the ground and dies, it remains only a single seed. But if it dies, it produces many seeds.   —John 12:24

[Jesus] commanded us to preach to the people and to testify that he is the one whom God appointed as judge of the living and the dead. All the prophets testify about him that everyone who believes in him receives forgiveness of sins through his name.   —Acts 10:42–43

Friday

HIS LEGACY OF PRAYER

While they were stoning him, Stephen prayed, "Lord Jesus, receive my spirit. . . . Do not hold this sin against them."   —Acts 7:59–60

Reflect On: Luke 23:44–49

Praise God: For his grace.

Offer Thanks: For the words of Stephen as he died, innocent, at the hands of bloodthirsty men. Thank God for Jesus' sacrifice for our sins and his unfailing love for us, the guilty ones whose sins sent him to the cross.

Confess: Any eagerness to receive applause for your obedience rather than to be completely satisfied with God's approval for your service—public or private.

Ask God: To give you the discipline to be prepared for whatever special commission he has for you—to have your mind and your heart properly prepared.

Stephen's life was a startling example of godliness in the face of many difficult assignments. He submitted to the power of the Holy Spirit and performed miracles in Jesus' name. He served indigent and broken people. He stared death in the face as he courageously defended his faith before a hostile crowd of men who hated him. And he pleaded with his Father to forgive those who spilled his blood.

God in heaven, thank you for your saving power. Thank you for the example of this man whose bravery and faithfulness changed the world. Please forgive me for my lack of discipline to prepare and courage to stand for you. Teach me to follow you in such a way that those who see me, hear me, and know me are introduced through my life to the living God. I pray this in Jesus' name. Amen.

PAUL

His Name Means "Little"

His Work: Paul was a Pharisee, possibly a member of the Sanhedrin, who was transformed by a visitation of Jesus on the road to Damascus to become a radical missionary for Christ.

His Character: His intensity about life was matched by his faith and love for Jesus Christ.

His Sorrow: The memory of his hatred of Christians and his sanctioning of their punishment, floggings, and murder.

His Triumph: Paul spread the gospel to the Gentiles.

Key Scriptures: Acts 9; Paul's letters

Monday

HIS STORY

Saul of Tarsus gathered provisions for the trip. Not only did he need food and clothing for himself, but no man would ever venture out on such a journey without assembling a caravan complete with guides and servants. Maps were scarce; bandits along the way were not. He was headed for Damascus from Jerusalem, an expedition that would take at least ten days to complete.

Saul's heart pounded with anticipation. This was an official visit, sanctioned and funded by the Sanhedrin. As a Pharisee, and possibly even a member of this elite council, Paul had made his case to Caiaphas, the high priest.

"Please commission me to travel to Damascus," Saul petitioned. "I've received word that there is a band of Jesus-followers who have infiltrated the synagogues there. Let me go so that I can arrest these troublemakers and return them to Jerusalem for trial."

Caiaphas was impressed with Saul's boldness and didn't hesitate. "You've made a sound proposal," he said. "And you are the right man to do this. You may go. I'll prepare documents for you to take. You have my blessing." He hesitated, knowing the extent and danger of the trip Saul was about to take. Like a concerned parent, he furrowed his brow and focused his eyes on Saul, "And may the God of our fathers go with you."

Saul was flattered by the high priest's affirmation and buoyed by the confidence he expressed. He bowed before Caiaphas and, as he stood, embraced him, kissing him on both cheeks.

"May God be with you," Caiaphas repeated.

"And also with you," Saul replied.

The journey was arduous but uneventful. In spite of the potential for attacks by traveling thieves, all went according to plan. By late afternoon on the ninth day, the caravan crested a hill and saw the city of Damascus in the distance. It was a beautiful sight. The men let out a collective shout. "Damascus!" they hollered. "Damascus on the horizon!"

It had been almost two days since they had left Caesarea Philippi—and any semblance of civilization—two days of toughing it out through the foothills of Mount Hermon and across the desolate Syrian Desert. The sun was slowly descending toward the western mountains, and its rays flooded the city with light, outlining it against the late afternoon sky. Seeing Damascus in the distance was cause for celebration.

Saul was very pleased. His journey was coming to a close, but his assignment was only beginning. His mind raced. Suddenly, directly overhead, a light appeared. Like a descending star, its brilliance beamed against the evening sky. The men stood aghast as the light continued to fall, but their shock turned to terror as they realized the light was coming toward them. There was no time to run—no place to hide— so they shielded their faces from the glare and held their breath.

The light came to rest on top of Saul. He was completely surrounded by it. It looked as though he was on fire. Saul fell to the ground in a panic. How could he ever survive this?

"Saul!" A voice thundered from the light.

The Pharisee covered his head with his arms.

"Saul!" the voice repeated. "Why are you persecuting me?"

Saul prepared to die. But conscious thoughts continued to stream through his mind. *What is this?* he wondered. *Who is this?*

"Lord, is that you?" Saul whimpered, afraid to hear the answer. A devout student of the old covenant, Saul had read of encounters like this. Many of the men in the caravan were also familiar with the stories of Moses and Elijah and Jonah. They were terrified.

Then the voice bellowed out again, "I am Jesus, the one you are persecuting." The ground shook.

Jesus? Jesus! Saul repeated to himself. *How can this be?* He peeked out into the light and saw what looked like a form of a man shrouded in the light.

"Get up," Jesus said. "Go into the city and someone will meet you. He will tell you what you must do."

Saul opened his mouth to speak, but he was unable to make a sound.

And then, just as suddenly as the light had appeared, it vanished. The men unshielded their eyes and saw Saul still crouched on the ground. Saul looked around and saw nothing but blackness.

"I can't see," he whispered. "I can't see," he said again, this time loud enough for his companions to hear. "I'm blind," he shouted. "Someone help me. Help me!" he repeated.

The men quickly gathered around Saul and lifted him to his feet. Once they had gained their strength and composure, they continued on toward Damascus, taking their blind leader by the hand. Their destination was the home of a man named Judas on Straight Street. When they arrived, Saul was inconsolable. For three days he would not eat or drink and hardly spoke a word. A lifetime of study and deep-seated convictions had been dashed in a single moment. Every one of his relationships, whether with friend or foe, had been forged by these beliefs.

On the fourth day he had a visitor. "Brother Saul," the kindly voice of a man named Ananias spoke, his hands resting on the disheartened Pharisee. "Jesus has sent me to touch you so that you can see again. The Holy Spirit has come to fill you, and I am going to baptize you."

At that moment, Saul could see again. Looking up into the face of his new friend, Saul stood and embraced Ananias. A new sense of calm took control of Saul's heart, assuring him that God would provide whatever he needed to accomplish the purpose for which he had been made.

Tuesday

A LOOK AT THE MAN

Stopped in His Tracks

Except for Jesus himself, no one in history had a greater impact on the formation of Christian doctrine and the setting up of the church than Saul of Tarsus—the apostle Paul.

But before Saul met Jesus on the road to Damascus, the thought of carrying such a distinction could not have been more abhorrent to him. Saul was a zealous Jew. His singular mission in life was to preserve the integrity and traditions of his religion, and he was ready and willing to eliminate anything that threatened it—by any means. About this he was shamelessly passionate.

Born in Tarsus, Saul was the son of parents who wanted their son to be grounded in the laws, the orthodoxy, and the traditions of Judaism. Such training was not available in Tarsus, so they took him hundreds of miles to the south to study in Jerusalem. As a young man, Saul sat at the feet of the great teacher Gamaliel.

"Anyone who is hung on a tree is under God's curse," Gamaliel read to his student from the fifth book of the Law of Moses. "You must not desecrate the land the LORD your God is giving you as an inheritance." Saul believed that the law was truth, and he had known the details of the trial and crucifixion of Jesus of Nazareth. As far as he was concerned, Jesus was cursed. In addition to his beliefs about Jesus, Saul was also apprehensive about the growing number of Christians, especially among the Jews. This pollution had to be cleansed.

A short time before Saul's journey to Damascus, Peter and a handful of disciples had been brought before the Sanhedrin, of which Saul may have been a part. They were charged with healing the sick in the temple courts and teaching people about Jesus. Furious about the disciples' endeavor, the high council listened to their defense.

"Kill these traitors," one of the Pharisees shouted. "Yes, we must destroy these heretics," shouted another.

But Gamaliel, now an old man, stood and spoke. "Leave these men alone! Let them go!"

Saul was shocked. Hadn't this same wise man etched the law into his head as a youth? Now was he telling the Sanhedrin to ignore the law?

"We've seen these movements come and go," Gamaliel continued. "If its purpose or activity is of human origin, it will fail. But if it *is* from God, even we will not be able to stop them; we'll be fighting against God, and we will fail."

Gamaliel's speech persuaded the Sanhedrin to forgo the execution of Peter and the other disciples; yet to assuage the anger of those who pressed charges, the Sanhedrin ordered the disciples to be flogged. They hated these followers of Jesus and despised the words they spoke. And the sound of the forty lashes slicing the backs of these conspirators from an adjoining room delighted each one of the great assembly.

"Do not speak in the name of Jesus again," the disciples were ordered as they reappeared, now bloodied and bruised, before the Sanhedrin. But from the looks on these offender's faces, not a single member of the council believed that they would obey.

Saul had never seen such resolve. This made him hate them all the more.

And in just a few days, the members of the Sanhedrin, with Saul in their midst, were able to vent their rage as they took Stephen outside the city and crushed his body under a volley of stones.

Now Saul was faced with the unthinkable. The disciples had been right. Stephen had been innocent—murdered in cold blood. Jesus *was* the very one spoken of by the prophets. What was he to do?

Saul—later on the island of Cyprus asking to be called "Paul"—spent the remainder of his life answering that question. In fact, he went straight to the synagogue and began to preach. "Come to Jesus," Paul preached to those who had gathered. "He is the Son of God.... Repent and be saved."

The priest in Damascus sent word to Caiaphas. "Good news: Saul has arrived in Damascus. Bad news: He's talking like a lunatic."

Before his martyrdom at the hands of Nero, Paul spread his "lunacy" throughout the known world. Through his love for Jesus, his compelling preaching, and his imprisonments, the fires of revival were ignited by this crazy man—once the gospel's great adversary, now its tireless champion.

Wednesday

HIS LEGACY IN SCRIPTURE

Read Philippians 1:1–21.

1. Paul had a unique perspective on suffering. He knew that God not only met him in a dramatic way on the Damascus road, but he also used the pain inflicted on the disciples and Stephen to get Paul's attention. Now Paul was suffering. What was his attitude about his "chains"?

2. When have you ever witnessed this kind of perspective and grace in suffering—either in your own life or through others? Describe that experience.

3. Because he knew that many believers were praying for him, Paul expressed his hope that he would "never be ashamed." What did he know about that? Some people run and hide when they're ashamed. What did Paul do?

GOING DEEPER

Read Romans 8:1–4.

4. It's one thing for a relatively "good" person to speak of "no condemnation." But Paul's sinfulness could only be described as heinous. Not only did he have the blood of the martyrs on his hands, but he wore those stains like badges of honor. What does "no condemnation" mean to such a man?

5. Everyone has sinned. So what does "no condemnation" mean to us?

6. Paul was a professionally trained law-follower. For him, nothing was more supreme than this. But then he met Jesus. Summarize, in your own words, how this encounter radically changed Paul's belief system.

Read Romans 5:20.

7. Until his fateful journey to Damascus, Paul loved the law. It was by his adherence to it that he was "saved." Now he had a different view of the law. Its purpose was to identify—and increase—our sinfulness and our desperate need for God's mercy and grace. How does this truth affect our goal to be "good Christians" by being "good"?

One more thing: Read Hebrews 10:16. Which is more challenging to obey: the law etched on tablets or the one written on our hearts?

Thursday

HIS LEGACY OF PROMISE

No New Testament person has given us more insight into his thinking, his beliefs, and his convictions than the apostle Paul. Although learning about the events of his life is fascinating, listening to what he said and wrote is even more significant.

Paul's life is a study in seeking—and finding—freedom. The law doesn't promise it. Radical religion doesn't provide it. Good works don't earn it. Only the grace given to us through the shed blood of Jesus Christ bestows on us the freedom we long for. By faith alone we receive that gift of grace.

Promises in Scripture

All have sinned and fall short of the glory of God, and are justified freely by his grace through the redemption that came by Christ Jesus.

—Romans 3:23–24

We are more than conquerors through him who loved us. For I am convinced that neither death nor life, neither angels nor demons, neither the present nor the future, nor any powers, neither height nor depth, nor anything else in all creation, will be able to separate us from the love of God that is in Christ Jesus our Lord.   —Romans 8:37–39

It is for freedom that Christ has set us free. Stand firm, then, and do not let yourselves be burdened again by a yoke of slavery. . . .

You, my brothers, were called to be free. But do not use your freedom to indulge the sinful nature; rather, serve one another in love.

—Galatians 5:1, 13

For it is by grace you have been saved, through faith—and this not from yourselves, it is the gift of God—not by works, so that no one can boast.

—Ephesians 2:8–9

Friday

HIS LEGACY OF PRAYER

"[I'm] confident of this, that he who began a good work in you will carry it on to completion until the day of Christ Jesus." —Philippians 1:6

Reflect On: Philippians 1:9–11

Praise God: For his persevering grace.

Offer Thanks: For the gift of his Son, the gift of faith to believe, and the gift of the Holy Spirit to fill us with himself.

Confess: Your shortsightedness and your unwillingness to thank him in every circumstance.

Ask God: To fill you with radical, life-changing love for him.

Paul was the last man to have the privilege of calling himself an apostle, having seen Jesus in person. And his encounter with the Savior can only be described as miraculous. From that moment on, all Jesus' appearances are by way of us—this band of believers Paul called Jesus' "body." And now our call is to be "Jesus" to a lost and broken world. May we, by his power and grace, do just that.

God in heaven, thank you for your Son who came to earth to save me. Thank you for your grace. Please forgive me for complaining when things don't turn out as I planned. Fill me with your Holy Spirit so that when others see me, they see you living in me. I pray this in Jesus' name. Amen.

About the Authors

Ann Spangler is an award-winning writer and author of many best-selling books, including *Praying the Names of God* and *Praying the Names of Jesus*. Her most recent books are *The Tender Words of God* and *Sitting at the Feet of Rabbi Jesus* (coauthored with Lois Tverberg). Her fascination with and love of Scripture has resulted in books that have opened the Bible to a wide range of readers. She and her two daughters live in Grand Rapids, Michigan. For information on Ann, visit www.annspangler.com. If you would like to invite Ann to speak to your group, contact her at annsdesk@annspangler.com.

Robert Wolgemuth is the owner of Wolgemuth & Associates, Inc., a literary representation agency, and the author of *She Calls Me Daddy*, *The Most Important Place on Earth*, and other bestselling books. He and his wife have two adult daughters and five grandchildren. For information on Robert, visit www.robertwolgemuth.com.

Women of the Bible

A One-Year Devotional Study of Women in Scripture

Ann Spangler and Jean E. Syswerda

Women of the Bible focuses on fifty-two remarkable women in Scripture — women whose struggles to live with faith and courage are not unlike your own. And now this bestselling devotional study book has been updated and expanded to enhance its flexibility, usefulness, and relevance for both individuals and groups.

Small groups will especially welcome the way the Bible studies have been streamlined to fit the unique needs of the group setting.

Vital and deeply human, the women in this book encourage you through their failures as well as their successes. You'll see how God acted in surprising and wonderful ways to draw them — and you — to himself. This year-long devotional offers a unique method to help you slow down and savor the story of God's unrelenting love for his people, offering a fresh perspective that will nourish and strengthen your personal communion with him.

Women of Today Can Find Inspiration and Encouragement in the Lives of the Women Who Lived in Bible Times

Women of the Bible:

52 Stories for Prayer and Reflection

Ann Spangler

These are the inspiring stories of fifty-two female characters in the Bible taken from the popular book *Women of the Bible.*

Women of the Bible: 52 Stories for Prayer and Reflection is a weekly devotional offering contemporary Christian women an opportunity to study the lives and legacies of fifty-two women in Scripture. Some — such as Eve and Mary — are prominent and well-known biblical figures. But even the lives of the lesser-known women—such as Tamar, the daughter-in-law of Judah, who disguised herself as a prostitute — offer provocative and fascinating stories. What shines through in this inspirational book is the author's respect for these gritty, intelligent, and occasionally flawed women.

Each woman's life story is briefly recounted in an enchanting storytelling voice, helping readers see how these ancient stories still have meaning centuries later. Included is an introductory section listing each woman's name, her character, her sorrow, her joy, and Scriptures pertaining to her life. Then her story is told, followed by a section outlining her legacy of prayer.

Available in stores and online!

Women of the Bible:

52 Bible Studies for Individuals and Groups

Jean E. Syswerda

These are the inspiring stories of fifty-two female characters in the Bible—and a unique resource for individuals or groups interested in studying them—taken from the popular book *Women of the Bible*.

Women of the Bible: 52 Bible Studies for Individuals and Groups is an abridged edition of *Women of the Bible*, specifically for those who want to delve more deeply into the life of each woman. Features include:

- the main Scripture passages that tell the story of each woman's life
- space for readers to record their thoughts
- a list of lesser-known women in the Bible, making this a complete list of all the women in the Bible
- timelines and charts

The stories of these biblical women offer encouragement through their failures as well as through their successes. God acted in surprising and wonderful ways in their lives, just as he continues to act in the lives of Christian women today.

Available in stores and online!

For information on Ann Spangler,
visit www.annspangler.com

If you would like to invite Ann to speak to your group,
contact her at annsdesk@annspangler.com

We want to hear from you. Please send your comments about this
book to us in care of zreview@zondervan.com. Thank you.

ZONDERVAN.com/
AUTHORTRACKER
follow your favorite authors